CASEY'S
LAW

CASEY'S LAW

IF SOMETHING CAN GO RIGHT, IT SHOULD

AL CASEY

WITH DICK SEAVER

FOREWORD BY
JACK VALENTI

ARCADE PUBLISHING • NEW YORK

To Ellie,

whose love and devotion made it all possible

FIRST EDITION

Library of Congress Cataloging-in-Publication Data

Casey, Albert V.
    Casey's law : if something can go right, it should / Albert V. Casey ; foreword by Jack Valenti. —1st ed.
        p.   cm.
    ISBN 1-55970-307-5
    1. Management. 2. Problem Solving. 3. Success in business. I. Title
HD31.C3565 1997
658.4—DC20   95–12716

Published in the United States by Arcade Publishing, Inc., New York
Distributed by Little, Brown and Company

10 9 8 7 6 5 4 3 2 1

BP

Designed by API

PRINTED IN THE UNITED STATES OF AMERICA

CONTENTS

FOREWORD

WHEN AL CASEY TOLD ME he was writing his memoirs, or perhaps more accurately, putting on paper the lessons he has learned from the business worlds he has inhabited and commanded — railroads, newspapers and books, TV, major airlines, banks — as well as from acting as United States postmaster general and head of the Resolution Trust Corporation, I told him I would pay him the highest compliment accordable to an author: I would buy his book at full retail price!

In a corporate world largely colored gray, Albert V. Casey is resplendently bright. In truth, he is one of a vanishing breed of great business leaders who can use wit and humor as both shield and mace. He is a man who understands the basic frame of the human condition, for he honors the individual dignity of those working under him and treats them with a warm affection that is both unfeigned and unpretentious. Most of all, he has an instinct for the future.

Put another way: there are countless men and women who can dissect a financial document, who are artisans of the spreadsheet and architects of shareholder enhancement, who can organize and administer and "do" board meetings. But there are too few CEOs who can walk the factory floor or the office corridors and achieve genuine rapport with the men and women who work there, earning their respect and inspiring their pride and loyalty. Al Casey can.

How do I know? Well, try fifty years of observing Al Casey — sometimes intimately, sometimes from afar — navigate the treacherous tides of the business sea.

It was on a crisp autumn day by the side of the Charles River that I first met Al Casey. We were both new students, part of an all-veteran class at Harvard Business School just after the end of the Second World War, eyeing one other warily as we met for the first time. It was a truly formidable class made up of restless intellects, the most tirelessly energetic and fiercely competitive group of men I have ever known. We were all graduates of the nation's finest universities and, having returned from combat in faraway places, eager to reclaim our lost years. The pace never slackened in the classrooms or in the study groups in which we worked until late in the evening, discussing each new case about the travails of a corporation. The conversations we had over lunch in a rickety old barn of a wartime-era cafeteria had only one pace: full speed ahead. We had no time to waste. We had to catch up with our futures. Among these young primal forces, not one of whom would choose to be less than a leader himself, Al Casey was dominant. His illuminating intellect, his brawny wit, and his ability to inspire affection among those with whom he worked put him at center stage.

Throughout his career Al proved that you could be tough-minded *and* friendly, that business environments could be competitive *and* fun, that you could watch the bottom line *and* enjoy a good laugh. Were there a Business Hall of Fame, Al Casey ought to have his statue placed there, and in a place of honor. But a caveat to the sculptor: make sure you carve a wide, all-embracing smile.

JACK VALENTI

ACKNOWLEDGMENTS

I should like to express my thanks to a number of people who contributed to shaping this book. First, Libby Scott, my longtime executive assistant, whose dedication and intelligence have helped me immeasurably not only on this project but throughout the past twenty-five years. Bob Erburu, Phil Williams, and Chuck Schneider furnished me with many details about Times Mirror and refreshed my recollection. Bill Roelle and Rick Aboussie were equally generous in helping me re-create the complex details of the Resolution Trust Corporation, and Sally Kearney aided greatly in the description of that operation. Bob Crandall and Gene Overbeck refreshed my memory on much of the tumultuous 1970s and 1980s at American Airlines. Dear friends Dave Myrick, Bob McLean, and Frank Coyne helped fill in the Southern Pacific blanks. A special word of thanks to Pat Patterson, who inspired me to undertake this book, and to my children Peter and Judy, who were in their own way a further inspiration. Finally, the late Jack Garrity, to whom I am indebted in more ways than I can say, clarified many aspects of life as we lived it together not only during my eventful stint as postmaster general, but also at the RTC. I only regret that Jack, who died in 1996, will not be here to read these pages.

CASEY'S
LAW

1

GROWING UP IN ARLINGTON

FOR DECADES, if not centuries, the inevitability of failure has been associated with a mysterious, no doubt depressive, Irishman named Murphy, who has steadfastly maintained that if anything can go wrong, it will. I never set out specifically to disprove Murphy. Instead, during nearly fifty years in business, including stints as the head of the Times Mirror Company and American Airlines, and several years in government service, I discovered what I have come to call Casey's Law: If Something Can Go Right, It Should.

Too simplistic? It's essentially an attitude difference, consistently viewing the glass half full rather than half empty. But it's even more than that. Problem solving often means taking risks, sometimes multimillion-dollar risks, but risk taking is inherent in making progress, in moving forward. Murphy followers have a built-in excuse. "See," they say, shrugging or throwing up their hands, when something goes wrong, "we told you that wouldn't work."

We should accept that mistakes happen in the process of decision making. Errors abound in business, government, sports — everywhere. But we can learn from our errors. Even Brooks Robinson, the Hall of Fame third baseman for the Baltimore Orioles, made an error now and then. The next day he would take extra infield practice, so that he didn't make the same error twice.

It has been my good fortune to be employed in various executive capacities by five very large corporations and twice by the U.S. government. This book is based on what I learned playing with the big boys for big dollars. I have some strong opinions,

especially on the subject of corporate ethics and corporate structure. I'd like to demonstrate that living by your principles can indeed work to your advantage in the corporate environment.

I also believe in simplifying situations, whenever and wherever possible. Throughout my business life, I did my best to avoid
getting bogged down with details in the decision-making process
or with issues that were not absolutely essential to the question or
problem being reviewed. In several of my jobs, but perhaps most
notably during my brief but tumultuous stint as postmaster general, a plethora of details and paperwork threatened to drown me,
and I took dramatic steps to fend off the flood. So should, in my
opinion, every business and government leader worth his or her
salt. One method I devised, early in my career, was to cut down
memos to a minimum. Read some you've sent or received six
months ago — or six days ago — and more often than not you'll
conclude your company could have done without them. Most of
the time, when my memo restriction was ignored or circum-
vented, I'd respond with a pithy — some might say curt — handwritten note, penned directly on the offending document. In my
eleven years with American Airlines, I never once wrote or dictated a memo, and still managed to turn the company around.

I used the term *business leader.* In every company, I have found
there are both leaders and managers, whose respective goals and
attitudes differ radically. Both types are vital to success, and each
must have a clear vision of his or her role if any business is to grow
and prosper. When starting a job, I found it helpful to trace the
longer view of one's goal and mission. For one of the great clogs
preventing a company from running smoothly is not having a clear
vision of what needs to be accomplished. Leaders need to send
clear messages; managers need to hear and understand exactly
what is required or expected of them. About which more later.

My long-standing quarrel with Murphy derives from my
conviction that negative attitudes breed negative results. I can tol-
erate explanations of why something didn't work if I truly believe
one gave it a best shot. But I can't help but dismiss people who

come to me assuring me Plan A won't work before they've even tried it, or who offer ready-made excuses. It's important not to confuse being *negative* with making *mistakes:* honest mistakes often derive from calculated risk taking and tough choices. I've always believed we learn more from our mistakes than from our successes.

As we all endeavor to keep pace with the rapid changes in our lives, both personal and business, we need to be reminded to think clearly and calmly, even in crises. Crises are usually problems that have been allowed to fester, unsolved, for too long; one way to decrease, and even eliminate, them — thereby prolonging your life — is to identify and deal with problems sooner rather than later. It takes some training, but the exercise is well worth the effort.

CEOs or any department heads who use their positions effectively will find that their power increases as they exercise it wisely. So generally will their company's profit. There is an intimate connection between power well used and profit, a kind of intrinsic partnership that in my experience is totally positive.

I have never worked for a boss that I did not like and respect. Also, I have always subscribed wholeheartedly to the thesis that the fastest way to get ahead in the corporate culture is to get your boss promoted. How can you do that, you might well ask? Read on.

I have resigned three times to accept more important positions, each time with greater pay and authority. But remember, this world is round. It is important when you leave one job for another to do so in as friendly and acceptable a fashion as possible. In my case, I count among my best friends the people in the companies I have left. When you are moving around in the corporate scene, my advice is never to slam a door so hard that you can't open it again. My father taught me that.

You don't have to be mean to be tough. You can make difficult decisions and still be compassionate. But to make things go right, you have to remember that the most important person in the world is not yourself, and that holds for everyone in the company, starting with the CEO. During my first days on the job as president of American Airlines, one of the young managers came up to me in the corridor of the New York headquarters, wished me well in my new job, and made a pyramid with both his hands.

"It must be an awesome feeling," he said, "being at the top of this huge pyramid, with so many people working for you and counting on you."

He was referring to American's thirty-five thousand employees. Gently, I took his hand pyramid and turned it upside down.

"That's the way I see the pyramid," I said. "With me at the bottom, working for all the people above."

A dozen years later, when the man retired, he wrote me a moving letter, thanking me for having helped him ascend the corporate ladder — actually he had helped himself — but specifically remembering the incident in the corridor when I had turned his hand pyramid upside down.

There are no easy, cut-and-dried formulas for business success, but dealing with people has to rank among the most important. Though she was always urging me to get good grades, my mother also, by her example, showed me that listening and paying attention to other people was essential.

My wife, Ellie, used to tell me, "Al, you're smiling, you're laughing, you're telling Irish jokes. But all the time you're testing the other person's reactions. And then you figure out how he or she feels. You're always evaluating people." She read me better than anybody else.

The families of both my mother and father had come to the United States after the Irish potato famine in the 1840s. My mother's family settled in Maine, my father's in Boston. Their parents had nothing when they arrived, but by the time I came around my paternal grandfather owned several tenements in the Roxbury section of Boston, where I was born.

In 1923, when I was three, our family moved from Roxbury to Arlington, Massachusetts, across the Charles River. A large truck farm extended all the way from Churchill Avenue to Highland Avenue, directly opposite the high school. That farm was only a block from our house. Up the street was Menotomy Rocks Park, with playgrounds and the delightful Hill's Pond.

When I was growing up, life in my hometown, as in the rest of the country, was rosy. With World War I behind us, America was a land not only of plenty but of seemingly unlimited opportunity. There were gains in production, a stock market boom, stable prices, low taxes, a balanced budget, a strong dollar. Automobiles were becoming commonplace; radio entertainment was expanding.

My father, who had an identical twin brother, always regretted that both he and his brother were denied college educations, especially because their father, my paternal grandfather, was quite well off. But my grandfather believed young men should work, not fill their minds with book learning. Still, Dad put himself through Lynn Classical High School, where in addition to absorbing a fair amount of book learning, he also studied building construction. Shortly after graduating, he founded the construction firm Casey & Darcy, and by the time we children came along, my parents had a sixteen-room duplex on Bartlett Avenue with a maid, a gardener, and a chauffeur.

In the mid-1920s, when I was five or six, my father was the victim of a terrible accident: a drunken Harvard student out celebrating his twenty-first birthday ran into Dad with his car. Seeing the car careening toward him, my father instinctively raised his left leg, but the student's car caught his right leg between his running board and a parked car, pulverizing the thighbone. He had ninety-eight stitches in that leg, and a permanent silver plate was inserted to replace the crushed bone. The leg was horribly discolored from ankle to hip for the rest of his life, and every Friday afternoon for the next quarter-century — until he died — he went faithfully to the Lahey Clinic for treatment for ongoing circulation problems.

Dad was an avid sportsman and, despite his accident, continued to play ball with my older brother John and me, and take us to as many sporting events — especially baseball — as he could find time for. He was equally proud of his two daughters, Eva Marie and Norine, and like my mother constantly stressed to all four of us the need for and virtues of education. Until I was nine, ours was a close-knit, storybook family. It seemed the idyll would never end.

Then came the fall of 1929 and all the rules changed. The October stock market crash was followed by other equally unsettling events. The Smoot-Hawley legislation, which restricted international trade, and bills requiring increased taxes to "balance the budget" had as much to do with the chaos in the 1930s as anything else.

Arlington in the thirties was a microcosm of the country. Our Massachusetts veterans marched on Washington, we saw professional men selling apples on the corner, the gloom of empty manufacturing plants, the banks shut tight. We entered the "alphabet" era of FDR: the NRA (National Recovery Act), WPA (Works Progress Administration), PWA (Public Works Administration), CCC (Civilian Conservation Corps). There were new bridges, roads, public parks, post offices, and other make-work efforts; waste and benefit abounded.

The Depression sowed the seeds for Social Security and federal medical programs and contributed to widespread unionism. In Arlington, in 1932, 650 men sought jobs in a single day at the unemployment office. Many town officials rebated part of their salaries because people had defaulted on the taxes that were supposed to pay their salaries. In those days, there were no food stamps or organized welfare. Families helped their own. Churches did their best to aid their parishioners. But there simply was not enough money available. Many Arlington homes were sold for back taxes. As the shoe and textile plants moved south, many small home businesses sprang up to make ends meet.

But despite all the economic distress that struck America in the fall of 1929, the Casey family was still relatively untouched as we entered the 1930s. My father's construction business, Casey & Darcy, was obviously affected, but it was still intact, and his excellent reputation as a builder seemed to promise that the Caseys would sail through the Depression, not unscathed perhaps, but without the kind of personal and financial disaster we saw all around us. For years my father had built schools and hospitals and public buildings throughout the Boston suburbs. Then in 1930, everything fell apart: almost overnight his company collapsed when his partner neglected to purchase public liability insurance for one of the company's construction sites, Whidden Memorial Hospital in Everett. One Sunday, a boy who had trespassed on the work site fell and was gravely injured. Though I was too young to remember the precise nature of his injuries, the boy's family sued and won. The suit wiped out the company: my father lost everything. I watched my father, a forty-year-old man who till then had been prosperous enough to have servants, now work part time as a postal clerk, sorting mail in the Arlington post office. His two four-hour shifts per week paid him $1.25 an hour.

Though only eleven at the time, I was old enough to see and understand what was happening to my father, who was changing before my eyes. I would come home from school to find this formerly energetic, optimistic man sitting on the parlor sofa, smoking a cheap cigar and reading *Argosy* magazine. He had to ask my mother for spending money. My father was broke, but even worse, he was a broken man. His self-confidence destroyed, he found it increasingly difficult even to look for a job. Eventually he found one as a construction inspector for the state, but he was never again the same bouncy, happy-go-lucky man I had known.

After my father lost his business, my mother, a strong woman, had to become even stronger. She enrolled in the educational administration department at Boston University. Even when we literally did not have a dime and the house was about to be sold for back taxes, she did not break. Realizing my father could no longer support us and provide for our education, she announced the opening of a new school in the fall of 1933, the Bartlett Elementary School, named after the street we lived on in Arlington. She had no school facility, but she had an idea. If she could make it work, she'd find the quarters to house the idea. The "idea" was simple but ingenious. In an era when millions of people were dirt poor, the notion of opening a private, tuition-paying school doubtless seemed ridiculous. But Mother also understood we were living in a very special neighborhood, a stone's throw from Harvard and several other important universities. She notified the faculty and posted notices on the bulletin boards of MIT, Harvard, and Radcliffe, announcing the opening of the Bartlett School, which, she stated, was a school "for gifted children only." Almost immediately several professors enrolled their children, since, of course, they were convinced *their* children were gifted. My mother had also learned that to start first grade, a child needed to be five and a half years old by September 1, but to enter the second grade a child simply had to be able to read. So in the school's early years, Mother had more than her share of very young, very gifted second graders! But her idea worked: in the fall of 1933, twenty children were enrolled in Bartlett, including my sister Norine. As for the school's quarters, the parlor of our house was ample for the first year's needs.

Mother worked very hard at her business, the school, but she never neglected her children. As we were growing up, she kept us busy helping out at her school and at home with the chores. Over dinner, she would tell each of us her objectives for us. To me she said, "You'd make me so proud if you got good grades." I never earned terrific grades. I always passed, but both my sisters and my brother were straight-A students, and Mother thought there was no reason I shouldn't be, too.

"But, Mom," I'd respond, "I think it's just as important to be president of the student council."

"That's important, too," she would say, "but good grades mean that you have applied yourself, that you've worked hard."

Getting along with people was just as important as good grades, I insisted. "Why do you think I go down and cut Miss Bennett's grass for thirty-five cents?" I argued one night. Miss Bennett was my Latin teacher. "I probably wouldn't pass if I didn't cut her grass."

"Al," Mother said, clearly distressed, "what an awful thing to say. You're challenging that woman's integrity."

Whatever his failings, my father, too, insisted we all get a good education. And indeed we did: John went to MIT and did brilliantly; I went to Harvard, Norine to Wellesley, and Eva Marie to Regis. John, though only seventeen months my elder, was mistakenly enrolled in school a year early, so was always two, and sometimes three, years ahead of me.

Thanks to my mother, whose determination to make things right was unswerving, we were somehow able not only to survive but to prosper. (*Prosper* is perhaps the wrong term, but thanks to Mother's iron will and positive spirit, we never felt deprived or depressed.) Her school grew rapidly, as more and more parents discovered their children were gifted. Each year we gave up one more room of our house to make place for another classroom. Eventually the school took over one side of the house; even the former coal bin was overrun and turned into a music room. When the school occupied all seven rooms of that side of our three-story duplex, we moved to the other side. Before long, the invasive school usurped a number of rooms there as well. Later, the ever-growing school was relocated twice into vacated public school buildings in the neighboring town of Winchester.

Despite the fact that it was gradually taken over as a school, my family home in Arlington has remained a fixture in my life for most of the century. I lived there for twenty years, and since leaving home I have returned more than two hundred times to visit my family, to tour the neighborhood, to reminisce. My sister Norine, who took over the Bartlett School from my mother, still lives there today.

When I was in junior high school, my best friend was a neighborhood boy named Don Currier. A good student, Don was shorter than I and not as tough. One day he came up to me and said, "Al, Quentin Stevens has been transferred to our school and he's a known bully. That's why they're kicking him out of his other school. We want to set him straight from the first day. We got together and decided we needed somebody to knock his block off as soon as he gets here. We all voted for you."

"Why me?" I said. "Quentin Stevens is one tough turkey. I know him from Sunday school. Besides, you know I'm not the best fighter in school." I wore glasses that were always getting broken, and it was not from dropping them by mistake.

"But you're the *tallest*," Don said. And I was. "Al, the first time Quentin comes into the playground, just tackle him and that will be it."

Quentin's going to kill me, I thought. He's *way* tougher than I am. But now that my school friends had set me up, I had no choice. Or did I?

That week at Sunday school I took Quentin aside and said, somewhat nervously: "Quentin, I hear you are coming to our school. Everyone there is saying you're a bully. Everyone *expects* you to be a bully. You should prove that you're not, and I'll help you. If you want, you and I will be friends."

On my way home I wondered if Quentin really believed me. I couldn't sleep that night, worrying about what might happen to me the next day. When I did fall asleep, Quentin would suddenly appear in my dream, breathing fire, and I'd wake up in a sweat.

Before school the next morning, Quentin came over to my house. I saw who it was through the window and didn't want to answer the door. But I knew I had to.

"Al," Quentin said as I opened the door, "I've been thinking about what you said yesterday." Then he suddenly cocked his fists in front of his chest, as if he were going to start a fight.

I recoiled, and Quentin, still the bully, gave a broad smile.

"Just kidding," he said. And we went down to the playground together, already buddies. I never did have to fight him. But I had learned something: if you sense you're going to lose, you must recognize the need to compromise or neutralize your adversary's advantage. Fact was, if I'd taken on Quentin as my schoolmates wanted, he'd have knocked my block off.

*   *   *

When I was seventeen, I spent the summer working at the A&P in nearby Scituate. Since it was several miles from home, and I had to be at work early, I found a room in a nearby boardinghouse, proud to be on my own for the first time.

One day my mother got a call from her brother, my uncle Fred, who asked her if she knew where her son was living.

"In a boardinghouse," she said. "And he's paying his own rent," she added proudly.

"Try again," said my uncle.

She called me, and I was perplexed by her concern.

"I don't know what the problem could be," I said. "The room's very reasonable. My landlady, Bonnie, is very nice. Of course, I do get home pretty late, but she leaves the door open for me, and I've never seen anyone going in or out."

"Is that all?" Mother asked sternly.

"Well . . ." I paused. "She did say if there was a tie on the banister I shouldn't come upstairs, but should sleep on the couch." Whenever the tie was on the banister, a dollar was deducted from my weekly seven dollars' rent, which as far as I was concerned made sleeping on the couch definitely worthwhile.

The boardinghouse, it turned out, was a brothel. Poor mother, I thought she'd never recover: her own son living in a whorehouse!

When I was not at the A&P, I worked nights at the newly built local movie theater. I first helped install the seats, and when it opened I became an usher — seven nights a week. Every Sunday, I worked on a "Sunday-tripper" fishing boat, preparing bait on the trip out and cleaning the decks on the trip in. I also sold Singer sewing machine oil door-to-door for fifteen cents a bottle. And Band-Aids: I bought them wholesale and peddled them, also from door to door. The markup was 100 percent. But my best deal was shoestrings: I paid two cents a pair and sold them for ten cents! Early on, I began to get a clear fix on how middlemen prospered.

I didn't know it then, but I was also beginning to learn the basics of Casey's Law: if you want things to go right, you can't sit back and wait for them to happen. You have to steer things in the right direction.

Growing up in the shadow of Harvard, I dreamed of attending that venerable institution. And of course my mother constantly reminded us children how fortunate we were to live in the same neighborhood as Harvard and MIT and only a few miles from Wellesley College. At the start of my senior year, I filled out all the application forms and wrote an eloquent letter giving all the reasons why I should attend Harvard. To my dismay, I was turned down. I could have settled for another school, but my heart was set on Harvard. I decided the only thing to do was to spend another year studying hard and getting those better grades my mother kept talking about. I had saved up enough money to pay for part of the tuition at a nearby prep school, New Preparatory School, the following year, where indeed I did work very hard and got good grades. I passed my college boards, and this time Harvard accepted me. To be fair, Harvard also accepted eighteen of my New Preparatory classmates. To be fairer, only four of us graduated. That prep school, filled mainly with rich kids, many of whom had been expelled from the name preparatory schools of New England, was adept at getting the kids accepted. But though many were called, few were chosen. From that experience I learned not to take no for an answer if there was the slightest possibility of turning it into a yes. Most of us have to learn that lesson several times before it sinks in.

2

WORKING THROUGH HARVARD

URING MY UNDERGRADUATE YEARS at Harvard I took a
number of jobs. Our family still had little money, and it
was a real strain to put my older brother John through
MIT at the same time. My tuition was four hundred dollars a semester, and I had to earn most of it. I ran errands, delivered papers
and, on holidays, the mail. The pay was fifty cents an hour, and I
was delighted to get it.

One of my jobs was, once a month, to drive Harvard's Oldest
Living Graduate, who was in his nineties and lived in Cambridge,
to the cemetery. He wanted to visit with and talk to his classmates
each month, he said, and they were all at the cemetery. My fee?
Fifty cents an hour. One day the elderly but oh-so-sprightly
gentleman told me he wanted me to drive him to Woods Hole in
his car. He was on his way to spend the summer on Martha's Vine-
yard. His offer: five dollars.

"Mind now, I'm paying you only for the drive down, young
man," he warned. "I'm taking the car on the ferry to the Vine-
yard."

"Excuse me," I said, "but how will I get home?"

"That's your problem, Albert, not mine," said Harvard's Oldest Living Graduate. And indeed it was. In any case, I hitchhiked
home without much difficulty, five dollars richer.

Speaking of summer holidays, each June, President James
Bryant Conant of Harvard would move north to New Hampshire
for two or three months. Mrs. Ryan, who worked in the Harvard
employment office, was entrusted with the job of packing him,
and enlisted me to help. From the looks of the van, you'd have

thought he was moving out, never to return. Among other things, he always took his skis with him; none of us could ever figure out why, since he dutifully moved back to Cambridge in the fall, together with his skis.

Another college job was driving school children from the town of Winchester to Browne & Nichols, a prep school just up the Charles River from Harvard. Every morning between seven thirty and eight I would pick up my charges and deliver them to school. Then I would return at the end of the day and drive the children home again, for which I was paid the princely sum of six dollars a week per child.

One job I particularly enjoyed, for all sorts of reasons, was supervising the ushers at the Harvard football games. I had been an usher there myself as a high school kid. There were 120 ushers at every football game, whose "pay" was to see the game for free. During my freshman, sophomore, and junior years at Harvard, in 1939, 1940, and 1941 respectively, I worked my way up through the usher hierarchy, and by the time I left to go into the service I was top dog, earning seventy-five dollars per game, a truly meaningful sum. But I did work for my pay. At ten o'clock every Saturday morning when there was a home game, I met the 120 ushers and laid out the assignment for each. It was the first time I had been in charge of a number of people, and though I won't say it was overly challenging, the job did require planning and supervision. There were twenty sections in the stadium, and each section had a head usher (whose pay was five dollars a game) to whom five to six ushers reported (whose pay was a free ticket).

Closing up three libraries every night was another job; they were all in Harvard Square on the second or third floors above stores. I had to go up with my set of keys starting at nine thirty, turn out the lights, and lock the doors. In truth, that Einsteinian task had been given to the Harvard quarterback George Heiden, as part of his "merit" scholarship no doubt, and he had conned me into doing it for him for the usual fifty cents. I also used to spell three different custodians in the Harvard houses, or dormitories, for half an hour each evening so they could go and eat their supper. All these odd jobs paid relatively little, but to paraphrase Everett Dirksen: a couple of dollars here, a couple of dollars there, and pretty soon you're talking about real money.

Most afternoons I drove the little red motorboat called the *Harvard Pup,* assigned to the 150-pound crew coach Harvey Love. While the snow and sleet were swirling about, I was bundled up in a nice warm coat, in contrast to those poor preppies trying to make crew, all sitting there in their shorts, freezing to death in their shells on the Charles River.

It may sound from all the above that I had little time for classes, which was not true. I was a serious, though not brilliant, student. But I learned as much from my various working experiences as I did from my formal education. All those jobs proved to be excellent discipline for me, reinforcing another of my mother's basic precepts: time is very precious.

In 1940, when I was a sophomore, my brother, John, had already graduated from MIT and was working for the propeller division of Curtiss-Wright in Buffalo, New York. The aerospace companies, which were gearing up in a hurry because of the threat of war, had hired John and a number of his MIT classmates straight out of college. John and his friends had rented a house in Buffalo, which they called Locksley Hall. They had all chipped in and leased a Piper Cub, which they took regular turns flying every morning (yes, they all *did* have their pilot licenses).

One weekend I went up to Buffalo to visit John with a classmate whose father was driving him home from school. I spent the night at my brother's house, and was planning to hitchhike back to Harvard the next day, since I didn't have the money to take a train or bus. John's day to fly wasn't until the following Tuesday, but because of my weekend visit he wanted to take me up.

"Have you ever been up in an airplane?" John asked me.

"No," I replied.

"Would you like to?"

"I'd love to!"

We asked the fellow whose turn it was to fly that morning, a Saturday, if he would swap with John. "I'd like to take my brother up for a little spin," John explained. "Would you mind swapping?" The fellow said that unfortunately he had to be away on Tuesday, so he couldn't use John's day. "But I'll take your brother up," he offered magnanimously. I took John aside and asked him whether this guy really knew how to fly.

"He's the best pilot of the group," John said. "I'd rather have you go up with him than with me."

So I climbed into the Piper Cub, which was about as big as a coffee table, just a wing and an engine, and we took off. It was a two-seater: one person sat behind the other. The cockpit windows were Plexiglas, and two of them were broken. The "runway" was a bumpy field where the plane was kept, and the takeoff was so rough I was afraid I'd jar my teeth loose before we were airborne. After we'd been flying for a while my brother's friend yelled above the roar of the motor, "So, what do you think of *that*, Al?" he said.

"I think it's great!"

Then John's friend turned the plane's nose down and let it rip for a couple thousand feet before pulling up. "How do you like *that?*" he yelled, grinning from ear to ear.

"Terrific!" I yelled back. "If this is the way it goes, then this is the way it goes."

So he brought the nose up to make a power stall, which strains the engine and causes it to quit, at which point the pilot dips the nose down and the propeller catches, like push-starting a car.

"So what did you think of *that*, Al?" he said.

"Wonderful," I yelled, but I wasn't feeling quite as chipper as I sounded.

He did another stall, but this time, heading down, the propeller failed to catch. As the ground grew alarmingly closer, with still no motor, John's friend eased the nose upward and flew the plane like a glider. Meanwhile, down below, my brother was watching with growing dread. "What am I ever going to tell Mother?" he later told me he was asking himself. "Hey, Mom, I sent Al up in our plane with a friend of mine, and he died in a terrible crash."

The fellow flying the plane (I hardly dare call him a pilot) said, "Hold on tight. We've got to go down now. We have no choice." And down we started. There wasn't a chance in hell we were going to make it back to the airstrip, I figured, and wondered if the reckless "pilot" had any idea where he was heading. As the earth came closer, I worked up my courage to ask.

"See that farm down there?" He pointed. "I'm going to try to land in the farmyard."

I was sure we were going to hit the high tension wires I saw rushing toward us, but somehow we managed to sneak under them. Barely. By maybe two inches, in my impartial judgment. The propeller never did start, so we made what was called a dead stick landing in the farm field. We bumped like hell, but nothing was broken, and the plane finally jiggled to a stop. I climbed out, my knees like jelly.

"Nice landing," I said. John, who had followed our flight with fear and trembling, rushed up, hugging me and kissing me as if I had come back from the dead — which, in a sense, I guess I had.

Flying with John's friend taught me to calculate a little more carefully the pros and cons of a situation before plunging into it. I was damn lucky not to have been killed. I was still pretty much a kid, and when you're young life seems to stretch endlessly before you, and risks are part of the game. But there's a fine line between being foolhardy and taking risks. Part of wisdom, I later realized, was learning how to differentiate between the two. My young "pilot" had been foolhardy — which means, literally, "crazy bold" — taking unnecessary risks without weighing the possible consequences.

I learned a lot about Murphy's Law in the summer of 1941, when I worked as a dining room and cocktail waiter at the Cliff Hotel in

North Scituate, Massachusetts, a beach community twenty miles south of Boston. The hotel was owned by the Summers, a Boston family.

The maître d', a Monsieur Roger Boderat, was a former professional boxer from Belgium. He hired ten college boys to help prepare the hotel for the summer (it was closed during the winter months). The work was backbreaking: we had to mix and pour cement; lug furniture out of storage, scrape it down, and paint it; and restore the warped and broken flooring.

Getting the place in shape took three weeks, and we worked twelve hours a day, seven days a week. In return, we were given room and board, plus twenty dollars a month throughout the three summer months, waiting on tables.

Nearly every evening during this preparation and cleanup period there were class reunion dinners. The hotel charged the class chairmen fifty dollars each night for our services as waiters. And in return for our noble efforts, we each received a dollar in pay, while Roger Boderat kept forty dollars for himself. Anyone who complained about the seeming disparity was fired on the spot.

Most of us toed the line because we needed the work, and we had been looking forward to a summer of pretty girls and big tips. The kitchen crew were all African Americans and kept similarly in line by Cookie, a large man who had a habit of waving an oversized chef's knife for emphasis whenever he issued an order.

As much as we detested Monsieur Boderat, there were times, most of them unscheduled and unplanned, when we got our revenge. The first occurred while we were serving one of those class dinners, and it involved Jim Logan, a brute of a young Irishman from Dorchester who had a football scholarship to Wake Forest. There was a set pattern for traffic between the dining room and the kitchen: you always stayed to your right in order to avoid traffic coming in the opposite direction. One night Big Jim, carrying a tray loaded with ten large glass water pitchers, thought he would take a short cut. He started through the Out door only to meet a fellow waiter barreling in. The class speakers were in full sway when the ten water pitchers soared — several feet it seemed —

into the air and landed on the floor, most of them — nine out of ten, as I recall — shattering into thousands of shards. The thunderous noise brought the festivities to an immediate standstill and Boderat running, his look implying that the guillotine would have been too kind and swift a fate for Logan. But taking a closer look at Logan's size and stature, the wise maître d' decided that, indeed, discretion was the better part of valor. So he limited his penalty to a heavily accented, but nonetheless scathing, verbal assault.

While none of us was ever slated to make the Waiters Hall of Fame, some of our little group were downright awful, which had the virtue of driving Boderat up the wall. On Sunday we always had three entrées: steak, chicken, and lobster. One Sunday a neophyte waiter, whose name I have long forgotten but whose misfortunes I remember well, took orders from his four tables, then went to the kitchen and ordered all the steaks for his tables and dutifully brought them in: one for this table, two for that, and so on. Back to the kitchen he went and ordered all the chicken requests, which in due course he proudly if not promptly delivered to the various tables; then a third trip to the kitchen to order the lobsters. Needless to say, the steak eaters were long finished by the time the chickens arrived, and by the time the lobsters put in their belated appearance, dessert and coffee had already been served to the steak and chicken folk. Monsieur Boderat decided, without too much introspection, that the guilty waiter was clearly not cut out for this high calling and dismissed him forthwith, with a flurry of French that, had the poor lad understood, would doubtless have destroyed his self-esteem forever.

At one point I was put in charge of the outdoor buffet, which was alongside and a floor below the dining room and main kitchen. We were tempted to pass trays of food and dirty dishes up to a colleague in a dining room window, but it was outlawed for all the obvious reasons. The long, legal route led out the back door of the kitchen and around a walkway to a patio, a long trek. On my tour of duty, lunch had taken longer than usual, and we decided to hurry with the cleanup. I leaned out a dining room window and told a buddy, Paul Lamothe, to pass me up the dirty dishes. All went well until he passed up a particularly heavy load — just as Monsieur Boderat appeared on the patio.

Paul had trouble lifting the load. I leaned out as far as I could to grasp the tray.

Monsieur Boderat glanced up and shouted, in his heavy Belgian accent: "Paul, vat in de world are you *doing?*"

Paul, stung by the words of the master, let go of the tray, which I was still grasping precariously. Try as I might, however, I couldn't lift the damn thing or even keep the tray on an even keel. Dishes and glasses started to slide off, slowly at first, then faster and faster, plunging like misguided missiles onto the concrete patio below for what seemed an eternity. Unfortunately, none struck the apoplectic maître d'.

If I had not been the favorite waiter of the hotel owner, I too would have been discharged on the spot. As for Paul, I saved his skin by declaring magnanimously to Monsieur Boderat that it was all my fault. "I cannot tell a lie," I protested, wondering if in Belgium they had ever heard of young George's legendary cherry tree. "It was all my doing."

Boderat fumed but, aware of my relationship with the Summers, restrained himself — no easy task.

During that memorable summer at the Cliff Hotel, I learned from Roger Boderat that while it's fine to push people hard, never push them beyond the breaking point.

In fact, Roger had not only been pushing us unmercifully but also constantly taking advantage of us. One night we waiters gathered in solemn assembly and took a blood oath to get even. Our only problem was we hadn't the faintest notion how. But we bided our time, waiting for the occasion to present itself. Labor Day weekend, with time running out, we finally decided to act. On Monday evening Mr. Summers hosted a particularly lavish dinner in the cocktail lounge, called the Bamboo Room by the customers and the Bad Booze Room by the help. There were about eighty people at the dinner, and the waiters brought drinks to their tables from a service bar set up in a hallway behind the cocktail lounge bar. As usual, Roger was shouting at us in the service bar hallway while bowing obsequiously to the owner's family whenever he was in the lounge. We had put up with him for three months plus, and this was our last chance. When monsieur made the tactical mistake of resurfacing in the hallway where all ten of us had gathered, without preparation or even a signal we picked him up and carried him over our heads back into the lounge, where we deposited him smack on top of the crêpes suzettes he had been lovingly preparing at the owner's table.

Vast confusion followed, and the police were called in, though finally no charges were pressed. When we reconnoitered at the end of the evening, knowing we would be leaving the next morning, we all agreed to sign a pact: the next time any of us saw Roger we would kill him, no matter where, no matter when.

Years later, when I went to work at the Times Mirror Company in Los Angeles, Harry Volk, then chairman of Union Bank, invited me to lunch at his club in the Union Bank Building on the corner of Wilshire Boulevard and Western Avenue. Wouldn't you know, barely was I seated when I looked up to see, approaching our table from the dark recesses of the room, none other than Roger Boderat, who was then the maître d' of the club. It had been more than two decades since we had seen each other, but there was instant recognition on both our parts. Alas, because of my earlier pledge, I was forced to kill him on the spot, thus spoiling my inaugural lunch at Times Mirror.

At Harvard a lot of us were speeding up our studies to finish college before we were drafted. I was the class of 1943. War was declared early in December 1941, so during the second semester, in the spring of 1942, I began doubling up on my classes, then attended the summer session so I could finish college early. Like many of my classmates, by the fall of 1942 I had compiled enough course credits to graduate — in my case, with a degree in economics. But I had to take an oral exam, because the school was waiving certain other requirements for my degree. Three Harvard economics professors questioned me in a building across the street from Adams House.

One of the professors was John Dunlop, who would later serve on several labor commissions under President Kennedy. Professor Dunlop had taught me in a course called Ec. 81, Labor Economics, which was the history of the labor movement. To complete that course, I had written a paper about the Reuther Plan, named after United Auto Workers president Walter Reuther, who proposed converting existing automobile factories to war production. To write my paper, I had actually contacted Mr. Reuther personally, and this evidently had made a big impression on Professor Dunlop. He liked students who showed unusual initiative.

During the oral exam, I could tell from Professor Dunlop's expression I was not doing very well. In fact, I was doing damn poorly. I was nervous, and Professor Dunlop was clearly disappointed that I was not demonstrating the kind of ability I had shown in Ec. 81.

Suddenly, the building next to Adams House caught fire. Two of the professors headed for the window. We could hear the fire engines clanging up the street and people shouting. Professor Dunlop did not move. Instead, he reached over, put his hand on my shoulder, and said, "Stay here, Al. I admire what you're planning to do, volunteering for the armed services, but I'd like to know what particular aspects of economics we could question you on so that you could give a better account of yourself than you've given so far today." So we discussed parts of the labor economics course he had taught me, including the Reuther Plan. When the other two professors returned from their rubbernecking interlude, Professor Dunlop said to them, "I'd like to take over the questions for a bit, because I had Al in one of my classes."

I answered the rest of the questions brilliantly.

Long after I had forgotten what I learned in Professor Dunlop's course, I remembered the relationship we had established. Professor Dunlop knew that, in his course at least, I had been a conscientious student. He also knew that conscientious students can get nervous in an oral exam and not give a good account of themselves. He and I had a relationship. Without that relationship, I might have failed my exam, perhaps graduated a year later, and probably not have been able to return to Harvard after the war to attend business school. When I was CEO of Times Mirror and, later, American Airlines, I still remembered Professor Dunlop, who clearly did not believe in Murphy's Law. In my oral exam, something was going wrong; he decided to make it go right.

Before I headed off to the service, I went over to the Harvard Business School admissions office one September afternoon in 1942 and filled out the application forms. I was accepted on the spot, since, because of the war, there were relatively few applicants. When I went back the next day and explained that I wanted a deferment until after the war, the dean of admissions rose to his feet and flung out his arms. I figured he had studied in France and was going to give me a Gallic embrace. "It's a noble thing you're doing," he told me. "You can rest assured: there'll always be a place for you at Harvard Business School."

Boy, that was easy, I thought as I left the dean's office. I went home and told my mother, with considerable pride, that I had been accepted to Harvard Business School as soon as the war was over.

"Did you get that in writing, Albert?" she asked. "I mean about the deferment?"

"Of course not, Mother. The dean gave me his word."

As usual, Mother was right.

3

THE ARMY, POKER,
AND SOUTHERN PACIFIC

B ACK IN THE DAYS when I was making seventeen dollars a
week at the A&P in Scituate, I used to risk part of my
paycheck — not to mention the potential wrath of my
mother — by leaving horse bets in the milk bottles. If I go to the
track today, I always use the same system I taught myself as an ado-
lescent. I do not bet on the horse that at post time has the biggest
improvement in odds from the newspaper morning line. I bet on
the second, third, and fourth horses that have the greatest change
from the morning line, and I bet them across the board. It cost me
eighteen dollars, six dollars for each horse. Nine times out of ten
I won, but not a lot because seldom did all three horses pay.

In the army, which I entered shortly after passing Professor
Dunlop's exam, I played cards religiously every noon, usually for
nickels and dimes but sometimes for more.

Actually, just getting into the service was a struggle. I first
tried to enlist in the navy in Boston and was turned down because
I couldn't pass the eye exam. I suffered from progressive myopia, a
condition that defies the laws of nature: your eyes get worse until
you're twenty-nine, then they get better (today I have better eyesight than ever). So I went down to New York and tried again
there. Someone had told me that they were so lenient there that if
your body was warm, you were in. Not so. Again I was turned
down because of my eyesight. So I went up to Buffalo and made
a third effort. Three strikes, Casey; so now what do you do? I finally traveled to Westfield, Massachusetts, near Springfield, where
I was able to enlist in the army reserve — whose physical require-

ments were much less rigorous than the regular army's — and sign up for a six-month radio repair course. Every weekend I would take the train from Westfield back to Boston to see Ellie, the young woman I had fallen in love with.

Her full name was Eleanor Welch, and she was the sister of a close friend of mine at Harvard, Andy Welch Jr. Andy was a year behind me — class of 1944 — but we had taken a number of classes together and enjoyed each other's company. Andy was a handsome devil and very charismatic. He was the class secretary, the highest position to which a student could be elected by his classmates. But it was not Andy who introduced me to Ellie. One day at the end of my junior year, a friend of mine, Larry Corbett, asked me if I would go on a blind date with a girl he knew.

"Sure," I said. "But I don't have a car."

"That's okay. I'll pick you up and bring your date with me," he said.

My parents were curious to meet the young lady. I was embarrassed, explained this was a blind date, that I hadn't met the girl myself. But when Larry arrived, he and my date walked up to the house where my parents and I were sitting on the front porch.

"Hi, Al," Larry said, "I'd like you to meet Eleanor Welch. And Ellie, this is Mr. and Mrs. Casey."

My mother looked at the girl — who, I confess, had taken my breath away — and said, "You aren't *Andy* Welch's daughter, are you?"

"Yes, I am," replied Ellie (no one addressed her as Eleanor). "Why do you ask?"

"Because I knew your father many years ago. In fact, we once went out on a date together!"

I didn't see Ellie again until the fall, because I was working — that was my infamous summer at the Cliff Hotel — but as soon as I got back to Harvard I called and asked her out again. I was totally smitten with Ellie, who was only seventeen, and I never went seriously with anyone else. At a mature twenty-one, I was already sure I was going to marry her.

The army reserve was lenient about overnight weekend

passes, so virtually every Saturday afternoon I'd take the train from Westfield to Springfield and on to Boston, where Ellie would pick me up in her Dad's 1939 Nash. I'd usually arrive in Boston about eleven, and we would drive over to the Somerset Hotel on Copley Square to have a drink before the bar closed down at quarter to twelve. Going back on Sunday, there were no trains to Westfield, so I had to hitchhike from Brookline along Route 9. Ellie and I were very much in love, and although we wanted to get married we decided it would be best to wait until the war was over. Besides, Ellie was still very young, her parents reminded us.

Fortunately for me, Ellie's father was a Harvard man, class of 1913, and lived and breathed "for fair Harvard." He commended me on the wisdom of my choice of college, adding, "Frankly, Al, I couldn't imagine my daughter marrying anyone who wasn't a Harvard man."

Upon completion of the radio-repair course, my fellow reservists and I were inducted into the real army at Fort Devens, Massachusetts, and assigned to the Signal Corps at Fort Monmouth, New Jersey. After basic training, we were given a battery of aptitude tests, as a result of which I was assigned to a cryptography class, where I learned how to encode and decode army messages, as opposed to cryptoanalysis, which is the breaking of enemy codes. I liked cryptography, learned it quickly, and soon became an instructor. The army was faced with constantly changing needs, however, and suddenly I was shipped off to a ninety-day immersion course in Italian, then transferred to Pine Camp, near the Canadian border, to guard Italian and German prisoners.

While at Pine Camp, New York, fellow PFCs (Privates First Class) Timmy Murphy, Bob Maguire, and I took off without formal, or even informal, permission, to go home for Mother's Day. Surely, we figured, the army wouldn't mind our going to visit our mothers! The real reason for the trip in my case was to see Ellie, whom I hadn't seen for weeks. During the Mother's Day weekend, everything on the trip to Boston went off without a hitch, but coming back to Watertown — the closest stop to Pine Camp — we were picked up on the train by the military police who, discovering we were AWOL, carted us unceremoniously back to camp, where they turned us over to the Pine Camp MPs, who locked us up for the night. Languishing in our cell, I asked Timmy and Bob what they thought would happen to us.

"I heard the MPs talking about a court-martial," Timmy said.

"We were only gone *two* days," Maguire lamented. "Is that so serious?"

Well, it turned out the army, which didn't seem to have an Irish sense of humor, thought our peccadillo was a grave matter, and though we were not court-martialed, our cases were turned over to the company commander.

I was terrified. The proceedings were brief and abrupt. We tried to make a case for Mother's Day being extenuating, but the army would have none of it. The company commander who presided was probably against apple pie, too. Be that as it may, Murphy (no relation to the Murphy of the Law) and Maguire were transferred forthwith from Pine Camp and dispatched to the Philippines.

"As for you, Casey, you're confined to quarters until further notice," the company commander said. That sounded ominous, I thought: where could they be sending me that would be worse than the Philippines?

As it happened, at that time I was playing second base for the camp baseball team, and the team was doing well. Since there was only one month left in the season, the brass had apparently decided not to break up a winning team. In any case, by the time the baseball season ended, the army's personnel requirements had changed again, the memory of my crime and punishment had apparently been more than offset by my batting average, and thanks to my college education and a reasonably high IQ test score, I was assigned to officer candidate school at Fort Monmouth, New Jersey. It struck me as rather odd, even unfair, that I was being rewarded for a military misdemeanor, but who was I to question higher authority?

From my milk-bottle horse-betting days, you may have gathered there is a bit of gambler's instinct buried — none too deeply — in my genetic makeup. Poker, too, held an unmistakable fascination for me, and throughout college, as well as during my army stint, I played often and long. Not for any great stakes, but there's an undeniable aspect of poker that carries over into your business life: you learn to read people, you exercise your mind by keeping close track of the cards, you learn when to hold 'em and when to fold 'em (good money after good versus good money after bad), and you learn the power of bluff* and when to call a bluff.

In my post-army years, when I was out in the so-called big world, I continued playing poker with friends and business associates. There were many memorable poker nights (remember: socializing with business friends has — in addition to the pleasure of the event itself — a bonding effect that often carries over into your work). I remember two such poker nights especially.

Perhaps the one I remember most vividly is the night I won $11,000. That night I had two queens and two sixes in the first four cards. Opposite me was a very nice fellow from Dallas, a wealthy oil mogul named Paul Meek. We were playing seven-card stud. In this game you get two cards down, four up, and the final card down. I assumed he had two clubs down, since the first up two cards were clubs, and he bet heavily after receiving his fifth card, also a club.

While we continued betting and raising each other's hands, our tall stacks of red, white, and blue chips were quickly depleted as the pot grew to cover most of the table's center. However, in this game each player also had IOU chits he could pull out, sign, and throw into the pot as he wished.

Paul's sixth card was also a club, so it was obvious, the way he was betting, that he already had a club flush. At that point those who had not already dropped out folded. However, their interest in the pot remained keen. Then Paul made a terrible mistake; he made a bet of only two hundred dollars as we drew the last down card. One of his clubs showing was a six, which meant that my only possibilities were the last six or one of the two remaining

*See chapter 5, the episode I could have called "Bluffing Nelson Rockefeller."

queens. I threw in two hundred dollars to call him and he said, "I guess I should have bet two thousand dollars." If he had, I would have dropped out; but for two hundred dollars, I had little to lose and a lot to gain.

"You damn well should have, but you didn't," I said. On the last card down, I had caught the case six (the last six), which gave me a full house, sixes and queens. And I knew what he had.

"I'll bet another five thousand dollars," I said.

"Good God, Al, you know what *I've* got, but I don't know what *you* have," Paul said. "Why don't you bet the way I did?"

"Because you made a mistake," I replied.

He sat there, everyone watching and wondering what Paul was going to do. "I couldn't go home with this crowd if you faked me out," he finally said. So he put up $5,000 to call. And I won $11,000.

"That's dirty pool, Al," Paul said. "I let *you* stay in the game for two hundred dollars."

"That was your mistake," I replied.

You sometimes get caught in such situations. Paul *had* to call. And when you do, you've got to be prepared to take the loss. But I've never, in my many years of play, some for high stakes, lost more than $7,500 a night. That was always my loss limit.

One of the greatest insults I suffered was overhearing two friends talking about my poker addiction.

"That damn Casey," said one to the other, "He plays poker half the night."

"I heard that remark," I intervened, "and I resent it. I play poker *all* night."

Perhaps my most memorable all-nighter — certainly my most successful — was in 1982 at the A Bar A, a ranch in Wyoming. There were several games going on simultaneously, and I moved from one to the other. It seemed as if I could do no wrong that night, as I won pot after pot at one table, then far more than my share at another. Unlike my night with Paul Meek, I never won big, but I won steadily. As dawn broke, I stuffed my winnings — which consisted of a jumble of greenbacks and IOUs — into my pockets and headed home. I had no idea how much I had won, but the next afternoon, when I resurfaced, I counted $7,000 in cash. Not bad, I thought. Then I counted the IOUs: $25,000, each signed by the debtor. I decided never to hound any of the losers; I did wonder, however, how many would pay up. To my surprise, every last one did, so my total evening's efforts had paid off to the tune of $32,000.

In business, as in gambling, you need to understand your strengths and limitations and, most important, have the confidence that your strong suits will carry you through a given situation. If you truly believe in them, your strengths will, almost always, overcome your limitations.

When I was a graduate student or army lieutenant, playing poker for peanuts, I of course never dreamed I would one day be playing cards with the Speaker of the House, Tip O'Neill, or negotiating to buy a television station from a former president of the United States, Lyndon Johnson. However, I had a certain conviction that I would succeed at whatever I did, a belief instilled in me early on by Mother and reinforced through many subsequent experiences. Nor was that a dream. Or a boast. Anything truly interesting in business — or life — is a gamble. The trick is not to think you're going to win all the time. What makes a winner is winning more times than losing — and the higher your percentage above .500 the better. There are of course times of caution, of hedging your bets, but those whose whole life is based on caution never, in my experience, come out on top. I've been lucky to win more times than I've lost.

As soon as the war was over, Ellie and I were married, on August 25, 1945. It was a small wedding, with only the families and a few friends present, at Saint Theresa's Church in West Roxbury. Tempering our happiness was the sad fact that Ellie's older brother, Andy Junior, who had joined the navy two years earlier and volunteered for the submarine corps, had been declared lost at sea the previous March. It was a rainy, blustery day; in fact, the weather was so bad our planned flight to New York was canceled, and we took the train, a crowded, five-hour trip. I was still in the service, with only a three-day leave to get married, but we had booked a room at the Roosevelt Hotel right next to Grand Central Station and had a wonderful night of dinner and dancing at the Starlight Roof of the Waldorf Astoria. The next day we went to Long Branch, New Jersey, where I had rented a two-room apartment.

On Monday, two days into married life, I bid Ellie good-bye and went on field maneuvers for three weeks. Though the war was over, the armed forces were taking no chances. I hated the idea of leaving Ellie behind, if only for a few weeks. But Ellie took it in good stride, and left me with a kiss and a smile. That, I was to learn, was to be her stock in trade through the years: time after time the demands of my job forced me to cancel plans she'd been counting on, and never once was there a rebuke or reproach. Always the understanding smile, which was the visible, outward sign of her nature but also a measure of her love, for she knew that I would never willingly upset our well-laid plans unless I was absolutely forced to.

My last army assignment, in August 1946, was running a separation center at Camp Atterbury in Indiana. From there I wrote a letter to the Harvard Business School announcing that I was about to be discharged and would be entering the fall class, as had been promised to me four years earlier.

A few days later a letter came back.

Dear Mr. Casey:

Thank you for your letter of August 14th.

I'm afraid we cannot accept you in this year's class. In fact, we are inundated with applicants who, like you, are returning from the service. And frankly, Mr. Casey, they are more qualified than you.

Sincerely,

Stanley Teele
Dean

I was irate. A promise was a promise. As soon I was discharged I rushed back to Cambridge and at nine in the morning plunked myself in the dean's office.

"I'm sorry, the dean can't see you," his assistant told me.

"I'll wait," I said. And I did, for two hours, until the dean, probably fearing for his safety, if not his life, agreed to hear my story. I explained the promise made to me in 1942.

"Ah," Dean Teele said, "but the man who made it is retired now. He lives up in Maine."

"Call him," I insisted. "I'm sure he'll remember."

We talked another fifteen minutes, on all manner of things. At one point, Dean Teele stood up, stuck out his hand, and said: "Welcome to Harvard Business School."

My father-in-law, Andy Welch Sr., owned the Hemingway House in Eastham, on Cape Cod (in New England houses are often known by the name of the previous owner, rather than the current one). This was the summer of 1947, when Ellie was also at Harvard, working in the English department's graduate literature program. Her father would pick Ellie and me up every Friday afternoon in the summer and drive us to Cape Cod for the weekend. One weekend when we were on our way to the Cape, Ellie's father went on at great length about how much Harvard meant to him and said his class was going to have a reunion clambake on Sunday morning on the beach in Dennis.

"Most of the people there, Al, will be of my generation," he said, "but I'd really like you and Ellie to be with us," he said. "Other people will be bringing their children. You'll have a good time."

"We'd love to," I said.

The night before the clambake, Ellie and I went to a humdinger of a party. I overimbibed to a startling degree, so that the next morning, when it came time to go to the clambake, I was in no condition to be sociable. It was suggested, not very subtly, that I walk a decent distance down the beach and stay there until the party was over, at which point someone would come to fetch me.

Oh, how my head was splitting!

I walked down the beach about half a mile, found a log, and sat down. I did absolutely nothing but sit there, feeling miserable in mind as well as body. As much as my head hurt, my pride hurt worse, for I could imagine what the Welches must be thinking about their new son-in-law.

Eventually a tall, patrician-looking man I'd never seen before came ambling along the beach. With all of us wearing shorts or bathing suits for the clambake, he looked a bit out of place: he was fully dressed, in a sports shirt, slacks, and a natty pair of shoes. To my surprise and embarrassment, he sat down on the log beside me and introduced himself.

"My name is John Walsh," he said. "Who are you?"

"I'm Al Casey."

"Oh, you're the fellow who married Andy Welch's daughter."

I was ashamed to say yes, convinced I was not in good enough shape to be considered part of the Welch family. But after we had talked for a few minutes I did confess that I was indeed Ellie's husband and that I was finishing Harvard Business School.

"You know, anybody who gets into Harvard Business School or graduates from Harvard Business School has to have a good enough brain," Walsh said. "But that isn't what's important to succeed in the business world."

Then he listed all the other characteristics he believed were needed to be a successful businessman. The first and most important was compassion for others. This went hand in hand with understanding, which was in turn linked with vision. Finally, Walsh said there was a fourth quality, which struck me as different from the others. And that was not to do things in the same way all the time.

My mind was not on what I might call "red alert," hardly in the best of shape to receive and assimilate this imparted wisdom. And although I would have preferred to be the only bump on the log, I did my best to appear conscious and, hopefully, attentive.

"What do you plan to do after you graduate?" Walsh asked suddenly.

I shrugged, my mind thrashing to find some bright, intriguing response that would duly impress my friendly inquisitor.

"Look for a job," was the best I could come up with.

"I'm in charge of the Wall Street financial office in New York for Southern Pacific Railroad," Mr. Walsh said. "How'd you like to work for us when you graduate? We're looking for a bright young man to join us."

Through the haze of the setting sun, not to mention my man-made inner mist, I groped to understand: Mr. Walsh was offering me a *job?*

"Of course, sir, I'd be delighted to be considered —"

"Not considered, Al. I'm *offering* you the job. But there are a few caveats. First I want to suggest a few courses I'd like you to take during your final two terms. If you take these courses, the job is yours."

"You really mean it?" I asked incredulously.

"Well, I expect you to make good grades in those classes, of course, but from what I've heard I don't think that should be a problem for you," Mr. Walsh reassured me. In fact, in business school I was working hard and doing well, much better than I had done as an undergraduate. I couldn't believe my luck. All my classmates were just beginning to look for a job; to sew up mine eight months in advance of graduation would be an unbelievable coup. And with a company like Southern Pacific to boot!

Walsh told me to study public utility regulation, transportation, and finance, the three areas he wanted me to focus on. Finance was no problem, because I was already majoring in it. However, I certainly wasn't interested in transportation. And the last thing I wanted to study was public utility regulation. But I recognized that following his advice was a small price to pay for the guarantee of a job.

A few months before I was due to graduate from business school, I called John Walsh. Was the job offer still good? Of course it was; he had given me his word. How was I doing in my three courses? Fine, just fine. Then you'll start right after graduation.

Toward the end of the year, I made an appointment to see Mr. Walsh in New York, to visit my future place of work and look for a place to live. The Southern Pacific office was on the twenty-second floor of 165 Broadway, on the corner of Cortlandt and Broadway. It was a very old-fashioned office — several workers had rolltop desks, and the filing system looked right out of Charles Dickens. I noticed, too, that there was a well-placed spittoon next to a man introduced to me as Mr. Barry, who, I noticed, made frequent and copious use of the gleaming brass cuspidor.

John B. Reid was the assistant to Mr. Walsh and would be my nominal superior, though I worked for everybody. My title: the assistant to the assistant to the vice president of finance. The pay: $375 a month, which translated into $4,500 a year. That made me the second-highest-salaried graduate of that year's Harvard Business School. The highest salary, $5,500 a year, went to an oil engineer who took a job with Exxon.

Ellie and I had come into New York by train on the twenty-seventh of December, just after the major snowstorm of Christmas Day, when twenty-seven inches fell. We stayed at the Roosevelt Hotel, our honeymoon hotel. With my salary, there was no way we could think of renting an apartment in Manhattan, but a friend of Ellie's dad owned a number of garden apartments in Baldwin, Long Island, where we rented a third-floor walk-up one bedroom for $65 a month.

Having secured a place to live, I formally joined Southern Pacific in February 1948 — about an hour and a half after I received my MBA from Harvard — and stayed with the company for thirteen years, eleven on Wall Street with Walsh and Reid, and two at the home office in San Francisco following Walsh's untimely death.

Southern Pacific Railroad was a consolidation of many rail lines, notably the Central Pacific, which teamed up with Union Pacific for the first transcontinental rail line; the Texas and New Orleans, which ran from El Paso to New Orleans, and from Dallas to Brownsville, Texas; the Saint Louis Southwestern, which ran from Dallas to Saint Louis; and of course the Southern Pacific itself, which ran from Portland, Oregon, to El Paso and had two lines the length of California, one along the coast and another through the San Joaquin Valley. In the nineteenth century, and well into the twentieth, the company was enormously wealthy but also had widespread political influence, by reason of the important roles played in the making of modern America by its founders: Collis Potter Huntington, Mark Hopkins, Leland Stanford, and Charles Crocker. In addition to the rail lines themselves, Southern Pacific also had important operations in the fields of oil pipelines, land development, warehousing, and — perhaps in part as a defensive measure rather than by conviction — trucking.

At Southern Pacific I learned many business lessons, particularly an understanding of stock brokerage firms and investment bankers. Our office serviced the company's stock and debt holders, that is, it paid interest on bonds, dividends on stocks, and transferred stock certificates. Also it raised funds through bond and equipment trust issues.

In those days, a company listed on the New York Stock Exchange had to have a stock transfer office located south of Canal Street. Most companies appointed commercial banks as their stock transfer agents; however, many large firms, such as AT&T, U.S. Steel, Bethlehem Steel, and almost all the railroads, were still doing their own transfer work, keeping records of changes in ownership of the company's securities.

Besides a small sales office in Rockefeller Center, the Wall Street office was Southern Pacific's only branch office in the East. In addition to the regular stock transfer and interest payment duties, all the company's odd jobs ended up in our hands, such as filing required reports — monthly, quarterly, and annually — to the Securities and Exchange Commission and the New York Stock Exchange, arranging for the sale and closing of bond issues, making final settlements on matured bond issues. My early years at Southern Pacific provided me with an unbelievable variety of business experiences. Since I was the first new employee in the

New York office since 1939, I constantly volunteered to take on all possible assignments. I often didn't have either the experience or training to undertake half the tasks I volunteered for, but I brought a willing attitude and put in a lot of overtime. I attacked the problems facing me from every possible angle, often looking to case studies I had read as part of my MBA program, to find parallels or seek guidance. I took nothing for granted, challenged every assumption built into the situation at hand. And John Walsh, a gentleman as well as solid businessman, always made himself available for counsel or advice.

We were not permitted to fly because flying was a competitive form of transportation, so I traveled extensively by train across the United States — from New York through the Sierras to the West Coast, and from Portland, Oregon, to New Orleans — writing property descriptions for new bond issues. Later, I was often directly involved in the sale and closing of new bond issues. And I was required to fill out periodic reports to the Securities and Exchange Commission, disclosing redemptions, sales, and purchases of stocks and bonds.

In 1951 or 1952, I became aware of a clever conspiracy devised by one of our paying tellers and a woman who worked in the auditing office. When someone came by to cash in bond coupons, the teller would verify the bank's count and draw a check to redeem the coupons. To cancel the coupons, the teller would punch holes in them and string them. However, the teller would fold some of the coupons in half before he began punching them. As he passed through the stack of coupons he would studiously miss the folded ones, thereby not canceling them. He would place a colored rubber band around the bundles that were not completely canceled, as a signal to the woman in the auditing office, who would remove the coupons and, a few days later, present them for payment again. She and the teller were splitting the proceeds 50–50.

When I caught on to what they were doing, I immediately reported the matter to John Walsh, who fired both of them before turning the matter over to the proper authorities. I wish I could say I was impressed by the ingenuity of those two, but in fact I could only wonder how anyone could so betray the trust that had been placed in them.

There were some problems that defied solution, including the search for the holder of a $100,000 bond of Pacific Electric Railroad (a subsidiary of Southern Pacific that provided commuter service to the Los Angeles area). When a bond issue is sold, temporary paper bonds are issued until permanent, engraved steel ones can be made. The steel bonds are later exchanged for the temporaries. Looking over some original work papers, I found out that that group of bonds had been sold in 1910. In the records, opposite temporary bond number T37, the letters H S A were written in pencil. The preceding and succeeding bond numbers were purchased by a man named Henry Huntington, who was the nephew of one Collis P. Huntington, a very wealthy easterner who had moved west years before. (Collis's widow, by the way, who had refused to move west with him, married Henry after her husband's death. Henry built a Park Avenue–style mansion for her in San Marino; today it houses the Henry E. Huntington Library and Art Collection, which contains two of Gainsborough's most celebrated paintings, *Pinky* and *Blue Boy*.) I learned, by a little sleuthing, that Henry had an abiding interest in the Hispanic Society of America and had contributed regularly to that organization. Which leads me back to the mystery bond. I presumed that Henry had earmarked the bond to go to the HSA, but after extensive, unsuccessful searching we had to ask Chemical Bank, the trustee, to return the $100,000 that we had put up to settle the maturity. If the rightful owner ever made a claim we guaranteed to pay it. So far as I know, the bond is still out there, waiting to make someone a very happy man or woman.

Speaking of a happy man and woman, the only shadow over our happy marriage was the discovery that we couldn't have children. When I was nine or ten years old I was repeatedly X-rayed for a troubled appendix. In those days, doctors were not yet fully aware of the consequences of X rays. Before Ellie and I were married I had been tested and told it was "highly unlikely" I could become a father. Ellie knew this, but it made no difference. We decided to adopt. We put our names in at the Angel Guardian Home in Brooklyn, a Catholic orphanage where, we were told, there was a waiting list of a year and a half. We were disappointed, but late in 1951 we had Peter, who was then eight months old, and two years later Judy, who was five months. The Angel Guardian officials, who had visited us on several occasions before the adoptions to make sure that we were fit parents, made follow-up visits to monitor the children's progress. I'm sure some parents who adopt feel that such visits are intrusions, but Ellie and I were constantly impressed by the caring attitude of our Angel Guardian monitors.

On the home front, our lives were busier now — far busier — than ever before. But they were also much richer, thanks to the children. The only dark cloud was the death of my father. Around 1940, Dad's identical twin brother Henry had gone diamond prospecting in Africa, leaving his wife and son behind. He was not terribly successful; when he came home several years later, he brought with him scads of feathers and caps and arrows, but very few diamonds. Instead of reuniting with his family, he became a virtual recluse, supporting himself as a secretary for the Teamsters Union in Washington, D.C. In 1954, Uncle Henry suffered a stroke. My father went down to visit him and was devastated: seeing Henry, he kept imagining he was looking at himself. Henry died shortly after Dad's visit. When Dad returned to Boston, he suffered a stroke himself, and a few days later died at the age of sixty-four.

On the work front, I was extremely fortunate to have John Walsh as a mentor, though it took me a while to feel comfortable around him. Aristocratic in manner and bearing, he seldom smiled. He had grown up in Albany, where his father owned the best department store in that city. He could be strict in his dealings with others: he did not manage by terror, but he was very selective about whom he did business with. But because he was so highly regarded on Wall Street, working for him was not only a privilege, the advantage also redounded to his subordinates' reputations.

Twice a year, in February and August, John Walsh, John Reid, and I went round trip by train from New York City to San Francisco to attend a meeting of the company's board of directors. (The other two quarterly meetings, in May and November, were held in New York City.) I prepared for the San Francisco board meetings by jumping off at train stations as we headed west to send wires or pick them up. Traveling to and from the board meetings with Walsh was a great experience for me, as he and Jack Reid discussed financial matters, relating to both the company and the world at large. Walsh was a walking textbook, and I was an avid student of his knowledge. Through him I had my first insights into the operation of a large corporation, for railroads in those days were still very much Big Business. In any corporation you look for the opportunities and threats. And then, based on your assessment, you make a decision. Among the many opportunities was the transportation by rail of automobiles and automotive parts. Southern Pacific contracted with General Motors to provide the service (our competitor, Santa Fe, got Ford), and we in return bought General Motors diesel locomotives. The biggest perceived threat to the company in the waning days of the 1940s was the ominous rise of the trucking industry. Falling back on the old dictum that if you can't beat 'em, join 'em, Southern Pacific evolved the "piggybacking" concept, wherein the railroads transported trailers, especially on long hauls where it was cost effective for both parties, trucks and the railroads. But year by year one could see the steady erosion of the once dominant rail system: lumber, for one, which had been a railroad staple, began to lose out to the truckers, who had the distinct advantage of being able to send their trucks directly to the mills to pick up their loads.

John Reid, though a bit stuffy for my taste, was nonetheless kind and thoughtful to the young man I then was. He gave me endless assignments, and shared his tasks with me in various areas of finance. I always felt comfortable going back to him with a question about something I had not fully understood. He was patient and painstaking in clarifying ambiguities and answering questions. I never failed to tell people how good I thought he was at his job — not to curry favor but because I honestly appreciated his dedication and professionalism, and saw no reason not to spread the good news. I didn't know it then, but I was already putting into practice a basic business belief: always try to promote your boss.

One project he gave me I shall never forget. Southern Pacific would sell about three issues of equipment trust certificates a year, and the bid openings were in our office. Equipment trust certificates were a prime credit, as the ownership of the equipment stayed with an independent "trustee" until all the certificates matured and were paid off. While these were normally of ten equal annual maturities, there was an innovation in the 1950s whereby these became twenty semi-annual maturities. The problem was, there were no financial tables on Wall Street to determine accurately what the cost of money was to the issuer, which was necessary to calculate the winning bid, especially if it was close. Under Mr. Reid's direction, I compiled tables to determine the streams of cash for both the principal and coupon payments. A friend of mine at Salomon Brothers, William Morris, made sure not only that the tables got wide distribution throughout the financial community but also that they were labeled "Al Casey's Tables." They're still in use today.

One important advantage the railroads still enjoyed in those days was land: they owned millions of acres, especially in the West, from early government land grants, as well as vast amounts of waterfront property, served by "belt line railroads." In Nevada alone, Southern Pacific had holdings of some four million acres. Oil exploration companies, eager to gain access to many of these properties, paid substantial sums for the exploration rights, which provided the railroads with a fair amount of extra income.

Working with Walsh for a number of years taught me many things, among them that you cannot achieve goals by yourself alone. Walsh was a good and patient boss who delighted in sharing his experience with me and other young colleagues. He, like many other people at Southern Pacific, considered his company a privileged place to work, one of America's elite, as indeed it was. Theirs was not just a job; it was a calling, which created a certain imperious attitude, as I was to learn one day. No one at Southern Pacific ever thought of looking for another job: when you had landed in heaven, why look anywhere else?

I had enormous respect for Walsh. But I did have to learn how to recognize what was important to him. This was not always a matter of common sense, since another person's idiosyncrasies are not necessarily predictable or fathomable in a logical, coherent fashion. I always tried to make sure I understood my instructions, aware that words mean different things to different people. Walsh stressed that you must always be certain that those who report to you are crystal clear about what you expect of them. Everyone in business thinks he or she adheres to this rule, he was fond of saying, but few really do. He felt so strongly on that score that he always made me repeat, word for word, any instructions he had just given me, to make sure they were absolutely, unequivocally clear and that I had understood. There were times when I felt I was back in school as I repeated verbatim the "professor's" words. But in fact by so doing I rarely made a mistake carrying out his instructions. And I also learned how, in later years, to be crystal clear myself when it was I who was giving the orders.

Walsh had the habit of picking up a pencil and editing my letters, which I had carefully, sometimes painfully, drafted for his signature. One day when I placed a letter before him, he picked up his pencil and proceeded to make notes in the margin.

"Mr. Walsh," I said, "may I say something?"

"Al, just stay put till I finish."

Again I tried to interrupt him, and again he brushed me off. Finally he finished and said, "There, that's a big improvement. Now, what was it you wanted to say, Al?"

"Mr. Walsh, that was an *incoming* letter *to* you, not a draft of mine."

Without missing a beat, Walsh retorted, "Be that as it may, Al, the letter's in *much* better shape now."

After John Walsh's untimely death in 1953, I had increasing contact for the next four or five years with Southern Pacific chairman Donald J. Russell, a legend not only in the railroad industry but in American business. Russell moved the Southern Pacific controller, Bob Plummer, from our office out to San Francisco and put my immediate boss, Jack Reid, in charge of New York, naming him vice president, finance. Thus I was promoted, shedding my unduly lengthy title of "assistant to the assistant" for the more exalted "assistant to the VP."

Russell was an imposing man, a company man of the old school, someone who inspired both loyalty and fear. For some reason he took a shine to me — probably because I kept long hours and was totally devoted, qualities he admired and tried to instill throughout the company. In any event, in the mid-1950s he gave me a special assignment that proved to be as challenging as it was enlightening. The IRS had hit Southern Pacific with an enormous corporate back tax liability, based on the premise that Southern Pacific's "invested capital base" was grossly overstated and its wartime profits should be taxed at a higher rate than the company had used in its tax returns. During World War II, under the wartime "excess profits tax" provision of the tax code, a company was allowed a 7 percent return on its invested capital base, then was taxed at 90 percent on all subsequent profits. The invested capital base was defined as including the market value of all stocks and bonds at the time of their issuance; obviously, the higher the invested capital base, the larger the 7 percent return before the 90 percent tax kicked in. Given Southern Pacific's long history — going back to 1884 — and its far-flung assets, it had used an invested capital base that included a stock price of $100 a common share. The IRS maintained that since the common stock, when first issued, was selling for $22, Southern Pacific should have been using that figure. To buttress its argument, the IRS showed that during the mid-1880s, Southern Pacific stock had continued to be traded at more or less that same price. My task was to discredit that

1880s market price, by demonstrating that the stock was then being traded in a rigged market, as the only seller was Collis P. Huntington, one of Southern Pacific's founders, who was head-quartered in New York and whose job it was to "trade" the stocks on Wall Street. Back in those days, to effect same-day trading, the stock certificates had to be delivered to brokers, who would then attempt to sell them. Huntington delivered shares to the brokers in the morning, and in the evening took back the unsold shares. In other words, there was no real free market for the stock, since Huntington was controlling the supply of Southern Pacific stocks. On occasion, I learned, he also bought back his company's own shares to give the appearance of a free market.

For the better part of three years, from 1956 to 1958, I pored through the Southern Pacific books and records, including newspaper articles and financial reports, gathering data that would convince a mule. I spent weeks, if not months, at the New York Public Library on Forty-second Street searching for documents and stories that would buttress our position. It was a full-time job, and at one point I was detached from the main Southern Pacific office and moved into a separate office in the same building. Still, I had many of my previous duties to perform, plus other assignments that Donald Russell threw my way.

During those three years, I journeyed often to Washington to argue on behalf of Southern Pacific, and many were the days when I would take the train back to New York after an exhausting session with IRS officials and wonder whether we would ever prevail. For I had compiled an impressive dossier, demonstrating forcibly that the $100-per-share stock valuation was indeed fully justified. But it was one thing to convince a mule; it was quite another to convince the IRS, since millions of dollars were riding on its decision. Nonetheless, even then I was practicing, if not formulating clearly, Casey's Law (or at least an activist variant): If there was even the slightest chance I could make things go right (and best the IRS in the bargain), I was going to fight to the bitter end. And indeed, in 1961, after I had left Southern Pacific, the IRS ruling came down: Southern Pacific's position was upheld. As a result, the company saved $33 million — the amount it would have had to pay had the ruling gone against it. In today's dollars, that would amount to something in the neighborhood of $100 million.

In 1959, Russell finally decided to close the New York office essentially because a larger number of major companies, which till now had been handling their own stock transfers, had begun to give up that time-consuming task as banks moved in and offered more up-to-date, cost-effective services. We turned our stock transfer business over to Banker's Trust, which was a relief to all, especially me. Informing me of the closing, Russell said: "Al, I have high hopes for your future. I've followed your career over the past decade. I know how highly John Walsh thought of you, and how highly John Reid regards you."

I thanked him, unsure whether his praise was a prelude to the ax or an offer, for, after all, he had called to let me know they were closing the New York office.

"I'd like you to move out here," he said, "to the home office. You'll like San Francisco, and San Francisco will like you."

That night I discussed the move with Ellie. After eleven years in New York, we had made many friends we would hate to leave behind. And the children were happy in school, Peter in third grade, Judy in first.

"Al, I sense that you're ready for a move," Ellie said. "And I also get the strong feeling this is what you want to do. So let's go."

As Russell had predicted, we immediately liked San Francisco. Life was pleasanter, easier, a far different animal from the hectic pace of New York. But it was also less challenging on a day-to-day basis. We found a house we loved on Los Altos Avenue in Los Altos, a town adjacent to Palo Alto and Stanford University. The Santa Rita grammar school was right across the street from our house, and Ellie became very involved, almost immediately, with school matters, as well as settling into a new community: new friends, new doctors for the children and ourselves, new everything.

For the next two valuable years, I enjoyed the job and the environment. Russell became my second mentor. In San Francisco, I

carried over my SEC and New York Stock Exchange reporting responsibilities and added a number of new ones. I helped David
Myrick, special assistant in the treasurer's office, part of whose job
it was to respond to stockholders' letters; I worked at keeping the
corporate bank balances within guidelines; I was in close and constant contact with the law department regarding financing and
IRS litigation. Above all, I learned cash management, which was
to stand me in good stead the rest of my life. My most challenging
job during those two years was an eighteen-month-long effort to
work out an agreement between Southern Pacific on the one
hand and the City and County of Los Angeles on the other, to set
up a rapid transit service in the Los Angeles area. It never worked
out — can you imagine the change in the entire Los Angeles environment today if it had? — but the experience of working with
so many different people, all of whom had different mandates, priorities, and agendas, was eye-opening. By this time I had been
promoted to the exalted position of assistant vice president and assistant treasurer.

During those two years, I also learned that rotten apples were
not an exclusive East Coast commodity; the West had a few choice
examples of its own. The Southern Pacific office in El Paso, I noticed, was chalking up more overtime than any other place in the
country. And its bills for spare parts were also out of line with the
rest of the company. We sent the auditors in, who discovered that
fraud was being perpetrated on a massive scale. The overtime
checks were fraudulent; so were the invoices for spare parts. But
the El Paso manager, not satisfied with these deceptions, had gone
further and concocted phony invoices. With his ill-gotten gains,
he had built himself a warehouse on paper, which he was rapidly
filling with nonexistent goods and materials billed to Southern Pacific. What amazed me most was that it was all so flagrant, almost
as if he wanted to be caught. He had to know that sooner or later
the auditors would find him out. The man had a decent job, was
married, had a family, and enjoyed a certain standing in the community. I wondered then — and still wonder — what strange virus
caused him to trade decency for thievery.

As I was rounding out my second year in San Francisco — and, I confess, getting a trifle restless — I received a phone call from a man named Bill Johnson, who identified himself as the new president and CEO of the Railway Express Agency. He was looking for a chief financial officer and wondered if I might be interested. I said I'd been with Southern Pacific for thirteen years, enjoyed my work, thought I had a future there, and doubted I wanted to move. But at the same time, I suddenly wondered if, indeed, there was a future for me at SP. My immediate boss was still John Reid, who was only a few years older than I: if I were to move up, Reid would have to move up ahead of me. Or move out. And I wasn't quite sure there was much room for Reid to move up, judging from the existing structure. I invited Reid out for a drink to assess the situation. After work one day we took a cable car up to the top of California Street and went into the bar of the Huntington Hotel. Over drinks, we engaged in the usual small talk for half an hour or so — life, love, family — then I casually steered the conversation to Southern Pacific. Reid let it be known that he enjoyed his job, which was not overly demanding, and had few if any aspirations to move up the corporate ladder. Then he unleashed his salvo:

"I have sixteen years to go till I retire," he said firmly, "and I intend to stay at Southern Pacific the full sixteen."

I had trouble understanding that mentality: for me, a job had to be challenging to be interesting. And till now, for the most part, my work at Southern Pacific had been a daily challenge with a steep learning curve. I also found it hard to understand how anyone in his forties could be counting the years — if not the days — till his retirement.

When Johnson called back a few days later, I said I'd be willing to talk but explained that Southern Pacific was a very traditional, protocol-oriented company. I also didn't feel comfortable talking to Johnson without Southern Pacific knowing about it.

"Then who shall we talk to?" Johnson asked.

I told him my immediate boss was John Reid.

"Then I'll have our senior vice president, C. J. Jump, give Reid a call," Johnson said.

The next day Jump called Reid and told him that his boss, Bill Johnson, had authorized him to talk to me about an important position in finance at Railway Express. Would it be all right to talk to Mr. Casey?

"Go right ahead," Reid said.

A few days later I flew to New York, where REA had its headquarters, and met Bill Johnson face-to-face for the first time. I liked him immediately. He was a thoughtful, articulate man, and his hawklike features and probing gaze made you pay close attention to his every word. When he talked to you, you were the only person in the world. A lawyer who had earlier served as legal adviser to the Pennsylvania Railroad, he had just been appointed president of REA. It had been losing money for years, and he had been given the job of turning it around.

"I warn you," he said, "the job won't be easy. Till now the REA's been funded by the railroads it serves, but now it's on its own. No more subsidies. So raising cash, and cash management, will be a top priority."

He went on to outline some of the other problems and challenges, then said: "Mr. Casey, the job of CFO is going to be whatever you make of it."

I was excited. And despite my loyalty and attachment to Southern Pacific, I was ready to make a move. When you're ready to go, you don't listen; you hear only what you want to hear.

The first of my challenges was informing Ellie that, having so recently — two years earlier — carted my family all the way across the country, I was contemplating moving back east. Peter, ten, and Judy, eight, were happy in their new school and would again have to make serious adjustments in their young lives. I laid out for Ellie, in full detail, the REA nettles into which I'd be walking, thinking perhaps if I painted a gloomy enough picture she'd tell me she just couldn't move again so soon, and that would be that. But I should have known better.

"Al," she said, "I've seen you growing restless over the past several months, and I think you're chafing at the bit. If that's what you want, that's what I want."

My second challenge was to seek an audience with Donald Russell, to inform him of my decision. I went through my speech of devotion to Southern Pacific, gratitude for all I had learned over thirteen years, reminding him that this was the only company I'd ever worked for, and saying that in John Walsh and himself I could not have asked for finer mentors. He listened unblinking, his eyes fixed on my forced smile, and it was impossible for me to tell whether my words had touched him or whether a volcano was about to explode. After I finished, he sat there, saying nothing, till the silence of the room enveloped me like a winding sheet. Then, in stentorian tones that still echo in my mind today, he said: "Clearly, Al, the Southern Pacific brand is not burned deep enough in your back. I must say, I am terribly disappointed at your leaving." With that he turned his lordly gaze back to the papers on his desk, signaling that the meeting was over. I later learned that he subsequently gave explicit instructions that my name never be mentioned again in his presence.

4

REA: A LESSON IN CRISIS MANAGEMENT

I KNEW FROM MY PREVIOUS CONVERSATIONS with Bill Johnson that my new job would be anything but a picnic. Historically, what was then the Railway Express Agency had derived from the merging of four express companies: Wells Fargo, Adams, Southern, and American Express. When America entered World War I, these four companies had been united to assist the war effort and increase efficiency. After World War I, the companies remained together, and in 1922 formalized their structure. Seven years later, the company adopted the name Railway Express Agency. As the name implied, REA, like its predecessor companies, was an agent for the railroads; its job was to provide pickup and delivery service for packages shipped throughout the country, using the facilities and tracks of the various railroads.

The history of the express companies goes back to the 1860s and 1870s, when they were used to transport cash, for the sale of stakes and land claims in the West, as well as to meet payrolls and purchase supplies. On the return trip, the famous pony express and horse-drawn carriages, now part of legend, carried precious metals — gold and silver — to the East. For roughly a hundred years, the forerunners of REA had carried their packages on express cars located behind the engine and in front of the passenger coaches. REA was not a separate corporation however — the railroads owned all the stock — and its board of directors comprised the chairmen of the various railroad companies REA served. The board inevitably saw to it that the goals and needs of the railroads always took precedence over those of the express agency. They set the rates, determined the service, and hired the officials. Because the railroads, especially after World War II, viewed with alarm the rise of the trucking industry, they offered very attractive express rates, which were often uneconomical. As a result, the REA consistently posted losses, and each year the operating deficit was divided among the stockholding railroads, proportionately to the service (ton miles) each had provided. After World War II, and especially throughout the 1950s, passenger rail service in America was declining, both because Americans were embracing in ever greater numbers the gaudy output of Detroit's booming automobile business and because more and more people were turning to the airlines for their long-distance travel. Many small rail lines had gone out of business, and the major ones were holding on for dear life. The REA, which depended on a good rail system for its very existence, was suffering in direct proportion to the railroads' decline. Fighting for survival, the railroads, realizing that their mounting losses stemmed primarily from passenger service, petitioned the government to let them out of that business, their desire being to concentrate on the far more profitable freight business. Passenger service required better roadbeds and far more personnel: no passenger service meant no stationmasters, no conductors, less rigorous schedules.

At the same time, looking to save money, the REA board of directors — the railroad chairmen — decided in 1961 to bite the bullet and make the REA an independent company. All well and good for the railroads, but it was a little like a ship at sea cutting loose a lifeboat in the midst of a raging storm. In any event, on July 1, 1961, just three months after I arrived, REA became an independent company.

While I had known that I was taking on a challenging job, I had greatly underestimated how dire the situation at REA really was. With the railroads trying to get out of, or at least greatly reduce, their passenger service, we realized we could no longer be effective or competitive using the rails. Passenger service ran on regular schedules that REA could calculate and count on for getting packages from point A to point B; rail freight service was another matter altogether. We quickly realized that we would have to come off the rails and go on the road, which meant purchasing trucks, building terminals, getting route certificates from the ICC. For that we needed capital, and fast. But after forty years of losing money as part of the railroads, our credit rating was somewhere between poor and terrible. In addition, we had very few assets to pledge.

Meanwhile, and more important, before tackling all these problems, I had my family to resettle. Ellie and I decided we should rent a house to start, while looking for one to buy, and we had found a pleasant house on North Street, just off White Plains Road in Bronxville, New York, which we were able to rent for the summer. But we needed a permanent place before fall, because of the children's school; we didn't want to start them in one school and then move them a few months later to another. They'd already suffered enough dislocation in their young lives. We finally found a two-story house at 21 Echo Lane in Greenwich, Connecticut. It was a lovely location, and although the rooms were small they were adequate. Offsetting that minor drawback in convenience, the house had a glorious kitchen, which suited Ellie, who loved to cook, just fine. There was also an excellent school in downtown Greenwich, Saint Mary's, in which we enrolled the children before the end of summer. If the commute from Greenwich was twice that from Bronxville, all in all I felt we had made the right choice.

Bill Johnson and I would meet almost daily to update one another on the current REA situation and strategize, mostly about how to raise money: what I call a communications meeting. Our corporate headquarters was a building at 219 East Forty-second Street — a former stable for REA horses, but now in the booming real estate market a very desirable midtown property. We decided to sell it off, which we did, then leased it back. That gave us a little financial breathing room. We owned a fair number of railroad express cars, and while most of them had some debt on them,

at least on paper there was some equity there. Through my Southern Pacific days I had gotten to know the people at Equitable Life
Assurance Society of the United States, and I managed to raise a
few more million by convincing them that the market value of the
cars was in excess of the outstanding debt. We were fortunate that
Equitable held the debt.

In addition to our meetings during the week, we would also
meet each Sunday morning at Bill Johnson's house, which was also
in Greenwich, barely a mile from mine. We usually brought in a
senior officer to discuss his specific area, meeting around Johnson's
dining room table. Together we would run through the progress of
the previous week, confront the major problems facing us the following week, and, periodically, draw up the agenda of an upcoming board meeting.

At one of those Sunday meetings, I said to Bill Johnson: "You
know that facility we have on the west side between Forty-first
and Forty-second Streets, between Eleventh and Twelfth Av-
enues . . . ?"

"The package sorting facility," Johnson said.

"Right. Well, it occurred to me that if we could combine it
with the block of buildings one block down, which is owned by
the New York Central Railroad, we'd have a great piece of property to sell to the right buyer. Besides, it makes no sense to me that
we're using a prime piece of Manhattan real estate to accomplish
an extremely low-profit task that could be done elsewhere at a
fraction of the cost."

"You're right," Johnson said. "What do you suggest?"

"Let me talk to the New York Central real estate people and
see if I can convince them it's a good deal for them as well."

"Don't the New York Central tracks run under that building?" Johnson asked.

"They do, and we can't disturb them. But we'd have a free
hand above ground."

"How much is this little effort going to cost?" Johnson asked.

"A hundred and ninety thousand," I said. I had already paid a
visit to the adjoining New York Central property and checked the

roster of tenants: nineteen in all. "I'll offer each tenant the same option money: ten thousand dollars each, and attractive lease-sale prices. That should get them at least talking. And that way there can be no griping, because you can be sure the first thing they'll do is ask their next-door neighbor how much he got."

"And if we don't get them all to leave?"

"Then we're out one hundred ninety grand," I said. "But I think our chances are fair to good, and if we pull it off, we'll have raised several million."

"Are you by any chance a gambler?" Johnson asked, smiling. "Okay, let's go for it," he said, but added, "Remember, time is precious. And it's not on our side." I thought I was hearing my mother's voice. But I had to admire Bill Johnson's style: it had taken him all of two seconds to commit to the $190,000.

Before I approached New York Central, I visited the building again and checked out the bulletin board more closely: the tenants ranged from a major trucking company to sweatshops to the last kosher slaughterhouse in Manhattan. From the names on the board, many looked like small businesses, where the financial enticement to move might be attractive. But the last kosher slaughterhouse? The biggest tenant on the property was Gilbert Trucking, a local trucker famous for its transportation of "garments on hangers," a coast-to-coast business.

For several weeks I bypassed my office and went directly to the property, where I'd knock on the door of one of the tenants.

"Good morning," I'd say brightly. "Is your boss in?" Sometimes, as was the case with the Gilbert truckers, I'd deal directly with the owners, but most of the time I met with the managers, all of whom assured me they'd pass my offers on to their bosses.

I ascertained that the man to see at New York Central itself was Jim Boisi, the real estate vice president, and I made an appointment. In his posh office in the New York Central executive suite at Forty-sixth and Park, Boisi received me cordially, and I wasted no time making my proposal: REA would combine the two adjacent blocks — REA's and New York Central's — in order to attract a large-scale real estate development, for either a large commercial building or an apartment complex overlooking the Hudson River. From REA's perspective, the deal would generate a portion of the cash we so sorely needed to build terminals and purchase trucks. But it would also benefit New York Central, because the potential new development would surely command better lease terms for the railroad. Boisi liked my proposal, but he had some concerns.

"How are we going to handle the present leaseholders?" Boisi asked.

"Let me worry about that," I said. "There are nineteen tenants, and I'm prepared to see them all and offer them option money to negotiate leaving."

"Whose option money?" Boisi asked, doubtless sensing that I might soon have my hand in his pocket.

"REA's," I said. "We're willing to risk it."

Reassured, he gave me his blessing and asked me to keep him duly informed.

I trooped over to the property and continued my persistent door knocking. To the owners of each of the businesses I offered to pay, as agreed, ten thousand dollars in "earnest money" in return for a ninety-day option to buy out their leases. In other words, in return for ten thousand dollars, each of the leaseholders gave REA ninety days to negotiate the *actual* buyout of the leases. After the purchase of the leases, the former leaseholders would have to move, but they would be compensated at what I told them would be attractive prices.

As I had predicted, all the leaseholders were pleased to accept $10,000 with no obligation other than to negotiate a high buyout price of their leases. But the negotiations themselves varied greatly in complexity. Some lessees were ready to move; others held out for an extraordinary premium on the purchase of their lease. I worked with several real estate people to determine what would be a fair price for each lease, then used my best judgment, taking into account the size and solidity of each company, in making my offers.

Meanwhile, I had another equally urgent problem: finding a

developer for the property we were going to create with the combination of the two blocks. Several promising leads yielded no results; the process was taking so much time that some of the ninety-day options were about to expire, and I was increasingly concerned that the entire deal might collapse. Then one morning, as I was reading the newspaper, I hit on what struck me as an ideal solution.

The Greyhound bus company, I read, had just won the transportation rights from Manhattan to the 1964 New York World's Fair, which was to be held in Queens next to the newly constructed Shea Stadium. Maybe Greyhound needed a place in Manhattan from which to operate, I reasoned. But I knew no one at Greyhound. So I went down to the Greyhound terminal on Thirty-fourth Street, stood in the ticket line, and when I got to the window asked the clerk, "Who is your boss?"

"The woman down at the end, sitting at the desk," was the reply. I went down there and asked her, "Can you tell me who your boss is?"

"He's working upstairs in the general offices," she said.

So I went upstairs, somehow got in to see the second person's boss, and asked again who his boss was. Eventually, I found that the person in charge of all Greyhound operations in Manhattan for the New York World's Fair was a regional vice president named Ray Schaeffer, based in Cleveland. I called him and described the Manhattan property we were trying to create with the combination of blocks owned by REA and New York Central. He was immediately interested in the site for Greyhound and suggested he meet with me under the clock at the Biltmore Hotel in New York the next afternoon.

After that meeting, we visited the site. Schaeffer decided it was perfect for Greyhound's needs and immediately offered to go forward with a deal to lease the entire two-block package. But first we had to finalize a price for the leases that Greyhound would be taking over from New York Central's tenants, as well as purchase terms for the block owned by REA. In addition, we had to resolve a problem Greyhound raised about the trains continuing to run under the site. Where would Greyhound store its buses when they were not in use? Without even calling Jim Boisi at New York Central, I knew there was no negotiating on this point. The tracks could not be moved, and Greyhound would have to store its buses elsewhere. After consultation with the home office, Schaeffer informed me that Greyhound had worked out a solution to its bus-parking problem.

We resolved the buyout terms we were prepared offer each of the nineteen tenants, as well as the delicate matter of timing, which was crucial because Greyhound needed to get started on the facility it planned to build, to be ready for the opening of the World's Fair. I had to act as a go-between in the Greyhound-lessee negotiations, and I needed every single lessee's agreement to make the arrangement work. Day after day I argued and cajoled, flattered and enticed, until I had agreement on every last one, and we settled on a closing date. The closing was to take place at the First National City Bank at 399 Park Avenue, at nine A.M. On the appointed day, the august offices of the bank were invaded by as bizarre and motley a crew — the leaseholders themselves or their appointed representatives — as the place had doubtless ever seen. I could see by the looks on the faces of the vice presidents, as well as the tellers and guards, that they wondered if *these* people had really come to the right place.

At the closing, although I had presumably airtight agreements for all nineteen tenants, I found myself continuing to negotiate all day and far into the night, because some tenants had second thoughts, or felt the money terms to which they had agreed were suddenly too low or the time too precipitous. We were meeting right next to the office of Mr. Stillman Rockefeller, the bank's distinguished vice chairman, who was considerably upset that such a "boisterous" group had the audacity to use the conference room adjoining his office. What was more, I had a suspicion Mr. Rockefeller did not often see the likes of some of the tenants, and I was willing to bet a hundred to one that he had never before laid eyes on the owner of a kosher slaughterhouse. Be that as it may, as day turned into evening, and evening into late night, I arranged a standard form of power of attorney, and as each leaseholder grew tired and impatient, he would sign a power of attorney, giving me the final terms and conditions under which he would be willing to sign over his lease.

When at last all the leases had been signed over, City Bank, at Greyhound's instructions, drew up cashiers' checks totaling $3 million (10 percent of the total $30 million purchase price on the leases), made out to the nineteen recipients. To each check I attached my power of attorney to accept. At three thirty A.M. the deal finally closed, and I had a briefcase with the $3 million worth of certified checks in it, duly made out to the nineteen tenants but in my possession until the next day, since by then all the weary, and newly rich, small businessmen were home, snug in their beds. One of our children was sick, and I had promised Ellie I would make it home, no matter how late the closing.

As there were no trains at that late hour, I had arranged to borrow a car from my assistant, John Sibley, who lived in Manhattan. I headed out of the city along the New York State Thruway to Connecticut. About a mile short of my turnoff from the turnpike, the car ran out of gas. In my anxiety to get home, I had forgotten to check the gas gauge. Somehow I had assumed that any friend of mine would always have a full tank!

I took my briefcase, bulging with certified checks, and walked nervously for about a mile to an all-night Texaco station in Greenwich. I asked the night serviceman if I could borrow a container and buy a little gas so I could get the car started.

"Sure," said the attendant, reaching for a container. "That'll be four fifty for a deposit."

I fished in my pocket and came up with a grand total of a dollar and a half. During the course of the marathon negotiations I had completely emptied my wallet paying for sandwiches and drinks for the leaseholders and their representatives.

"Well," he said, looking at the reasonably well dressed but more than slightly rumpled man with, I thought, more than a smidgen of suspicion — after all, it was four A.M. and for all he knew I could be carrying stolen money in that briefcase — "I'll need four fifty. Not a penny less."

"What can I do?" I pleaded. I told him my name was Al Casey, but he was completely unimpressed. "Sorry, too many containers have never been returned," he told me matter-of-factly, then he brightened. "That briefcase of yours looks pretty valuable," he said, "I'm sure it's worth at least four fifty. Why don't you leave that with me?"

It wasn't even locked, but I made a split-second decision to trust the man. I handed him the briefcase, walked the long, dark mile back to the car, poured a couple of gallons into the tank, drove to the filling station, and gave the man back his container, proud not to be in the dubious category of those who absconded with Texaco's finest gas cans. I started to drive off when the night attendant hailed me.

"Hey, mister," he said, "aren't you forgetting something?" I was so tired I had forgotten to take back my briefcase containing the $3 million in certified checks!

Before I had been with REA for six months, I was directing the following departments: finance and accounting, law, purchasing, insurance, construction (which included land acquisition for eighteen terminals), public relations, and personnel — everything, in fact, except operations. Well, Bill Johnson had said that I could make of the job what I would. It's not that I had consciously sought to broaden my areas of responsibility. The situation at REA had forced me to think imaginatively every day: there was no going back to the files to see how others had done it. We had to make things up every moment of our working lives. Crises were not a sometime thing; they were an everyday occurrence.

As always, and despite all our artful measures, cash was a constant problem. One day when I was in San Francisco I learned to my dismay that we would not have sufficient funds to cover payroll; checks to the tune of $1,500,000 had been issued without the necessary funds on deposit. I was desperate, groping for ideas. Then a positive, pragmatic, and slightly overfetched idea took hold of me. I knew that Warren Hellman, the chairman of Wells Fargo Bank, was enamored of his company's rich history and rightfully proud of the Wells Fargo History Museum. I knew, too, that Wells Fargo had been one of REA's proud predecessor companies, and that in our warehouse we had a number of antique Wells Fargo ticket desks.

I was in San Francisco to determine what to do with some rail terminal space we were abandoning and to take care of a few other REA business matters. I made an immediate appointment with Hellman at the Wells Fargo Building and told him that I was pleased to report that we had found in our warehouse two old Wells Fargo ticket desks, which I wanted to contribute to his museum. Hellman beamed.

"That's wonderful, Mr. Casey. And how nice of you to remember the historical importance of those desks. Some people might just have thrown them out. Thank you very, *very* much."

"You're very welcome, Mr. Hellman. And in return I'd like something from you, if you don't mind."

"Certainly, Mr. Casey, what can we do?"

"I'd like one and a half million dollars put into our bank account tomorrow. I don't have any collateral, and let's not even talk about interest. But I'll give Wells Fargo the biggest lockbox in the western states. I'll give you the right to service all the REA checks west of the Mississippi." The lockbox offer meant that Wells Fargo would receive all the REA accounts receivable checks for the western states. A considerable windfall — but at no additional cost to REA.

Without a blink, Hellman said: "Mr. Casey, you'll have your million and a half in the morning."

I smiled, convincingly I hoped, for inwardly I was shaking. My request was born of desperation, yet I had not "taken" Wells Fargo; the desks had been my opening gambit, to create the right frame of mind in the chairman. But my lockbox offer was a good piece of business for Wells Fargo, too. Hellman never knew how desperate I was. As I was thinking these thoughts, Ralph Rebele, the Wells Fargo president, whom I knew, entered the room.

"Al, what are you doing here?"

Hellman explained that he had just granted REA a $1.5 million loan, without collateral.

"Is that true, Al?" he said to me, doubtless hoping I might deny it.

But before I could comment, Hellman added: "And Mr. Casey has just donated two of the nicest antique Wells Fargo ticket desks for our museum. Isn't that wonderful?"

I quickly shook hands with both gentlemen and beat a hasty retreat. What neither of them knew was that, without that infusion, REA would have been bankrupt the following morning.

Working at REA was a little bit like working on a high wire without a net. In fact, the Wells Fargo loan was but one of several. Most of the time we had to borrow without collateral. We would get what were called management, or M, loans, with the rates based on the banks' assessments of the corporation's management skills. We had M loans from Wells Fargo, Morgan Guaranty, First National City Bank, and several other banks. The purpose of these loans was, as I indicated, to build terminals and purchase trucks, so we could render ourselves independent of the railroads.

I represented to the banks, with the REA board of directors' full knowledge and consent, that there would be no dividends paid to our stockholders until we had established a sufficient record of earnings to substantially pay down our loans. However, in August 1963, when we reported a profit of $4 million for the fiscal year just ended — our fiscal year ended on June 30 — the board of directors decided they wanted to declare a $4 million dividend.

Just because you make a profit does not mean you have the cash on hand to pay the dividend; in fact, we did not have the cash. To pay a dividend, I would have had to go out and borrow the money. More important, paying a dividend would also be a clear violation of my personal representation to the banks.

The board knew full well my promise that I would not allow a dividend to be declared until we were in a much stronger financial position. Yet a very powerful board member, David Beven, financial vice president of Pennsylvania Railroad, spoke up at the board meeting and virtually demanded that the dividend be declared.

Since I was not a member of the board but only attended the board meetings ex officio, all I could do was explain why it was imperative that we not do that. It would be a violation of my word, and I would be unable to carry out my fiduciary responsibilities if my word were not worth anything.

Beven stared at me and asked, "Al, what is your salary?"

"Twenty-seven thousand dollars," I replied.

"Well, we're going to have an executive session on this subject. Will you please leave the room."

Something was wrong and I sensed it. How could the board not understand my position? How could it be so damn shortsighted?

A few minutes later, Bill Johnson summoned me back upstairs. Beven, the man who was so strongly in favor of the dividend, said imperiously, "Al, I've got great news for you. Your salary is now fifty-four thousand dollars a year."

I was stunned. I knew immediately what had happened while I was out of the room.

"If you're doubling my salary, it must mean that you've declared a dividend," I said.

"We have," Beven replied.

I thought again of all I had done for the company. I also thought of my family. But I was absolutely certain there was only one thing I could say to the board.

"In that case there's no way I can stay with REA," I announced. A hush fell over the room, followed by a few discreet coughs and murmurs. Maybe they thought I was bluffing. I turned and left. I never even went to clean out my desk. I walked straight out of the building, over to Grand Central Station, and took the next train home.

An axiom of Casey's Law: if you want something to go right, the foundation of your dealings with others must be total integrity. I emphasize, at the risk of sounding self-righteous, the word *total*. This is not a matter of blind allegiance to some idealistic code of conduct; it's simply that a lack of integrity — however seemingly innocuous or minor the deviation — will eventually come home to haunt you and your company. I resigned from the REA because I knew that if I stayed, I could not have looked at myself in the mirror the next morning. Or any morning thereafter for the rest of my life. I also knew that I could not have looked the next banker in the eye.

Throughout the trip home after I left Railway Express in August 1963, I wondered how I was going to support my family. We did not exactly have a lot of money stashed away. My REA salary had given us a decent living but was not enough for us to put any meaningful sum aside for a rainy day. I looked out the train window. As if to emphasize my plight, it suddenly started to rain. It was ten minutes to three in the afternoon. I picked up Ellie and said, "Let's go get the kids." They were still at school, in a Saint Mary's summer program. While we were driving to Saint Mary's, I told Ellie everything that had happened. Then Peter and Judy got in the car, and we went to a soda fountain where we ordered Cokes and snacks. I explained to the kids that, because of my business situation, we would probably be leaving Connecticut. If they had a choice, I said, where would they most like to go? The children said if they had to move — and they emphasized the *had* — they'd like to return to California. But did we really *have* to move again? We'd only been here two years, and really liked Greenwich. I held out the possibility that, if we moved to California, they might have their own swimming pool, which I suspect went a long way toward persuading them.

Moving, I realized, would be much more of a burden, once again, on my family than on me. Although I had been at REA only a short while, I had countless friends in the business world from coast to coast. But my family would have to start over, with the kids once again attending new schools, Ellie finding and putting a new house in shape, not to mention handling the lion's share of the move itself, since generally by the time we found a new house and sold the old one, I would be ensconced in the new job, and Ellie would be left with the task of overseeing the packing, shipping, and unpacking at the new location. The Church was always a great resource, helping her make new friends and find answers to all sorts of questions about the new community, but mostly it was Ellie's consistently positive attitude that made these wrenching moments appear so effortless. That day I was especially sensitive to everything my decision implied, but nevertheless I felt strongly it was time for me to go. After what had happened at REA, I wanted to put as much geographic and psychic distance between me and that company as possible. I had broken my back for REA — working seven days a week for two years — and in return been offered what amounted to a bribe to overlook the board's blatantly broken promise.

Bill Johnson called and urged me to change my mind. He apologized for what the board had done and then made me an offer he doubtless thought I couldn't refuse.

"For God's sake, Al, don't go. I know how hard you've worked for us. If you stay on three more months I'll resign, and you can run the company."

I thanked him but told him I had made up my mind.

I had been gone a scant two years from San Francisco and Southern Pacific, however, and decided the Bay Area business climate might not be particularly receptive to my return, because of Donald Russell's declaring me persona non grata. So we opted for the Los Angeles area. I wasn't concerned about finding a job there. In my entire working career I have never worried about such matters, not because I don't have reasons to worry like the next person, but because I believe that worry is a negative force. Worry is why people don't get what they want. You have to be confident, even when the odds seem stacked against you. *Especially* when the odds seem stacked against you.

Above all, I knew I wanted a company whose board of directors I could respect. And I wanted a company that was not unionized. To put it mildly, at REA I had not enjoyed dealing with Jimmy Hoffa and the Teamsters. Hoffa's union had thirteen thousand members in the REA, and another union, the Brotherhood of Railway Clerks, more than twice that number. Hoffa knew full well how vulnerable and financially precarious the new company was, but in negotiating a new contract he proved so intractable and bullying that I more than once came close to losing it with him.

"This isn't negotiating!" I exploded one day to Johnson. "This is intimidation, pure and simple."

I also wanted a company that had real growth possibilities and, hopefully, challenges. In my experience, the two generally went together.

Jack Vance, who ran the Los Angeles office of the management consulting firm McKinsey and Company, was working on the diversification program then underway at the Times Mirror Company, the West Coast communications company whose flagship publication was the *Los Angeles Times*. Vance had written a letter to several of his McKinsey partners throughout the country, informing them that Times Mirror was looking for a top financial person. "The person we're looking for," said Vance, "must have the following qualifications:

1. demonstrated financial capacity
2. exceptional skill in negotiating
3. demonstrated ability in handling diversity
4. ability to work well with people."

Among those he wrote to was Jack Garrity, a senior McKinsey partner in New York. Garrity immediately got on the phone to Vance.

"Jack," he said, "I have your letter about Times Mirror, and I think I have your man." He went on to outline my career to date and gave Vance my number in Connecticut.

Vance called and asked if I could fly out to California as soon as possible. I booked a flight the next day on American Airlines —

I always flew American — for Ellie and me. I had an appointment with the chairman of Times Mirror the following morning, but I also had two other job interviews lined up, and, since we were definitely moving to LA, I wanted Ellie to get the lay of the new land.

Two Times Mirror board members, Harry Volk, chairman of the board of Union Bank, and Frank King, CEO of United California Bank, had also long felt the company needed a strong chief financial officer. They had already started a job search of their own by the time I went to California, and both, hearing I had decided to live and work in LA, said they would recommend me to the chairman because of my broad and varied financial background.

During that same visit, I had also set up interviews with Litton Industries, manufacturers of electronic products, and Northrup Aircraft, both of whom were also looking for a chief financial officer. But my first choice was Times Mirror: it was a family-owned company, much admired in the community, with, I was told, a self-imposed mandate to expand and grow in the coming decade.

Although my experience in the communications business — newspapers, magazines, books, not to mention radio and that upstart, television — was nil, I felt my fifteen years in finance had well prepared me for the Times Mirror post. But as is the case with all family-owned businesses, the key question remained: how well would the chairman of the company, Norman Chandler, and I hit it off?

5

MY LIFE AND TIMES
AT TIMES MIRROR

AT MIDAFTERNOON, Norman Chandler received me at the Times Mirror corporate headquarters at First and Spring. As he stood to greet me, I could see that he was about my height — six feet — but a mite slimmer than I. At sixty-four, he was a handsome man with smooth white hair and chiseled features. I liked him immediately and thought he liked me as well. Given my background in railroads and shipping, however, I thought it important to level with him about my lack of experience in the newspaper business.

"That's unimportant," he said, shaking his head. "I can run a newspaper. My son Otis can run a newspaper. We don't want somebody to run the newspaper. We want somebody to run the finances of this company."

He went on to fill me in on the current corporate thinking, the necessity to diversify and to take some of the burden off the newspaper.

"Put me into other publications," he said. "Newspapers, magazines, books. Outside of LA. We're too concentrated in this geographic area. East Coast, West Coast, it makes no difference, so long as the company we're acquiring is solid and good at what it does. And the price we pay makes sense."

He filled me in on the company's acquisitions to date. ·

Our meeting went on for over an hour, and as I stood to leave, Mr. Chandler said: "You came very highly recommended by the McKinsey people, Mr. Casey. In fact, they give me the impression they think you can walk on water."

I thanked him and returned the compliment, observing that I had the impression a lot of people in LA felt the same about him and the Chandler family in general.

"Ah, the family . . . ," Norman said, his voice trailing away. "There are a lot of us, Mr. Casey, and as I expect you'll find out if you settle here, opinions about us vary. We Chandlers agree on some things but disagree on many, too. Including politics."

"What family doesn't?" I responded blandly.

"You should know, too, Mr. Casey, that all the Chandlers own Times Mirror stock, left to them in a very tightly monitored trust. And several — especially those who don't work in the business — are highly critical of their meager returns. So our incipient diversification program is meant in part to enlarge our asset base but especially our return to the stockholders."

"To get them off your back," I concluded.

Norman paused, assimilating my last sentence, and I realized that was not quite how the diplomatic chairman might have phrased it. But he broke into a warm smile and said, "Precisely, Mr. Casey. Precisely." Then turning back to our earlier conversation, he added, "You also have two friends on our board. Harry Volk of Union Bank and Frank King of United California."

That evening, Norman and his charming wife, Dorothy, invited Ellie and me to dinner. The only other guest was their son Otis, who had recently been appointed publisher of the *Los Angeles Times*. He was a strapping, good-looking young man, much given to fitness and fast motorcycles, but I could tell from his conversations about the *Times* that he was deeply committed to his new job and intent on making it a better paper. It was clear as the evening progressed that we all liked one another; perhaps more important, we all felt comfortable with one another.

During the dinner, Dorothy Chandler suddenly asked Ellie what her birthday was. Ellie told her: February twenty-eighth.

Then Dorothy turned to me and said, "And what's your birthday, Al?"

"Same day. February twenty-eighth," I answered. It was as if I'd tossed a bomb.

"February *twenty-eighth*," she said in a near whisper. "Both of you born not only under the same sign but on the same day! Amazing!"

It turned out she was deep into astrology, and that fortuitous conjunction held some deeper meaning that neither Ellie nor I could fathom. But we took it to be a good sign.

As we were leaving, Norman asked if he could pick me up the next morning at the hotel and drive me to the office. We agreed on a time: nine o'clock.

After chatting for a while in his office, Norman suggested we take a tour of "Times Mirror Square": the holding-company offices, the paper — both editorial and production, the employee lounge, the cafeteria, the executive dining rooms. Norman introduced me along the way to one and all — a tactical error, since no one knew who I was or why I was there. After the tour, Norman sent me to spend some time, individually, with three Times Mirror directors, in their respective companies. I knew two of the men, Harry Volk and Frank King, both bankers. The third, Tom Jones, was chairman of Northrop Corporation. All three meetings were pleasant and positive. After the last, with Jones, I returned to Times Mirror, where Norman was awaiting me.

"Mr. Casey," he said, "I'd like to offer you the job we've been discussing. Your title would be vice president, finance." He offered a salary of $50,000, which was fine, and outlined the responsibilities. I'd report both to him and, for some matters, to Ray McGranahan, the newly appointed executive vice president. "I very much hope you'll accept," he said. "We're off on a very ambitious new program, and I think you could contribute mightily to its success." He paused. "You'll probably want a day or two to think it over. I know you're considering a couple of other prospects."

"Mr. Chandler," I replied, "my wife and I discussed my various options last night, and my decision was made then. I'd be delighted to accept. When do I begin?"

"As soon as possible," he said. "Would September first be too early?"

"That's fine," I said, "but for the last two weeks of September I'd like to fly back to New York and assure the smooth transition of my responsibilities at REA."

"That's most unusual," he said. "Most unusual." Then he looked at me: "Al," he said, "I not only approve, I admire you for it."

The next day, back in New York, I put in a call to Bill Johnson, who again expressed regret that I had left. "But," he added, "I fully understand why you had to." I told him the purpose of my call was to see if I could be of help to my replacement and thereby ensure a smooth transition. Johnson said he greatly appreciated the gesture, adding: "Al, I can't tell you how profoundly touched I am that you're doing this. Especially after the way the board treated you. It renews my faith in the harsh world of business."

"Bill, my differences with the board in no way lessen my esteem for you," I said. "I know how tough a job you've got there, and *I* wouldn't feel right if I didn't brief my replacement. So you can say I'm being selfish."

"I've promoted John Sibley to your old position. I'll have him call you."

"This isn't something we can do on the phone," I said. "Tell Sibley to read all the files in my various areas and to prepare his questions. Since he's worked with me for some time, he's probably familiar with most of the problems."

"Has Mr. Chandler approved this?"

"Of course. Norman fully approves. . . . So I'll be in the office on Wednesday. I'll be too busy pulling together all the loose ends to prep Sibley during this trip. During the next few days I simply want to make sure that by the time I go back to Los Angeles at the end of the month, you're up to speed on everything in my areas. Then I'll come back specifically for Sibley."

"Al, I can't tell you —"

"Then don't even try." I laughed. "You'd do the same for me."

And it was true: in the reverse situation, I was sure Bill Johnson would have gone to bat for Casey.

During my stay in New York, I divided my time between helping Ellie prepare for the impending move and filling in Bill Johnson on every detail of my former job. Then, as August drew to a close, I boarded a plane and headed back to Los Angeles and Times Mirror, where I spent the next two weeks settling in and getting acquainted with both the people and the company organization and financial picture.

On September 15 I was back in the Big Apple, closeted with Sibley, filling him in on all my areas of responsibility and the overall situation of the fledgling company as I saw it. It was strange being back but not really back, yet I knew I was doing the right thing. Even though I felt I had been betrayed by REA, I believed — and still believe — that you should do your best to leave a job with good feelings all around. During the course of those two weeks I also saw a lot of Bill Johnson, both in and out of the office. Although our paths were parting, I admired him as a friend and valued him as a businessman. And I still do today.

My first day on the job at Times Mirror, Norman wanted me to meet Bob Allen, vice president in charge of acquisitions, and Ray McGranahan, neither of whom had I met before I was hired. My first stop was to see Bob Allen, whose office was a few doors down from Norman's. I introduced myself and told him why I was there.

I could see Allen's face fall till it was slightly below his knees. Only then did I realize that Norman had not yet told him I'd been hired — a major gaffe. I tried to turn on as much Irish charm as I could muster, but it clearly wasn't working. Inwardly I was upset, for as much as I liked and respected Norman, as a good executive he should have alerted his key people that I'd been hired. My surmise that Allen was miffed proved correct: within a couple of days he resigned.

My next stop was to meet Ray McGranahan, the executive vice president, who had arrived only a few weeks before me. Formerly president of Wilshire Oil, a Gulf subsidiary, McGranahan's role, it was explained, was to oversee the Times Mirror subsidiaries and plan their long-range development. He, too, I could see, had not had prior warning that Casey was coming to bat. Second major gaffe, Mr. Chandler. But unlike Allen, McGranahan did not seem angry or threatened by the news.

Aside from those first two encounters, the rest of our tour was uneventful. I met twenty to thirty key employees that day and got an immediate sense of loyalty and dedication from everyone.

The Chandlers not only had been one of Los Angeles's leading business families, but also were intimately involved in the city's cultural life as well. As I took up my new post, a great deal of time and energy were focused on the city's ambitious, spanking new Music Center, which was due to open a few months later.

One day in mid-October Norman called me in and said: "Al, I've got a problem. And when I have a problem, you have a problem. I'd like you to go see Mrs. Chandler at the Music Center. *She* has a problem, which she'll tell you all about."

The Music Center was Dorothy Chandler's baby. It sat on a hill overlooking the city, a gleaming, ninety-two-foot-high, glass-facaded building with fluted columns and a sculptured overhanging roof — LA's elegant answer to New York's Lincoln Center. I went to the Music Center and found Dorothy Chandler visibly upset.

"Norman asked me to talk to you about a problem you're having with the Music Center —" I began.

"Al," she interrupted, "very simply, we've run out of operating funds."

Dorothy Chandler, a major cultural fixture in Los Angeles,

had individually raised $19 million for the Los Angeles Music Center through her tireless fund-raising drives. There had also been a county bond issue of $15 million, and with that total of $34 million the Dorothy Chandler Pavilion was built.

However, it turned out that a not-so-minor problem still remained: the full $34 million that was raised had already been used up building and furnishing the Center, leaving no money for various preopening operations: rehearsals, costumes, salaries for the administrative staff and musicians, general overhead, and the considerable advertising costs associated with such an ambitious, not to mention prestigious, enterprise.

Although the Center had several hundred thousand dollars in advance ticket sales, under the law these were trusteed funds, which could be released only as the performances were given. But the trusteed amounts could be used as collateral, so the Center had borrowed $350,000 from the Bank of America. Then it had run out of cash again and had no more ticket funds to pledge as collateral. The Center asked the Bank of America for $150,000. The bank, however, was not only unwilling to provide the necessary additional loan but threatening to call the $350,000 already borrowed and spent. I asked Mrs. Chandler to give me the names of all the Music Center's board members and said I would make some phone calls to see if we could hold a meeting that same afternoon. I phoned the members, told them we had a very serious problem regarding the Music Center, and suggested we meet at five o'clock to deal with it. It was a distinguished group, which included Lew Wasserman, chairman of MCA (Music Corporation of America).

We convened promptly at five o'clock. Dorothy Chandler introduced me to everyone. "Mr. Casey is the Times Mirror's new chief financial officer, and I'm sure he can help us solve our problem," she said with an assurance I did not fully share. With that, I started to outline the full scope of the problem.

Before I was three sentences into my explanation, Lew Wasserman interrupted. "Wait a minute," he said. "Before you go on with your sad tale, let me just say that, following your call, I

stopped in at the Bank of America on my way down to this meeting and put my personal signature on a note for a half million dollars. Your three-hundred-and-fifty-thousand-dollar loan has been
resecured and you have one hundred and fifty thousand available
right now."

For once I had nothing to say. Well, very little.

"That's great, Mr. Wasserman," I said. "May I thank you on
behalf of the entire board. I strongly suspect, on the basis of my
brief involvement, that this has to be the shortest board meeting in
the history not only of the Music Center but of Los Angeles. This
meeting is hereby adjourned." Lew was a busy man and wouldn't
have wanted us to waste any time praising his magnanimous
gesture.

I did not see Lew often after that meeting, since we had no
other business relationships. It took me four years to get the
money together to pay off the half-million-dollar note that Lew
had signed. But one day I called him up and said, "Lew, I'm on my
way to the bank to make the final payment on the Music Center
loan you guaranteed and pick up the copy of your note. If you
don't mind, I'd like to deliver it to you and thank you personally
for what you did."

"Fine," he replied. "Why don't you come to the studio for
lunch?"

I stopped by the Bank of America, made the final payment,
picked up the note that he had signed, and drove over to meet Lew
for lunch in the Universal Studios cafeteria. I can't say it was an intimate lunch. Apparently everybody there either needed or
wanted to talk to Lew, the studio boss, so there was a steady stream
of people to our table. During that hour I met more Hollywood
stars than I have met during the rest of my life.

We ceremoniously burned the promissory note in the ashtray.
Then Lew said, "Al, I appreciate what you have done to make the
Music Center a success. If at any time you feel that my services
could be of help to you again, don't hesitate to call on me."

"I appreciate that kind offer, Lew," I said. But since I had seen
the man only twice in four years, I could not imagine when or un-

der what circumstances I might take him up on it. Nonetheless, I made a mental note of his offer.

For most of its corporate life, the Times Mirror Company had depended primarily on a single product, namely the Los Angeles Times newspaper. And this single product was sold, essentially, within a single market, the greater LA area. To expand its product line and its market, in 1959 Times Mirror had brought in McKinsey, which recommended — having been told by Chairman Norman Chandler his fears of holding all his eggs in one basket — that he buy a few more baskets. Norman had been convinced by McKinsey that there was a high probability there would be a recession in the next few years, and the newspaper, so dependent on advertising for its revenues, would be highly vulnerable. McKinsey's advice began to be implemented in 1960, three years before I arrived on the scene. To oversee the diversification effort, Robert Allen was brought in by Norman Chandler to acquire publishing companies outside the LA area. Part of the reason for diversifying was the pressure brought by the stockholders, of which there were only seven hundred at the start of 1959, including — as Norman had warned me — a number of Chandler family members who had inherited stock in the company but did not participate in its management, all of whom wanted to receive a greater return on their investment. In 1959, the company had revenues of $98 million and posted a profit of $4.8 million. More than respectable, at least in the newspaper business, but not overly impressive by Wall Street standards. Shareholders wanted faster growth and better profits. In the world according to McKinsey, diversification was the magic route to both.

Notwithstanding Norman's concerns for the future, the Times Mirror Company had enjoyed eighteen years of solid growth before I came on board. Norman, who was sixty-four when I arrived, had been chairman and president for more than twenty years. Although as head of a family-owned company he had no statutory requirement or, apparently, burning desire to retire, it was generally assumed that the mantle would pass before too long to Otis. But Otis had his hands full with the paper and little time, if indeed interest, in becoming involved with the diversification program currently underway. In my earlier conversations with Norman, he had made it clear that my appointment was based in large measure on his conviction that closer financial supervision was necessary both to evaluate and control the new acquisitions and to assess the worth and synergy of potential new candidates. The plan was to find companies that fit into the general classification of communications, which included books, magazines, television, and indeed other newspapers. As a first step, Times Mirror had acquired, in 1960, the highly respected New American Library of World Literature, the second largest publisher of paperback books in America. In the summer of 1963, it had purchased World Publishing, one of America's leading hardcover publishers of Bibles and dictionaries. And literally a month before I took up my post, it had finalized the acquisition of Matthew Bender and Company, one of the country's foremost publishers of law books.

In June 1963, in a move that ran counter to this expansionist strategy, Times Mirror had sold its only television station, KTTV, for $11 million to John Kluge, of Metromedia. During my first weeks there, I was reviewing the company's recent record and asked why it had sold KTTV, which struck me as a real growth entity. Probing, I found the real reason was emotional rather than financial: the sale had been prompted by the anger of the newspaper people, who were upset and irritated by the television station's continually scooping them on breaking news. The sale was a dumb move, and everybody knew it. John Kluge's Metromedia was going to keep on scooping the *Los Angeles Times* just as KTTV had when it was part of Times Mirror, only now the benefit — financial and other — would accrue to Metromedia. (Today KTTV is worth at least $400 million, which is what Rupert Murdoch's News Corporation paid for it in 1994.)

In May 1964, Times Mirror went public. Our 1963 earnings had been solid: revenues of $177.6 million, with a profit of $9.1

million, or $1.83 a share. This was almost double the revenue and profit of 1959. And from all indications, 1964 was shaping up to be the best year ever. But even the best-laid schemes of mice and conglomerates can go astray, as our acquisition of a small but highly prestigious company was to show.

While most of our planned acquisitions were in the area of communications, we occasionally ventured beyond that already broad category when a top-notch company caught our eye. In 1964 we bought Pickett Incorporated, a small company but a leader in the manufacture of slide rules, with sales of about $2.5 million a year. Slide rules were a widely used tool in architecture and engineering companies, and we also felt we could generate incremental sales through our textbook lines, especially in the elementary and high-school markets. Pickett slide rules were so highly regarded they were selling increasingly in Europe, even in Germany, which prided itself on precision instruments. "Buy quality," I had recommended, and I still believe that's a good place to start. Who could have predicted that, almost overnight, our proud product would be rendered obsolete by the invention of a better mousetrap? But that problem lay in the future.

The same year that we bought Pickett, I noticed, in going through the company's reports, that its inventory was building up, yet I was told it couldn't keep up with sales without paying considerable overtime. Common sense told me that it didn't sound right. Rising inventory and trouble meeting sales just don't mix or match. To check the figures, I sent over an internal auditor. Unbeknownst to me, the company's president, John Pickett, had arranged for a woman to spend the weekend with the auditor, presumably to help him understand the figures. She must have done a fine job, for the auditor came back and reported that everything at Pickett was fine. Really fine.

A couple of months passed, and still the company was reporting difficulty filling orders, coupled with a further increase in inventory. So I sent the auditor back, this time with a list of specific questions I wanted answered. When he arrived, John Pickett informed him that the woman he had been with during the previous visit was pregnant and needed an abortion, which, Pickett said, the auditor would have to pay for.

"I can't do that," replied the auditor. "First, I don't have the money. And second, if my wife ever found out it would destroy a happy family."

Pickett volunteered to pay for the abortion, but on one condition. He wanted a clean report to go back to me. Again the auditor returned and told me all was well. But a sixth sense told me he wasn't telling the truth. So I called in our outside public accounting firm and asked it to audit the company. Before long, the accountants reported back. "Mr. Casey," said the head CPA, "I'm afraid we've uncovered a case of massive fraud." Pickett himself had been taking money out of the company and had hidden his theft by misstating the value of the inventory.

I telephoned Pickett and asked him to be in my office the next afternoon. When he arrived, I confronted him with the story and told him to sit still while I drew up his confession. I asked my secretary to take it down.

I, John Pickett, have been flimflamming Times Mirror by extracting funds illegally from the company . . .

"Now, you sign it," I ordered Pickett.

He said that he had to see his lawyer.

"You sign it or you go to jail within twenty minutes," I replied, though I had no idea how I'd back up my threat. He signed.

"Now, that's the first step," I continued. "The next step is for you to get your ass out of that company. Don't ever show your face in that plant again." He pleaded with me, reminding me it had been his father's company before him.

"You should have thought of your father before you started milking the company," I told him.

"What about my house?" he said. I presumed that he expected me to take his general assets as well. I told him he could keep his house, and I didn't care what he did there, but he was never to set foot again in the plant.

We took the bonus we were to have paid John Pickett and offered it as an incentive to Dow Carpenter, the Times Mirror sectional group vice president to whom John reported. Dow should have uncovered the fraud but hadn't. My initial instinct was to give him hell, but realizing that my first responsibility is always to protect the assets of the company, I removed him from the position of group vice president and made him president of Pickett, as he was more familiar with the operations there than anyone else. I promised him the substantial bonus if he achieved certain objectives over the following two years.

Nothing in business is static; success is determined by what you do with the facts at hand, how quickly you recognize a new situation, and how decisively you act on it. Even though Dow had been negligent, his mistakes were not conscious — since he, too, had every reason to believe in Pickett's basic honesty; it had indeed been his father's company, and who would knowingly sully his father's good name, for God's sake? I believed, given the situation and the incentive, he would perform well. As it turned out he did, and for the couple of years he was there, Pickett did well. But as I just noted, nothing in business is static, and Pickett proved no exception to the (slide) rule. A few short years after we bought it, both Texas Instruments and Hewlett Packard introduced the handheld electronic calculator. Overnight, the Pickett slide rule became obsolete.

Nineteen sixty-four, an election year, gave me a chance to see how seriously people — or maybe only politicians — can sometimes take themselves. It was an election year, and both Nelson Rockefeller and Barry Goldwater were seeking the Republican nomination for president. Both were eager to get the endorsement of the *Los Angeles Times,* which, till Otis Chandler moved in as publisher, had been rigidly, even rabidly, conservative. In 1964 the family and stockholders all favored Goldwater, while the editorial types, headed by Otis, who was trying to move the paper to a more moderate editorial position, favored Rockefeller.

Rockefeller felt it would aid his case if he made a substantial donation to the Dorothy Chandler Pavilion and Music Center.

By this time I had been elected president of the Music Center — perhaps because of the now renowned brevity of my first board meeting — and we were soliciting "founder" donations of $25,000, primarily from major donors. So Rockefeller made a commitment to Mrs. Chandler for a $25,000 donation. He'd have to go see me to work out the details, she told him.

I had known Rockefeller socially but couldn't claim I knew him well. After leaving Mrs. Chandler, he came over to my Times Mirror office and announced that he had brought with him a painting, Picasso's *Blue Lady*. He was going to donate the painting to the Music Center, he announced, and in return he wanted credit for a $25,000 donation.

"Picasso's *Blue Lady* isn't worth twenty-five thousand dollars," I said, bluffing. I didn't know the painting's value, but I was sure it was *at least* the credited amount Rockefeller wanted. "If you give me four thousand in cash, I'll give you credit for a full twenty-five-thousand-dollar donation," I said.

"You don't know your ass from your elbow about what this painting is worth," replied Rockefeller.

"I'm telling you, Governor, it's not worth twenty-five thousand to me, because I need *cash* for the music center. Now, four thousand is a very modest amount, and I want four thousand in cash. Up front."

He finally agreed to give me the $4,000, plus *Blue Lady*. I told him he would have to deliver the painting to the Music Center. I didn't want any part of it at the Times Mirror Company because we would have had to insure it. He said he'd mail me a check for the $4,000, and I told him that as soon as I got the check and the Music Center had sent the receipt for the *Blue Lady*, he'd become a founder.

But I never said a word to Rockefeller about the newspaper's endorsement; I never played that game with anybody. Nor, to his credit, did he ask, though we all knew the reason behind his munificence.

"You can go back to Mrs. Chandler and tell her we have made a deal," I said.

But Picasso's *Blue Lady* never made it to the Music Center.

After he left my office, Rockefeller went back to see Mrs. Chandler, who had recently redecorated her living room. She decided to keep Picasso's *Blue Lady* at home. It looked beautiful on her wall, but I reminded her that she had to take out insurance for it.

"Insure it for how much?" said Mrs. Chandler.

"At least forty, maybe fifty thousand," I said. (By then I had been told by an art expert what the painting was actually worth.) She asked me to insure it under the Music Center coverage, which we did.

Even though Nelson gave us Picasso's *Blue Lady* and $4,000 cash, he didn't get the endorsement. And Mrs. Chandler got the painting, which stayed in her house for seven years.

Then one day my secretary announced that someone was bringing *Blue Lady* over to our offices. Mrs. Chandler had decided to redo her living room and the painting no longer fit into the new décor! We didn't want it, I said, adding that it should be delivered to the Music Center. The Picasso was the Music Center's property and should have been there all along.

By then Picasso had died, and, checking, I found the painting was now worth in the neighborhood of half a million dollars. When asked what I was going to do with it, I replied that I was going to sell it. The Music Center still needed cash.

I asked Franklin Murphy, who in 1968 had been brought in as the Times Mirror chairman, to call Armand Hammer, the head of Occidental Petroleum, and have him give me a call. A billionaire art collector, he owned a museum of his own and his brother operated the Hammer Galleries in New York.

When he called, I came right to the point. "Armand," I said, "we'd like to sell Picasso's *Blue Lady*, and I think it's worth about half a million dollars. Could you tell me what you think it's worth, Armand?"

Armand had no idea what its value was and asked me to send it on to his brother, who would get it appraised.

"Fine," I said. "One other thing, Armand. There is no commission payable."

"What the hell do you mean, Al? No commission?"

I explained to Hammer that the Music Center didn't pay commissions for the sale of art.

"But we're talking about forty-five or fifty thousand dollars!" he said.

I almost commented something to the effect that I thought billionaires would be above such petty concerns but wisely refrained.

"Sorry, Armand, but that's our policy. You should be honored to be helping us."

The painting was subsequently sold by the Hammer Galleries, and a Japanese buyer paid $450,000 for it.

When I next ran into Armand Hammer, he asked about the sale of *Blue Lady*. I filled him in, then said, putting on my most serious face, "I would have paid you a commission if you had gotten the full five hundred thousand." He was not amused.

That should have been the end to the story but it was not. Some years later, Ellie and I went to the 21 Club in New York one night with half a dozen other people. We sat upstairs around one of the big round tables at the head of the stairs. Near us, in the corner on the banquette, was Nelson Rockefeller and his wife, Happy. He had clearly been drinking.

He looked over and saw me, and I could hear him say to Happy: "See that man over there? He's the son of a bitch who made me pay him four thousand dollars *and* Picasso's *Blue Lady* to get credit for a twenty-five-thousand-dollar donation to the Music Center in Los Angeles. Then he went and sold it for half a million goddamned dollars!"

Embarrassed for my guests, I excused myself and went over to speak with him.

"Good evening, Governor. Nice to see you again," I smiled. "I simply wanted to let you know your figure is wrong. I really didn't sell *Blue Lady* for that much," I said. "It only brought four hundred and fifty thousand."

Now it was the governor who was not amused. "I told you he's the bastard who wouldn't give me credit for the lousy twenty-

five thousand without paying four thousand in cash," he repeated
to Happy, who looked more embarrassed than happy.

Rockefeller remained angry, but I had no apologies to make.
I may have driven a hard bargain with him, but all I did was take a
tough negotiating stance in an area where the value in question
was ambiguous, therefore vulnerable to negotiation. Rockefeller
probably thought by his gift to have "bought" the *Los Angeles
Times*'s endorsement, even though that quid pro quo was never
raised. If it had been, I would have tossed him out of the office,
governor or no governor. And his Picasso with him. For your integrity is worth more than all the Picassos in the world: it is, simply, priceless and irreplaceable. If you believe in who you are and
stand on that belief in your business dealings, you can, indeed,
move mountains.

Ray McGranahan, whom I had found to be highly ambitious and,
how shall I say, not exactly a team player, came into my office one
afternoon during that summer of 1964; he was steaming, and it
was not from the Los Angeles heat. He had often alluded to the
fact that he had taken the job with Times Mirror on the understanding he would be made president as soon as Norman retired.
McGranahan's assumption was that Norman would retire when he
reached 65 in September. I was far from certain that was Norman's
assumption. But on more than one occasion McGranahan had col-
lared me and bent my ear about the Chandler clan.

"Al," he said, "my best guess is that no one in this company
whose last name isn't Chandler can ever succeed to president or
chairman."

I responded that I wasn't at all sure that was true but reminded
him that, after all, the Chandlers still owned over 35 percent of the
company. But today he was out of control.

"Al," he said, "I've been here a year. I was made promises
when I came. I *demand* to be made president!"

I'd never liked the man very much; now I liked him even less.

"Ray," I said, "that's a stupid way to go about it. '*Demand* to be made president!' Why don't you discuss it with Norman in a civilized way?"

"I've tried . . . I've tried . . . ," he said. "He keeps putting me off."

"Sorry I can't help," I said, "but I think you're going about it all wrong."

One month later, McGranahan resigned.

One Saturday in October, Norman called me and asked me to drive over to his house.

"Al," he said, "I like the way you do things. It's been just over a year and you've already made your mark here."

I thanked him, not quite sure, but suspecting what the first act to this overture would be.

"As you know, Ray has left us, and we've yet to fill the position of executive vice president," he said. "Al, I want you to take the job."

I'd had a feeling that might be coming, and I'm certain my reply astonished him.

"Norman," I said, "I can't accept the position. I'm very happy in my present job." In fact, Otis was the heir apparent, and I didn't want to get involved in a family squabble.

"You'd also attend board meetings," Norman said, as if offering a carrot.

"I had more than enough problems with the board of directors in my last job," I said, "to last a lifetime."

"Nonetheless —" Norman began. I seldom if ever cut him off, but this time I did.

"Norman," I said. "You should give the title to Otis. He's the obvious choice, the logical choice."

"Otis has his hands full running the paper," Norman continued. "He hasn't got the time or the mind-set to focus on or carry out our diversification program."

"Norman," I told him, "I like my job. I like Times Mirror. I have the feeling that if I accepted, I'd be walking the plank in a matter of months."

"No, you wouldn't," he said. "I'd see to that."

"What does the board think about all this?"

"They're all for it, Al. A hundred percent."

With which he picked up the phone and put in a call to Tex Thornton.

"I'm here with Al," Norman said. "He wants to know what you think about his becoming the executive VP." With which he handed me the phone.

"Al?"

"Yes."

"It's very simple: you *have* to take the job."

And so I became, sincerely against my wishes, the executive vice president of Times Mirror in October 1964.

Otis Chandler, who had been out of town the day of my promotion, was both generous and magnanimous when we met the following week. He congratulated me warmly and said he wholly approved of the move. Perhaps when you're the chairman's son, you feel less threatened than most people in the corporate world. Or perhaps he was simply relieved that the work of implementing the corporate strategy would be on my shoulders, not his.

A few months after my promotion, several Times Mirror executives were invited to a *Fortune* magazine editorial board luncheon. The Chandlers came, as did the publisher and editors of *Fortune*. Henry Luce, the founder and chairman of the board of Time Incorporated, was the host. Twenty of us arrived on time for lunch, introduced ourselves, and waited for Luce in a long, rectangular room high atop the Time-Life Building in midtown Manhattan. I happened to be standing by the only door into the room when Mr. Luce came striding in.

"Hello there," he said. "I'm Harry Luce, chairman of the board of Time. What's your name and what do you do?"

"I'm Al Casey, executive vice president of Times Mirror."

"Fine, Mr. Casey, nice to meet you."

Then the great man went around the table and introduced himself to each of our management members and exchanged pleasantries with the Chandlers. I wandered the other way around the table, and suddenly found myself face-to-face with Luce again.

"Hello, I'm Henry Luce." He smiled. "I'm chairman of Time. What's your name and what do you do?"

"Well, my name's Al Casey and I'm the executive vice president of Times Mirror."

"Fine, nice to meet you, Mr. Casey."

Then we all sat down.

Norman Chandler was having his soup course when Luce said, "You know, Norman, one of the things that has always fascinated me is corporate organization." And Norman was just about to sip a mouthful of soup when Mr. Luce continued, "Tell me, why do you have *two* executive vice presidents?"

"But we don't!" Norman replied, nearly spilling the soup.

"Yes, you do. And they're both here today."

Overhearing the conversation, I raised my hand and said, "Mr. Luce, you met me twice: once at the door and once after you'd made the rounds of the table. Sorry if I confused you."

The fact was, I hadn't confused him; he simply hadn't been paying attention. But I thought diplomacy called for me to be magnanimous and take the blame for his confusion.

Henry Luce tested Casey's Law. If I had been flip or contentious with Luce, the consequences could have been serious. Often, in your dealings with others, you walk a fine line between respect and kowtowing. There are also times when you have to speak up, even when the matter may seem minor and the consequences of saying the wrong thing large. It may seem a small detail, but in business you cannot be intimidated by other people, however powerful. And you can be magnanimous without being obsequious.

*   *   *

Some time later, Henry Grunwald, the editor of *Time* magazine, organized a trip for a group of about twenty business executives to various cities in Europe, including Paris and Moscow. While in Hungary, Grunwald scheduled a three-hour meeting on a Sunday morning with the Budapest Chamber of Commerce, several foreign correspondents, and us visiting business executives.

I knew the meeting was going to be a complete waste of time. While exchanging pleasantries with the locals might be interesting, I didn't see how the meeting could be of any benefit to Times Mirror. Shortly before it was to begin, I looked Grunwald straight in the eye and said: "Excuse me, Henry, but I can't attend the meeting. I'm a Catholic, and I have to go to Mass this morning."

Grunwald, who did not like absentees, shot me an agitated glance but permitted me to leave. Then Vernon Jordan, who at that time was a law partner of Bob Strauss, later to be chairman of the Democratic National Committee, raised his hand and said, "I'm thinking of becoming a Catholic. I need to go to Mass with Al." Grunwald grew slightly redder, but he gave a permissive nod of his head as he let out an exasperated breath.

One of the press photographers with the group, not wanting to get stuck at the meeting either, raised his hand and said to Grunwald, "I think I should go too, so I can take some pictures of Mr. Casey and Mr. Jordan." Grunwald's face turned scarlet with frustration, and he banged his fist down hard on the table.

"All right," he said gruffly. "You're excused too, but that's it. No more!"

When we arrived at the cathedral it was almost completely dark inside, and most of the seats were taken. I turned to Jordan and whispered, "We'll go up to the front. There are always seats up there."

Jordan whispered back nervously, "But Al, I can't see where we're going."

"Just hold on to my shoulder, Vernon," I said.

As we walked up the aisle, Vernon, who is black, leaned in close to my ear and asked, "Al, why is everybody looking at me?"

I craned my head back and said softly, "I don't think they've ever seen a Baptist before, Vern."

Early in 1965, a few months after I had been made executive vice president, I called my mother and invited her out to see us and the children. Norman, learning of her impending visit, asked me to bring her to the Times Mirror annual meeting. Everyone got along, and Mother was clearly impressed by the suave, elegant head of Times Mirror. But impressed or not, she was always one to speak her mind. As we entered the hall, Mother was walking with Norman, with Ellie and me close behind. Although we had never discussed the specifics of my or any other Times Mirror executive's salary with Mother, she obviously had some idea of people's salaries in large corporations. I suddenly heard her saying to Norman in her dulcet Boston accent: "Mr. Chandler, if you don't mind I'd like to make a comment about what you pay your people."

Ellie gave me a look as if to ask if there was a quick way we could sink unnoticed into the ground.

"By all means do," said Norman.

"Well," she said, "it's my honest opinion that no one on God's earth is worth more than fifty thousand dollars a year."

Norman paused for a second, then I heard him say, very gently: "But Mrs. Casey, I pay your son Al more than that."

"I *know*," Mother said without further comment, as if she had just proved her point.

I looked over at Ellie. She had her hand across her face and was shaking. At first I thought she was hiding her face in shame, but then I could see she was trying to restrain her uncontrolled laughter.

For years thereafter, Norman would inevitably introduce me by saying, "I should like you to meet our most overpaid executive. How do I know? His mother told me so."

*   *   *

All the Chandler family's Times Mirror stock was held in a trust fund and could not be distributed until the death of the last member of a list Harry Chandler had put in his will. In the 1960s there were still people on the list who were only in their thirties. Therefore we devised a plan to increase the dividend so that the family could realize an appreciation resulting from the growth of the company. This dividend plan would also provide the Chandler family with current income, but board member Tex Thornton was adamantly opposed to paying dividends. He favored corporate reinvestment and subsequent stock price appreciation, and he certainly had a track record with Litton Industries to prove the wisdom of that strategy.

I was not on the board at that time but attended the meetings as executive vice president. I went to Tex Thornton and told him that he would be voted down.

"We'll see about that," he replied.

Then I visited with each director to ensure their commitment.

At the next board meeting, I presented the dividend plan, and Tex said, "Before you vote on this, I should like to say a few words." He was strong and persuasive, and the board promptly withdrew the dividend action.

At the conclusion of the meeting, Thornton came over and said to me, "Al, I hope you learned something today."

"I certainly did," I replied.

On the issue of the Times Mirror dividend, I had been naive to think that the board of directors would support me over Tex Thornton. However, I found a way around Tex and achieved the objective, although in doing so I strained relationships between the Chandlers, the other board members, and Tex to a rather unpleasant degree. Before the next board meeting, I arranged to buy a small company, Year Book Medical, that was in competition with one of Tex's companies, PDR (Physicians' Desk Reference Manual), and because of the conflict of interest, he was forced to resign from the TMC board. The dividend plan was then passed.

Several years later, I saw Tex at a hotel garage. There was an awkward moment as our eyes met, then I smiled and stuck out my hand.

"Let's put past differences behind us," I said to him. "I want to be friends."

Tex shook my hand, and we never again discussed what had happened with the board. But this strategy of letting bygones be bygones does not always work. Business is not a bed of roses. If you're a successful boss, you are inevitably going to make enemies.

When I received a promotion during my Wall Street days, the man who thought he should have been promoted ahead of me was bitter. If I got onto an elevator with him, he would get out. Not until we were reunited by chance in California did we reconcile.

Our diversification strategy was working well, and the recently acquired companies were pulling their weight both in revenues and profits. What was more, the feared recession, which Norman and Otis were concerned would adversely affect advertising revenues at the *Times,* had miraculously failed to materialize. Southern California was still booming, and so was the paper. Thus, our 1964 sales were just shy of $200 million, and our profits were $12 million, or $2.18 a share, a hefty 19 percent improvement over the previous year. Wall Street also liked what it saw, and we decided, early in 1965, to have a secondary stock offering, essentially to raise capital for future acquisitions. Given our twenty consecutive years of record revenues and four straight years of increased earnings, the offering should have been a breeze. But it turned out to be not only a pain, but uncommonly difficult.

With this offering, Times Mirror would be listed on the New York Stock Exchange. However, we had a not-so-minor problem: one stock exchange restriction forbade the listing of any company that has a large share of its stock in a voting trust. At that time, about one-third of the shares were held in the Chandler trust. Phil West, the man who ruled on stock listings, refused to waive that requirement. Bob Erburu, our general counsel, was eloquent and convincing, to no avail. In a final push, however, he persuaded West that the trust would be collapsed when the last family member on the list of nineteen passed on.

"All right," West relented, "if you'll guarantee me that."

"Absolutely," Erburu said, telling the truth as he always did. The only thing he forgot to mention was that with several family members on that list still in their thirties, that collapse might happen sometime in the next millennium.

The purpose of the secondary stock offering was to enable us to broaden our stockholder base. Since we issued treasury stock to acquire companies, it was also a means of offering liquidity to those who had sold their companies to us and had taken stock in return. Our varied holdings in communications, publishing, timber and paper products, and map and chart companies made Times Mirror's portfolio an attractive investment package. Because we were considered a good prospect, a solid and growing company, many investment firms wanted to be the sponsoring banker for the secondary offering. We were wined and dined by everybody, and on my own I decided to apportion the offering to several different companies. Paine, Webber, Jackson & Curtis in Boston; Goldman, Sachs in New York; Dean Witter in San Francisco; Stone & Webster in Chicago; and Blyth and Company in Los Angeles were selected to be comanagers of the deal.

When the senior partner of the Merrill Lynch office in Los Angeles, Milbank McFee, heard about our decision, he came to see me.

"We've got the right reputation, and we can achieve a wider distribution of the stock," he said. "We can meet *all* your objectives and standards," he stressed.

I explained that we wanted a major portion of the stock to end up in individual stockholders' hands; we did not want to have the stock held predominantly by institutions.

"We can also meet your requirements on that score," he promised. But I knew despite his promise that Merrill Lynch would place most of the stock with institutions.

"Thanks, but I'm going to do it my way and have several underwriters."

Now, McFee was a close golfing friend of Norman Chandler, so he phoned Norman to complain about this fellow Casey. Norman then called me and said, "Al, couldn't you see your way clear to do it Merrill Lynch's way?"

"Norman, this is my responsibility," I said. "Please let me do it my way."

I did offer Merrill Lynch the New York portion of the offering. And the New York officer made the same objection Norman's friend in Los Angeles did. "Why don't we just manage it single-handedly?" he asked. And he added a threat. "If we can't be the manager, we're not going to be in it at all, and that's going to hurt you."

"No way," I replied. It was a tough decision to make, because we had a lot riding on the outcome of the deal, and Merrill Lynch was so big and so powerful that their participation would have ensured that our stock offering would be fully subscribed. But since they couldn't have it all, they refused and bowed out.

While there was some risk in their nonparticipation, I felt that negative was more than offset by the broad participation of the other underwriters and the competition between them that I expected would result.

Nineteen sixty-five was another banner year for Times Mirror: revenues were up 19 percent over 1964, and earnings per share 33 percent. The stockholders were understandably happy, and, closer to home, so were the Chandlers. In January 1966, Norman, Otis, and I journeyed to New York, where we spoke to the Society of Security Analysts about the company's present and, especially, its future.

My concerns about getting involved in a family squabble had proven groundless. Otis and I got along fine, and he was continuing to do a bang-up job on the newspaper front. At the February 1966 board meeting, I was elected president of Times Mirror;

Otis was made president, newspaper and forest products. We both reported to Norman, thus avoiding any potential conflict between us. And both of us were elected to the seven-man executive committee of the board. At sixty-seven, Norman was effectively delegating to me the day-to-day operations and the future planning of Times Mirror.

Although this was my first job as head of a large corporation, over the previous eighteen years I had been observing closely how companies operated at the top and became convinced that most CEOs, and indeed most top executives, had too many people reporting to them. Sometimes it was because they didn't know how to delegate; again it was because they could not bring themselves to relinquish any of the authority, or power, vested in them. Whatever the reason, I had determined that if I ascended to the top job, I would make sure to simplify the reporting process. When Norman named me president, he said, in a memorandum to the staff: "Mr. Casey's appointment makes it possible for me to devote all my energies to the role of chief executive officer." I couldn't have agreed more. A CEO, while keeping tabs on all aspects of the company — from finance to operations to sales and marketing — needs time to plan, to envision, to explore, to compare. Saddled with minutiae, besieged by too many reporting parties, a CEO has no time for the bigger picture, for strategy and planning.

It was with these thoughts in mind that, almost as soon as I started, I simplified the reporting functions to what I thought was the practical minimum. Four people constituted the executive inner sanctum, reporting to the president: the executive vice president; the vice president, finance; the vice president, marketing; and the general counsel, or "corporate wastebasket," as I jokingly dubbed it.

I was familiar enough with the company's key executives to know whom I wanted as executive vice president: Bob Erburu, the general counsel. The then financial vice president, Dennis

Stanfill, had been vying for the same job, and when he didn't get it he resigned and went on to fame and glory at Twentieth Century Fox. So we needed a new financial officer. After extensive interviews, I narrowed the choice down to two candidates. I explained to them that we would have a six-month contest between them, to determine what field the company should enter or expand in. Whichever of the two men had convinced us to follow his strategic course of action would be appointed financial vice president.

One of the men was Ted Marks, a Harvard Business School classmate of mine who had extensive financial experience. He was also well known to everyone in the company. The other finalist was Phil Williams, also a Harvard Business School classmate of mine, who had been working in the mortgage servicing business. I hired both of them on a temporary basis, with the understanding that only one of them would continue with Times Mirror after the contest (the loser would not have wanted to remain). Anyway, I was convinced that in business as in life, it's better to spell things out from the start.

Oddly, given his financial background, it was Ted Marks who felt that mortgage servicing should be our priority. The servicing companies that do the mortgages for banks and for savings and loans send out the monthly bills or coupon books, record payments, and so on. Through computerization, there were all sorts of offshoots, such as mailing lists and benefit records. Phil Williams, whose background was largely in that area, did not believe Times Mirror should get involved. Williams wanted us to go into cable television, and he argued persuasively for his choice.

I weighed each case carefully before making my own judgment. I made both candidates come up with full presentations, including slides to illustrate their points. Each man had two to three hours to make his presentation, and they both really worked at demonstrating the many present and future benefits of their strategy.

After careful reflection I chose cable television. The vagaries of mortgage servicing worried me, and I saw cable television as the wave of the future — at least one of the waves.

Ted Marks was disappointed, said he thought I was making a

mistake, but took the decision like a man. But he asked me one favor: to take the slides and his presentation with him, since someone else might want to buy it.

"Of course," I replied. "Take it all with you."

He later presented his idea to the Wells Fargo board of directors, and they bought virtually the whole program. The resulting expenses, however, nearly broke the bank. The mortgage service business got so competitive that it became a commodity, and everybody was outbidding everybody else.

I was, needless to say, more than relieved to have made the choice I did.

There was another choice I made at the time that might have seemed less momentous but to me was vital. My secretary, Beverly Bechard, announced that she was getting married and would be leaving us. In my new post, I wanted a person whom I could trust, someone I could teach how to do things my way. There was a pool of secretaries who served various executives on an as-needed basis. One of the secretaries who impressed me greatly was a young lady, Elizabeth Scott, known to all as Libby.

"Miss Scott," I said, "I don't care whether or not you can take dictation or whether you can type ninety words a minute. I want someone I can teach to do things my way, someone I can trust completely."

In short, not only did Libby Scott fit that bill to a T for me at Times Mirror, she followed me from there to American Airlines and to Washington when I became postmaster general. In fact, she is still with me today. I do not exaggerate when I say that I would not have been able to write this book without her help, loyalty, and cooperation. Not to mention her wonderful memory.

In 1966, having business in San Francisco, I called on Donald Russell of Southern Pacific out of the blue. It had been five years since we had last spoken, and I thought he might refuse to see me. I was wrong. His secretary ushered me into the same office where I had announced my departure.

We shook hands, a bit awkwardly I admit, then I took a deep breath and said: "Mr. Russell, it has always bothered me that we left on poor terms. I still treasure my days with Southern Pacific and would like to make amends and have your friendship."

His barely audible response was to reiterate that the SP brand was not burned deep enough in my back, but then he said: "Al, it has also bothered me that we parted the way we did. By all means, let's be friends."

And from that day forward we spent many pleasant afternoons together playing dominoes or just talking at the Bohemian Club Grove, to which we both belonged. The Grove, situated some ninety miles north of San Francisco, is a great place to restore body and soul and meet old friends in an environment free of stress. Even though I had doubtless let too much time go by before making my gesture to Donald Russell, I had always known that one day I would. My suspicion was that if I had tried much sooner, a still unforgiving Russell might have turned me down. And once I had done so, it might then have been impossible to try again. It was all a matter of picking the right moment.

Over the next few years, Times Mirror aggressively sought to bring other related businesses under its corporate umbrella. It expanded further into book and magazine publishing, purchasing the well-known *Outdoor Life* and *Popular Science* magazines, and later *Golf* and *Ski* magazines; medical publishers C. V. Mosby and Year Book Medical; and the art book publisher Harry N. Abrams. As the company's need for newsprint grew, Times Mirror built an additional newsprint mill in Newberg, Oregon, and acquired forest product firms in the Pacific Northwest to provide the raw material for the newsprint mill, thus greatly reducing the company's newsprint expenses. In addition to our station KDFW-TV in Dallas, we later acquired cable television systems in California, New York, and Florida. We were not acquiring companies willy-nilly, however. Acquisitions can be a risky game, and without careful measures both of the intrinsic value of the new company and of its fit into the corporation, the potential for loss could be considerable.

When assessing each potential acquisition it was critical to determine why the selling stockholders were willing to sell. Sometimes the reason was heightened competition, lack of a worthy replacement for a retiring CEO, or, more than once, family disagreement among shareholders of a family-owned company; or it was loss of an important client or major supply contract. Until we determined this key element, whatever it was, we wouldn't bid for the acquisition, because we couldn't fairly evaluate the quality of the company's expected future earnings stream. The seller never provides a buyer with bad news. It's up to the buyer to ferret it out as best he can, through probing and proper due diligence.

We acquired some companies for cash, but in most cases we used unregistered treasury stock, also called letter stock. These are shares that have been authorized by the board of directors and the shareholders but held unissued in the company's treasury. The recipients of these shares receive dividends and can vote at the annual meetings, but they are not free to sell them until the shares have become "registered" by means of a secondary offering — which means that the issuing company must prepare an "offering prospectus" that covers these shares and includes a financial history of the company, a list of directors and officers, and a description of the company's business.

One way of ensuring continuity, I found, and buying ourselves a kind of insurance policy, was to sign up three or four of the key executives of the company to be acquired with three-to-five-year contingent bonus arrangements. I would offer them an attractive bonus if the forecasted results were achieved. The executives of the acquired company liked this arrangement because it ensured that I didn't plan to move in and start a wholesale housecleaning. I'd inevitably make it clear to them, however, that I had a firm grasp on the business's basics — from inventory to cash flow to obsolescence — so that there could be no chance their long and intimate knowledge of their company could ever be used to conceal or obfuscate.

Both *Outdoor Life* and *Popular Science*, which had been acquired in 1967, owned book clubs, with hundreds of thousands of members. And the book clubs, highly successful themselves, also helped the magazine. For once that much-abused and overused term *synergy* really seemed to be working.

We set sales and profit goals for each of these companies: in every instance we worked closely with the executives in assessing the company's potential and in targeting realistic goals. For most of them, we aimed for annual profit increases of 15 percent. Tough, but not impossible. I have always believed in incentives as a key to productivity and success. At Times Mirror I had my first opportunity to put that belief to work. If a CEO and the management team of any company met their targets, the reward should be substantial. At each Times Mirror company we instituted a quarterly "report card," where progress toward annual goals was assessed, and targets adjusted upward or downward if necessary — a kind of reality check. If our goals were met, employees could — and did — receive bonuses as high as 40 to 50 percent of their annual salaries. At first I ran into some opposition from the Chandlers, who were worried I was giving the store away, but as sales and profits soared quarter after quarter, that concern gave way to enthusiastic endorsement.

In each company, too, we installed my five-man executive team, that is, the CEO and his four key executives, and instituted weekly Monday-morning meetings of the top team. That one-hour meeting brought them all up to speed on the company's plans and problems and gave them the information they needed to pass on down the line. In addition, cloning a policy I had instituted at Times Mirror itself, I asked the CEOs of each subsidiary company to follow up the Monday-morning session with a one-on-one meeting, no longer than an hour, with each of his or her four key people once a week, where individual views and concerns could be aired candidly and openly.

One day in the mid-sixties I flew to Chicago to pay a visit to Year Book Medical, which was not meeting our profit goal. I had urged the people at Year Book Medical to come up with plans and projects for making the 15 percent goal, but strategize and scheme as they might, they seemed unable to approach, much less reach, the target.

"Al, we just can't do it," management said, shaking its collective head. "There's just no way we can come up with fifteen percent profit."

"I have an idea," I said half jokingly. "What you need is a book club, and we'll call it Disease of the Month."

They took my half joke dead seriously, and shortly thereafter started a club using that name. Years later, it is still going strong, a major success. Talk to doctors anywhere, they all know Disease of the Month. And by the way, Year Book Medical, thanks to its Disease of the Month, did manage to come through with its 15 percent profit increase.

In 1968, Norman Chandler, then sixty-nine, called me into his office.

"Al," he said, "I've made a decision that it's time for me to step down as chairman —"

As I started to interrupt he held up his hand:

"I have no intention of fading away. I'll remain as chairman of the executive committee."

"Will Otis take over?"

Norman shook his head. "No, Al, he won't. That would be my preference of course, but we Chandlers are not only numerous, we're sorely divided on many counts. For many of the Chandlers — what I call the 'other side' — Otis is far too liberal. Otis will be vice chairman."

"And as chairman?" I knew I was not in line for the job, nor did I want it. At this point it was more of a figurehead than an operational post.

"Franklin Murphy," Norman said. "He's a good man, well liked and respected in the community. And he'll not interfere with you in any way."

"A good choice," I said, "though I must say, Norman, I'll greatly miss working with you directly."

Franklin Murphy — Dr. Franklin Murphy — had been on the Times Mirror board for the previous three years. He came out of academe: at that point he was chancellor of UCLA, having come to California from the Midwest, where he was chancellor of the University of Kansas. He was on the board at the National Gallery of Art in Washington, D.C., the Bank of America, and the Ahmanson Savings Corporation. He was an impressive-looking man with a courtly air and a stentorian voice. A fine chairman.

The only problem was: how would I cope with having to work side by side with a Murphy for the first time in my life?

Our 1965 stock offering was so successful that, in 1971, we decided to do another, again essentially to fund our ongoing acquisition program. As before, while we acquired some companies for cash, in most cases we used unregistered treasury stock. Most of our deals employed this technique, a kind of corporate IOU that enables the holder to comply with the SEC rule against selling such stock except under certain circumstances. There is no rule against awarding the registration rights for the shares to be included in a subsequent secondary. The acquiring company, in this instance Times Mirror Company, does not want to grant a secondary to the selling company's shareholders, because during the preparation for, and the selling of, a secondary, the acquiring company must "stand still" for a reasonable period both before and after the sale of the shares. Since we generally were negotiating with at least half a dozen potential acquisitions for Times Mirror Company at any given time, we always wanted to pick the most propitious moment to have a secondary.

At the time of the new offering, Merrill Lynch, still upset at not having been the sole sponsor of the earlier offering, was seemingly still pouting. In any case, Times Mirror and Merrill Lynch were not on speaking terms. This is ridiculous, I said to myself. Times Mirror Company, a burgeoning publishing giant on the West Coast, not even talking to Merrill Lynch. I always try to repair relationships; it's a matter of principle.

By then my old friend Don Regan had risen to become head of Merrill Lynch. When I was at Harvard, Don Regan and I were copresidents of the Harvard Catholic Club. We parted company to serve in World War II, and after the war Don went to work for Merrill Lynch, steadily climbing the executive ladder. By the time I went out to Times Mirror, he was the senior officer at Merrill Lynch in New York. He went on later to serve President Reagan in a variety of posts.

I spoke first with the people who ran the Merrill Lynch offices in Los Angeles and New York. It was still their position that they get all of a deal or they wouldn't participate. Finally, in exasperation, I called Don.

"Don, I have nobody to have lunch with next Tuesday. I'm going to be in New York. Why don't you invite me to have lunch with you."

"What in the hell are you calling me for?" he said. "I don't understand. I don't hear from you in fifteen years, and now you call me up and say you want me to take you to lunch."

"That's right," I replied. "Maybe you should assume that if I've waited fifteen years to call you, I have my reasons."

"Okay," he said, but I wasn't sure he was convinced.

I took along Bob Erburu and Phil Williams. We were to meet Don in a very posh dining room in a downtown Manhattan luncheon club. The table was set for more than a dozen people. All the Merrill Lynch officers came in at the same time as we did, on time, except for Don. So we stood around making small talk. Nobody sat down. When Don went to a lunch for Merrill Lynch, nobody sat until he did.

"Let's sit down and have a glass of water or something," I finally said.

"We can't sit until Don sits. He has to be the first."

"That's the biggest piece of baloney I ever heard of," I said. "Does Don know that rule?"

"He instituted it."

Just then the phone rang, and we received a report from the front. "Don has left his office," the caller said. "He's approaching in his car."

A few minutes later there was another phone call, this time from the chauffeur. He'd left Don off at the ground floor of the club. So Don would be approaching the elevator. I couldn't believe this. Finally someone near the door murmured, "He's here, he's here."

"Don," I said, shaking his hand, "are you aware we haven't been able to sit down and have a glass of water, just because you weren't here?"

Rather than apologize, he said, "Al, you sit with me."

I realized Regan's employees were frightened to death of him. I was appalled. I could never have run an organization like that. Yet I knew that there were many companies, including giant corporations, where fear ruled the roost, and the CEO acted more like some potentate than a simple businessman. In any event, we worked out a deal together, and I gave Merrill Lynch some of our stock business, just as I had wanted to all along. Merrill Lynch still wanted to be our lead underwriter; instead, we made them one of the syndicate.

Don certainly wasn't imperious with me. I wouldn't have let him. I talked to him on the phone a couple of times after he left Merrill Lynch, but that lunch in New York was the only time I saw him for years. When I went to Washington as postmaster general, he had been secretary of the treasury under President Reagan before switching jobs with Jim Baker and serving as White House chief of staff. He called me as soon as I started work at the post office and said, "Al, I want you to join me for lunch at the White House."

And over a period of nine months he invited me to lunch several times. Don and I would always eat alone, just the two of us, in his office, because in the common lunch room he, as chief of staff, was constantly besieged by various staff members who wanted either the president's ear, an update on their favorite project, or some special favor.

In the early fall of 1971, Jack Valenti, president of the Motion Picture Producers and Distributors of America, called and suggested I talk with his old boss, former president Lyndon Johnson, about the possible purchase by Times Mirror of the Johnson family television station in Austin, Texas. LBJ, having decided not to stand for reelection in 1968, was back home on his ranch on the Pedernales River, west of Austin. The Vietnam War, which many in the country blamed on Johnson, was still raging, and his "retirement" was more like an ostracism. Most of the leaders in the Democratic Party shunned him; his ranch had become his Elba. And his health was failing, too; he had had several heart attacks, brought on, one suspected, by his presidency — beginning so tragically in Dallas when President Kennedy was assassinated, and burdened by social and racial unrest and an increasingly divisive war at the other end of the world — which had taken such a toll.

I had never heard of LBJ's television station, KTBC, but I learned a lot about it very quickly. And about the former president of the United States as well. Most important, over the next year, I learned more than I ever wanted to know about the art of negotiation. I had done a fair amount of negotiating earlier in my business life, but dealing with LBJ was a whole new ball game. First, he was his own negotiator; he deferred nothing to anyone. Second, he was always fully prepared on any subject. He genuinely worked at versing himself in the FCC rules; he knew what was happening in the Austin market; why there could be only one VHF station in the area; how to man and staff; how to sell advertising. On every aspect of KTBC, he was an absolute expert.

We didn't have much trouble with the size of the Austin market. We didn't have much trouble with the FCC rules or how to run the station. Our only basic problem was price: we just never seemed to be able to get together on the price. And the distance between our offers — my $8 million and his asking price of $12 million — seemed a gap I'd never be able to bridge. But the fact we were talking made me think he really did want to sell and, if I was patient, we just might eventually come to terms.

For half a year or so, I repeatedly called on LBJ at his ranch. Usually I flew in to Austin and rented a car and drove out to the ranch. As I approached the gates I always reviewed what I hoped to accomplish, but I soon realized it was folly to imagine I could set the agenda. LBJ was a superb negotiator, and although I had been in business twenty years, he sometimes made me feel like a rank amateur. He had an uncanny ability to keep a discussion going until he had the advantage. He also liked to celebrate his advantage with a Scotch and soda — or several — after which we would tour the ranch in the open white Lincoln Continental. If things were going well or he was in a good mood, it was "Al, this" and "Al that"; if he had some other problem on his mind or we were making no progress, it was back to "Mr. Casey."

Each time I visited him, usually on a Saturday morning, I would be ushered into LBJ's den.

"Good morning, Mr. President," I would say.

"Here, Al," he would respond. "Look at this." And he would hand me a small slip of paper. He did this every time we met. The paper inevitably contained three items, which were our agenda for that meeting. Once we had discussed them point by point, it was time for fun — lunch, a tour of the ranch, or a trip to Austin. LBJ also set the "fun and games" agenda. Once we flew to Bergstrom Air Force Base so the president could visit with "his boys," by which he meant the military men who had been loyal to him during the Vietnam War. I was told to leave my rental car at the ranch, and it was a month before it was returned to the agency.

One day the president and I were arguing during one of our negotiating sessions. Leonard Marks, his lawyer, listened in. In fact, President Johnson was negotiating with me with the advice of Marks, and they were both saying that they wanted more money, they wanted more beneficial conditions.

"Bull," I said. "I came down here, and you knew in advance what the conditions were."

The president looked hurt and pained. "I'm going into the bedroom," he said. And he did. He then screamed, "Leonard, come in here. And close the door!"

I could hear their voices without being able to understand what they were saying. They talked for a long time. Finally Leonard came out.

"Al, the president wants to see you in the bedroom," he said.

We went in together. There was Lyndon, supine on the bed with a small tank of oxygen, the plastic mask on his mouth.

"Al, I want you to know you're *killing* the president of the United States," he said, taking off the mask, then quickly putting it back on before I could respond. Then he removed it again briefly to add, "Leonard, don't you dare leave me."

I was crestfallen because I knew we were not going to make the deal that day. I had been outfoxed again.

Shortly thereafter, LBJ phoned me in LA: "Al," he drawled, "I need you down here. Tomorrow. I've got to do a favor for my ranch manager, Dale Malechek. He's just divorced his wife Brenda and needs to buy a house in Austin. I'm going to arrange for his mortgage money, in return for which he'll continue working on the ranch. I'd like you to fly with Lady Bird and me to Austin, to check out a house he had picked out. Of course, before we do, we'll continue our negotiations about KTBC."

I flew to Austin and drove out to the ranch. Lyndon and I continued our ritual dance for a couple of hours, had lunch with Lady Bird, then flew from the ranch — Lyndon had his own airstrip there — over to Austin. Dale's wife, Brenda, went with us, since she was Lyndon's driver. Kind of strange, I thought, being part of the elite contingent to find her newly divorced husband a home. But Lyndon would have no other driver, and besides, it was none of my damn business. Nor did my job description at Times Mirror include house-hunting for the manager of someone's ranch. But although this was a totally peripheral event, I knew that it was, in the complex LBJ scheme of things, part of the negotiating process.

We drove to a development of modest one-story brick homes. There were houses by the dozen, up and down the streets, very uniform in appearance. Almost impossible to tell one from the other.

LBJ had the address of the place we were to inspect. When we arrived, I told him I had nothing to contribute, so I would stay in the car. "No, you won't," he said. "I want your opinion. Mrs. Johnson and I, Brenda and you, will make the decision whether Dale gets this house or not," he said. I knew Lyndon consulted with Lady Bird on virtually all matters. A woman of enormous dignity and grace, with a keen mind, she always gave her husband good, practical advice. But first he wanted to be sure he was getting good value for his investment. He lined us up like so many strangely clad soldiers on the curb and lectured us.

"Now, hold all your opinions until we've completed the tour of the house," he said. We went in and discovered that the walls were purple and red. And there were mirrors all around the master bedroom. We inspected all the rooms, which were unfurnished, in great detail.

"Now remember, keep your opinions to yourself until we get outside," the president said.

Then he lined us up on the curb again and said, "Al, would you buy that house?"

"No," I said.

"Get in the car, Al," he ordered.

The others all agreed it was a fine house and LBJ should buy it. We drove back to the airport; not till we got there did Lyndon ask me why I was the only person in the group who would not buy that house.

"It was the only house on the street that had a one-car garage," I said. "All the others had two. If bad times come, and lots of houses go on the market, people will want the houses with two-car garages, not one."

"Why didn't you say something?" he said.

"You told me to keep my mouth shut and get in the car," I replied.

"Well, for God's sake, you don't *always* have to listen to me!" he said.

From then on he called me a two-car-garage guy.

Johnson had an all-consuming need to be the center of attention. That was why he became so personally involved in the negotiations for the sale of his TV station. His three-item list served two additional purposes. First, this method stretched out the negotiations, testing my patience and resolve. Second, it enabled LBJ to win a kind of victory each time we met, since he always asked for at least one thing he knew I could — or would have to — approve. For example, once he made a federal case about making sure that Lady Bird would always have a priority parking place in the station basement garage. Chalk one up for his side.

During our many visits, over the course of a year, President Johnson and I became friends. I could sense his mood as soon as I arrived. One day when I went to see him LBJ seemed distracted, not himself. I could see I didn't have his attention. We were making no progress on our three agenda items, and to make matters worse, he kept getting up and leaving the room, and by the time he returned we'd have to start all over again.

"Sit down, Al," he said rather peremptorily, I thought, when he came back into the room for the *n*th time.

"Mr. President, I can see I don't have your full attention, so we're not going to get anywhere today. I have a dinner engagement in Seattle this evening, and we both know you can't easily get from Austin to Seattle. So I need to get an early start."

"No," he said. "Let me tell you about what's bothering me. Al, I'm going to die soon, and they're going to bury me out there in the family plot under that big tree on the banks of the Pedernales." He motioned with his head toward the window.

"Heads of state from around the world will come to the service. The marines are going to shoot off their rifles. And there are going to be three speakers.

"My good friend, Governor John Connally, will give the first eulogy. He'll let his hair grow for three weeks beforehand so he can throw back his mane. And he'll raise his chin when he speaks, so the photographers can get a good profile."

I interrupted — not something you did easily or often with Lyndon Johnson. "John Connally's a friend of mine, too," I said. "He's a smart man. But how in heaven's name is he going to know in advance when to start letting his hair grow?"

LBJ stared at me. He put his hands on his chest, the way a preacher might as he reached the climax of his sermon.

"He'll know," he answered. "He'll know." Then he continued mournfully: "My friend the Reverend Billy Graham will be the next to speak. He'll be wearing his long robes. He'll be very dramatic, swaying this way and that. And he, too, will say grand things about me.

"Then our German minister from the little Baptist church down the road will speak. I brought him over here this morning. I told him I was going to die, and I showed him where I'm going to be buried. I told him heads of state are going to come, Billy Graham is going to come, and Governor Connally is going to give the eulogy. And then I said, 'But it's you, Pastor, who's going to close the ceremony.' So I said to him: 'What are you going to say?' And this is what he answered: 'Lyndon Johnson was a man of the people, a child of the sod, he loved his family, and he was a good neighbor.' Not a word about what I did to raise the status of the poor and the black people of this country, not a peep about all the work I did for civil rights. Nothing about what I did for undeveloped nations or the spread of education. So I said to him: 'No, no, no, Pastor. That's not at all what I had in mind.'"

"Mr. President, why don't you level with him? Tell him what you'd like him to say."

"Well, Al, I've got him in the next room. But I need some help putting down my ideas."

"This is a very easy problem to solve, Mr. President. You and I can sit down right now and write your eulogy, and then you can give it to your pastor."

And for the next hour that is exactly what we did. LBJ and I tossed phrases back and forth to each other, and when we had reached a consensus or settled on a felicitous phrase, I would write it down. Johnson went on at great length about his devotion and loyalty to his predecessor, doubtless because the manner in which he had come to the presidency carried with it, in his view and that of many other Americans, a taint, and he felt a bounden duty to erase it. He waxed poetic, too, about his contribution to bettering the lot of American blacks, an accomplishment all the more important because of his southern heritage and background.

"Al," he said, "I want some especially felicitous phrases about my education programs. People have short memories, but history, I'm sure, will give me full credit for that."

So we wrestled with phrases about the importance and value of education in our society, and LBJ's commitment to it throughout his five years in office. Then we moved to his long and loyal service in the Congress, where he had spent many of the happiest and most productive years of his life. And of course we mentioned in glowing terms the vision and accomplishments of the Great Society, of which he was most proud.

When we were finished, I handed the handwritten pages to him to read over and approve. He would read two or three lines, then nod approvingly, sometimes murmuring, "Yes, that's right. That's exactly right." He especially liked the references to the Great Society, which we had decided ought to open the eulogy. In fact, he liked the whole thing so much he wanted to deliver it himself, which I told him might pose a slight problem.

"Now, Mr. President," I said, "why don't you go into the next room, give it to your pastor, and have him read it. When you're satisfied, come back, and we'll resume our negotiations."

After quite a spell, the president returned and said, "He's got it down perfect, Al. He's going to be just fine. I really appreciate your help. That's a great load off my mind."

"Great!" I said. "Now, what's on our list today? What are the three things?"

"There are just two today. The eulogy was one, Al. The other is, my children have to get a higher rent for a land lease under the KTBC television tower."

I agreed to the request, and minutes later we were in the white Continental, with a Scotch and soda in hand, cruising around the ranch. I never did make it to Seattle for dinner.

I often left the ranch after a day's negotiations feeling I had made no progress. To make matters more complicated, Jack Valenti had made me promise "to pay our great president" 5 percent more than we would have paid anyone else. It was a difficult promise to keep, because LBJ's asking price was $4 million more than our initial offer. At one point we were so far apart we didn't see each other for a good six months. But I never gave up hope. Eventually we raised our offer to $9 million and he accepted. It was a fair price, and both sides were satisfied. We finally closed on the deal in late October 1972.

Several months later the president did, as he had so sagely predicted, die. Ellie and I, together with Gregory Peck and his wife, flew to LBJ's ranch for the funeral, as guests on the chartered plane of Edie and Lew Wasserman. And as LBJ had also predicted, there were many heads of state present. And the marines did shoot their rifles. And Governor Connally had miraculously let his hair grow for three weeks. And the Reverend Billy Graham appeared in his flowing robes. Each speaker eloquently set forth how much President Johnson had done not only for his country but for people everywhere. Finally then, the local pastor stood up to speak. My pulse quickened as I waited to hear the eulogy I had written with the president.

"Ladies and gentlemen," the pastor intoned, "Lyndon Johnson was a man of the people, a child of the sod, he loved his family, and he was a good neighbor." Then he sat down.

I looked at the heavens, fully expecting to see President Johnson's wrathful hand emerge from the rain-filled clouds to smite the neglectful pastor. But no hand emerged, and only I knew of the omission, which seems to illustrate again the truth of the old saying about the best laid schemes of mice and men. Even the most powerful men cannot control everything.

That negotiating experience taught me that if you want to reach your goal, you have to really know the people you are doing business with, as I got to know LBJ. Over the long months of our negotiation I made a friend in President Johnson, and he in turn learned to trust me. He was willing to sell the family jewel, but only at a fair price and, I sensed, to a buyer he liked. Our friendship did not mean he let the station go for less than it was worth. Nor would I, despite our newly forged relationship, have paid more — well, maybe 5 percent more — than I thought it was worth. There were many times over the long months of talks when I heard Murphy whispering in my ear, "Forget it, Casey, this will *never* work." But Casey's Law prevailed: the Johnsons were pleased, and the Times Mirror made a good investment. Today, KTBC is worth at least $50 million.

Despite Phil Williams's convincing presentation advocating the rich future of cable television, it was not until 1972 that Times Mirror finally made the plunge. We decided to enter that largely uncharted world for two reasons: one, we thought it was a wave of the future; and, two, we wanted to challenge Jack Kent Cooke, the high-profile owner of the Los Angeles Lakers and the Los Angeles Kings. A very successful businessman, Cooke controlled a company called Teleprompter that was also just getting into cable television. Both Teleprompter and Times Mirror invested in cable television in Hillsborough County, which surrounds Tampa, Florida; we were told it was an excellent testing ground for cable because of the demographics. The only problem was, I didn't know about Cooke's investment nor he about ours. Whether our dual investment was pure fluke or the result of some smart but less than scrupulous cable entrepreneur selling us both on the area, I have no idea.

In any case, before long I discovered that the system we had in Hillsborough County wasn't meeting financial expectations; we just weren't getting the necessary cash flow. That's critical in cable, because of the substantial initial investment. You need cash back fast to begin repaying the investment. And it wasn't happening.

Before we could sell cable television subscriptions we had to have all the necessary receivers fitted and cables hung from utility poles or buried underground. We also had to purchase an advance supply of conversion boxes to rent to our customers.

The problem was, our cable group in Tampa was not meeting its targets. We would draw up a plan, which was reasonable and realizable, and month after month we would have a significant shortfall. I couldn't figure out why. So I decided to hop on a plane to Tampa and check it out personally. To my shock and dismay, I discovered we weren't alone in Tampa: there was a competing cable system, licensed by the city of Tampa and owned by Jack Kent Cooke. Now, parallel cable systems in residential areas make no economic sense. It was like having parallel streetcar lines. Under such circumstances, there was no way we — or Cooke — could ever make any money.

I had brought along my trusty Polaroid camera, and I scoured the section of the city where the dual systems were installed, snapping pictures of both. The Polaroid snapshots were grainy, but the evidence was plain to see: in addition to the duplicate thick power cables strung tightly along the top of the poles and the phone lines slung loosely lower down, the photographs showed two thin black television cables, one belonging to Times Mirror, the other to Cooke's company. There were parallel underground installations as well, which I could prove but not document on film.

Cooke was a very independent man. To take but one example, when he couldn't come to a satisfactory agreement with the County of Los Angeles to build a stadium to house his two sports franchises, he simply went out and built the Forum himself.

I knew he was tough and proud, not an easy one to deal with. Still, I had no choice and put in a call to his office, simply saying I needed to see him on a "fairly urgent matter."

I went to see Cooke at his Los Angeles office, which was in the Forum, and told him, without further ado, that both of us had installed competing cable systems in the same county.

"Don't ask me how it happened," I said, "but it did. So now one of us needs to sell out, or neither of us will ever make any money."

He did not like threats.

"I can't believe what you're telling me," he said.

"Jack, here are the pictures," I said. "And here's your manager's name and phone number. Put him on the speakerphone, and you and I will ask him some questions."

"Al, if I didn't respect your company so much, I'd tell you you were nuts," he replied.

But he called the manager and told him about the pictures I had taken of the competing systems.

The manager had never told Cooke about our system. His boss hung up after a brief conversation, and by the look on his face I surmised that the man would soon be pounding the pavement.

"It's clear one of us has to buy the other out, or we'll both go under," I said. "I'll take either position. I'll buy you out or I'll sell to you."

Cooke stiffened visibly and answered imperiously: "Al, I *never* sell. I'll buy *you* out." We discussed terms, and I agreed Times Mirror would receive about $6 million, which I had calculated was a good price based on the information we had available. At that time, a purchaser would pay $125 per actual/potential subscriber. In a negotiation, I always do my own calculations. As they say on Wall Street, he who writes the check writes the deal. Cooke wanted to pay for the purchase in Teleprompter stock.

"I'm not going to give you the stock for less than seventy-two dollars a share," Cooke said. "Divide the six million by seventy-two."

"I can't agree to that," I said, "since the stock is currently selling for forty-two dollars a share."

Cooke asked me what I *would* do, and I replied, "We'll pick a week in the future. You can pick the week, I don't care when it is. Between a year and a half and two and a half years from now, and whatever the price is then, that will be the price in our deal. You pick the week."

"Something funny's going on, Al," said Jack. But he agreed on two years.

"Fine," I said.

Now, two years is a long time in a deal like this. Typically, you go from six months to a year.

We signed that deal on August 16, 1972, and on August 31, 1974, Teleprompter, by reason of its borrowing restrictions, could not issue equity in that amount, so Times Mirror accepted $6,000,000 of notes and 60,000 shares of stock as a bonus.

In 1971, Jim Chambers, the publisher of the *Dallas Times Herald,* which Times Mirror had purchased a year or so before, invited me to be his guest at the Gridiron Dinner in Washington, D.C. It was my first Gridiron Dinner, an annual affair attended by many luminaries of the sports, communications, and political worlds, and I enjoyed it greatly.

In Washington I was staying at the Madison Hotel, and the morning following the sports bash, Jim had a breakfast obligation at another hotel. The plan was that after breakfast he was going to swing by with some other people and take me to the White House, where the Reverend Billy Graham was slated to conduct a service in the West Wing.

On my way down to the lobby to wait for Jim, I found myself riding alone in the elevator with Billy Graham.

"Reverend Graham, I'm very pleased to meet you," I said. "My name's Al Casey. I've heard you speak on the radio and in church several times. And I greatly enjoyed your eulogy for President Johnson in Austin."

"Thank you very much," replied the famous clergyman. "It's nice to meet you, Mr. Casey."

It was quickly apparent that he was also waiting to be picked up. Graham and I were the only ones in the lobby area. In a short time, we had exhausted all our common points of interest. In fact, we had doubtless said whatever we were going to say in the elevator coming down. So we sat and looked at each other and talked about the weather and watched people coming and going in and out of the hotel. I said how much I had enjoyed the Gridiron Dinner.

"I'm glad you did. It's a very festive occasion, isn't it?"

I averred it was, then we lapsed into silence again.

"It's a nice day, isn't it?" said Billy Graham.

We were really having a difficult time finding common ground, but for about fifteen minutes we struggled on, with long periods of silence between further idle, if not inane, comments.

Fortunately, both our rides came along at about the same time, and in separate cars we headed for the White House. I went into the West Wing with Jim Chambers's party and sat down. President and Mrs. Nixon arrived, and we sang some hymns. President Nixon then said he imagined Billy Graham would give an outstanding sermon. And he did.

Afterward, the chief of protocol stood up and said, "Now folks, please stay in your seats. The president and Reverend Graham will meet you in the East Room." That large, gracious room is where most White House receptions take place.

Jim Chambers grabbed me by the arm and said, "Come with me, Al. I know a shortcut. Go over toward the outside wall where all those windows are."

There was a line of doors along the outside wall that, if you knew the way, you could slip through, thus evading the crush of the main corridor, down which the people were streaming to line up to say hello to President Nixon and Graham.

In about two minutes we came out into the East Wing reception area, where the president and Billy Graham were standing. We walked up to a marine who was standing beside the president.

The marine asked our names and then gave them to the president. Jim, knowing both men well, smiled, shook hands, said, "Good morning, Mr. President. Good morning, Reverend Graham," and was on his way to the coffee and donuts.

As he left, the marine said to me, "Remember now, you must never leave the president alone. You must stay with him and talk to him until the next person comes along."

Unbeknownst to me, there was another marine at the door leading into the room from the main corridor. Seeing me alone there with the president and Billy Graham, he assumed a highly personal conversation was taking place, so he held up all the other guests, allowing none of them in. Meanwhile, the marine had introduced me to President Nixon, and I spoke with him briefly. "What do you do, Mr. Casey?" the president asked, glancing nervously over my shoulder at the doorway.

"I'm president of Times Mirror, Mr. President." At that he brightened.

"Ah, the *L.A. Times.* My earliest supporters," he said, but I could sense his thoughts were elsewhere.

I didn't have much else to say, but I didn't dare move on because the marine had told me to stay put. So we talked a bit about the service and the sermon and the weather. Finally Nixon said, "Reverend Graham, I would like you to meet Albert Casey."

"Of all the people in Washington, I have spent more time today with Albert Casey than any other person," said Graham pleasantly, which only led the president to raise his esteem of the previously little-known Mr. Casey a notch or two higher. Maybe even three. Obviously, a dear friend of Billy Graham was a friend of his.

Then, turning to the marine beside him, the president said, "For some reason your colleague seems to be holding up the crowd at the door. Please tell him he should start letting the people in."

That was the memorable day when I had, for all the wrong reasons, both President Nixon and Billy Graham all to myself.

6

LEAVING TIMES MIRROR

IN THE SUMMER OF 1972 I received a phone call from Mr. X, a big gun on Wall Street and a member of a very prestigious public accounting firm. I had never met the man personally, but he was, I knew, a fairly close friend of Otis Chandler. In fact, if I recalled correctly, Otis and he had gone big-game hunting together on more than one occasion. On the phone he was pleasant enough.

"Mr. Casey," he said, "I understand you'll be in New York sometime in the next few days, and I wonder if we could get together."

I'd be happy to, I told him, and asked if he could tell me what business he cared to discuss, in case I needed to bring along any information or materials for him. Although I have a reputation for being pretty relaxed and — after several years in California — even "laid back," I always like to be mentally prepared for any meeting. And given Times Mirror's ongoing acquisition program, I assumed he probably had a business he was interested in selling us. The man's response was evasive, however, but we agreed to meet for breakfast the following week at the Waldorf Astoria. I decided to check with Otis to see if he had any inkling what his Wall Street friend might have in mind, but Otis said he had no clue. I thanked him and said I'd bring him up to date after our New York meeting.

At eight sharp the following Wednesday morning I met with Mr. X at Peacock Alley in the Waldorf. We exchanged the usual pleasantries for a few minutes, then, presumably pressed for time and cutting to the chase, Otis's friend said: "I suspect you know that I'm a member of the Committee for the Re-election of the President."

"I know a fair amount about CREEP," I said, "but —"

"We prefer not to use that unfortunate acronym," he cut in.

"I understand," I said, waiting for what I suspected was going to follow. For I had heard, secondhand admittedly, some stories about the committee's fund-raising tactics that had not exactly warmed my heart. I had only hoped they were untrue, or greatly exaggerated, as politicians are wont to do from time to time.

"I'm sure you understand how vital it is for this country's future that President Nixon be reelected," he began in what sounded more than vaguely like the opening of a canned speech. "And to make sure that happens, we need money."

"Presidential campaigns have certainly become expensive these days," I sympathized. "If you're looking for my personal support —"

"No, Mr. Casey, that would hardly warrant a breakfast at the Waldorf, would it? Not to mention our valuable time," he added, glancing at his watch.

Remembering the prices on the Peacock Alley menu, and figuring my planned personal contribution to the presidential campaign, I quickly calculated that at best Mr. Wall Street would be breaking even.

"Mr. Casey, what we're looking for from the Times Mirror is a five-hundred-thousand-dollar contribution. Given the size of your company, and the Times Mirror's long-standing support of President Nixon, that should not strike you as excessive, I'm sure."

In fact, the *Los Angeles Times* had not only backed Nixon; the Chandlers, among his earliest supporters, had probably done more than anyone else to make his career, from his first congressional campaign on.

Interestingly, although I was taken aback by Mr. X's number, I was not totally surprised by the tack the conversation had taken. For while Otis had not known why his friend called me, I had had a suspicion that the meeting might be more politics than business.

I looked at the man squarely and said: "Sir, whether or not

the number is excessive is beside the point. But unless the law has changed since I last checked, such a corporate contribution would be illegal. So I'm afraid I'll have to decline." I could see the man's affability vanishing like water down the drain.

"How can you use the word 'illegal,' Mr. Casey, when we're discussing the president of the United States?"

"Mr. X," I said, feeling more than a trifle queasy at this point, "the law regarding campaign contributions is very clear. And 'illegal' *is* the proper term, president or no president."

"I believe, Mr. Casey, you're being very shortsighted." He shook his head slowly in what I took to be a reflection of disgust at my amazing stupidity.

"Mr. X," I said with a smile, "till this point in my life I have never broken the law. And I'm not going to start now."

"Mr. Casey, I think you should know that your friend and colleague Otis Chandler could be in serious trouble with the SEC. I could, you realize, have the SEC investigate him . . . which might prove very embarrassing."

"That sounds to me very much like a threat," I said.

"You may take it for what it's worth, Mr. Casey. I should also tell you that I could, if you persist in your position, have President Nixon fire Franklin Murphy from his position on the Foreign Intelligence Advisory Board."

Franklin Murphy, who for the past four years had been the chairman of Times Mirror, I knew cherished his political position on that committee. A man in his mid-sixties, with a long, distinguished career behind him, Murphy would be distressed if my breakfast "friend" made good on his threat. I shook my head, desperately searching for some wittily devastating rebuttal with which to puncture Mr. X's political balloon. But all I could come up with was:

"That's a crock of baloney, and you know it!"

He reddened, pushed back his chair, and rose haughtily from his seat. "In that case, Mr. Casey," he said, "you and I have nothing further to discuss." He paused. "But if I were you, I'd talk to Murphy and Otis before you close the door on this." He thrust out his hand, presumably to have it shaken, but by now my Irish was up, and I kept my hand on the white tablecloth where it belonged.

"I'll certainly inform them of our meeting," I said.

He turned and strode out of Peacock Alley, leaving me (of course) with the check.

Back in California I called on Otis to report about my meeting with Mr. X.

I went down to his office — Otis almost never came to see me in my office, except when for some reason he'd come up to see his father, whose office was down the hall from mine. I gave him the full rundown, and my blunt negative response. In fact, I wanted to see how Otis would react to the man's threat.

Otis listened without visible reaction, then shook his head. "We really don't need an SEC investigation, Al, do we."

"No," I said, noncommittally, "who the hell does?"

"It could be embarrassing, to say the least. I mean, Jesus, the newspapers would go to town on the story. And think of my kids, all the finger-pointing at school, that kind of thing."

"Are you telling me I should not have turned the man down?" I said.

"No, no," Otis hastened to reply, "you did the right thing, Al. Absolutely." But despite his reassurance, I could see as I left the room that he was deeply upset.

I then asked Franklin if I could see him for few minutes, repeated my Peacock Alley story, and informed him of Mr. X's unveiled threat. To my surprise, I could see immediate tears welling in his eyes.

"Jesus, Al! They really want to humiliate me, don't they? They know how much being on that committee means to me."

Again I asked my key question: "Do you think I was wrong to turn the man down cold, Franklin?"

"No, no," he said, the tears now running down his cheeks. "You did the right thing, Al. It's just that . . . They're really playing dirty pool, aren't they?"

"Which is why we should have nothing to do with them," I said.

And like Otis before him, Franklin Murphy, as I left his office, looked more upset than I had ever seen him.

For a moment, I wondered if I had been precipitous in my reply to Nixon's envoy. Not wrong, but hasty. Perhaps I should have consulted with Murphy and Otis before conveying the company's official position. But to me the man's threat was so blatant, and the required answer so clear-cut, that not to have responded on the spot would have been tantamount to equivocation. A matter of basic ethics.

At the risk of pontificating, ethics has constantly to be at the core of your business. To compromise it in any way, or on any level, is to destroy the very fiber of your business. Perfection being not of this world, I am well aware that this is easy to say and far more difficult to do. But I also know that when one compromises one's integrity, no matter how great the temptation or grave the threat, the price to pay is overwhelming. I'm not referring here to out-and-out dishonesty, such as I painfully uncovered at Pickett Incorporated, where the man had gone so far over the edge that he had ruined his life forever. No, I mean day-to-day ethics, which has to start at the top and permeate all levels if an organization is to grow and prosper.

Later, when the sordid revelations about the tactics of the Committee for the Re-election of the President were made public, the news media had a field day. The fact that Times Mirror had been dunned by CREEP and turned it down redounded greatly to the benefit of the company and certainly enhanced its reputation. Both Otis Chandler and Franklin Murphy were quick to take credit for standing firm, as well they should. By that time I was no longer part of Times Mirror, having decided, some time after this unpleasant incident, that it was time for me to move on.

I realized that I had gone about as far as I could there and had fulfilled my mandate to help Times Mirror diversify and solidify its financial health. Although president of the company, I was still only number two at Times Mirror, and I suspected, since it was still very much a family enterprise, that I would never be number one. It wasn't a matter of ego; it was simply that after twenty-five years in business I had a desire to run my own show. I was fifty-three; I felt I had earned my stripes as an executive in a variety of companies and businesses. But, as was the case when I left the Railway Express Agency for Times Mirror, I had no idea exactly what I would do next.

For better or for worse, but I suspect for better, I had never filled out a résumé in my life. Now, in the fall of 1973, I let a few friends know that I was "looking around" not just for a job but for a position that, in my mind, would be the culmination of my business career. There was no urgency, I stressed, since I knew I could stay at Times Mirror as long as I liked, but I was available for the right post.

Geography had never played a major, or even minor, role in my career. In fact, looking back, the only thing I could determine was that I seemed to be very much a bicoastal fellow. I had started with Southern Pacific in New York, then moved to their San Francisco office, bounced back to New York, then moved west again in 1963 to Los Angeles. If the past was any indication, it was perhaps time to move back east.

In September 1973, my old friend Jack Garrity, who had been instrumental in sending me to Los Angeles ten years before and who was now head of McKinsey's D.C. office, called and said: "Al, if it's true you're contemplating leaving Times Mirror, there is a post in government I want you to consider."

"What is it, Jack?"

"Conrail."

"Conrail! For God's sake, Jack, you mean you're really trying to get me into the bankruptcy business?"

That was a joke, but it was also the truth. Conrail was the government-owned agency that was a consolidation of eastern bankrupt railroads, the core of which comprised the Pennsylvania Railroad and the New York Central.

"I'm serious, Al. The secretary of transportation, Claude Brinegar, is looking for someone to head up the agency."

Actually, the plan was to name someone as head of USRA — those acronyms again! — the United States Railway Association, which Congress had set up to be the funding and oversight vehicle of Conrail.

"Would you come to D.C. and meet with Secretary Brinegar?" Garrity went on. "You'd be perfect for the job."

"Well," I said, "I have often thought of government service."

"Fine," Garrity said. "I'll set up an appointment."

I had a good meeting with Brinegar, a Nixon appointee who had formerly been a top economist with Union Oil. After consultation with the president and his chief of staff, Alexander Haig, Brinegar phoned me and offered me the job.

"This is an enormous challenge," he said. "The situation of the railroads in this country is, I needn't tell you, catastrophic. You'll have to deal with Congress, which funds the agency and will resist efforts to pour money into the railroads at this juncture. But unless we take drastic action to turn the railroads around, they're going to be a continuing drain on the whole economy for years to come."

I liked the idea of challenge, always had. I probably should have joined a circus when I was a kid and specialized in tightrope walking. No, the challenge didn't faze me a bit. What did bother me was that the post was subject to Senate confirmation, and therein was the rub: in the fall of 1973, Nixon and the Senate were in bitter conflict over Watergate, a conflict that was just escalating into a full-scale war. Nixon was refusing to release the famous White House tapes, and in retaliation the Senate was refusing to confirm any of the president's appointments.

When I met with General Haig at the White House a day or two after my meeting with Brinegar, he asked me to take the job *without* the confirmation of the Senate.

"General, the job already is rife with problems, in part because the USRA is going to be staffed by employees who have been cast off by the other agencies," I said. "I'm perfectly willing to take on the assignment, but without confirmation you get killed by your staff in Washington. So I must have the stature of congressional approval, or the employees will feel that I'm just passing through."

"The president would be immensely grateful," Haig pleaded.

"Not without the confirmation," I replied.

We agreed that Haig would make further efforts to convince the Senate that, for the good of the country, they should make an exception in my case. But the Senate turned his request down cold. Still, Haig wouldn't give up. He asked me to come by the White House one afternoon for a final discussion. We met in a room just outside the Oval Office.

"On the other side of that door," said Haig, pointing to the Oval Office, "is President Nixon. When I open the door, he's going to step out. He'll put out his hand, take your hand, and say, 'Congratulations, Mr. Casey. I want you to know you have my appreciation for taking on this enormous responsibility.' What do you say to that, Al Casey?"

"General," I said, "I say, 'Don't open the door.'"

He didn't. And I didn't take the job.

That same year, Bill Paley, the founder and longtime chairman of CBS, was looking for a replacement for the company's president, Frank Stanton, who was approaching CBS's mandatory retirement age of sixty-five. Stanton, citing the precedent of Paley himself, who was well over that age limit, was fighting to have an exception made for himself as well. But Paley, for whatever reasons, would have none of it. CBS had hired the prestigious executive recruiting firm (for us common mortals, read "headhunter") of Hedrick & Struggles to find Stanton's replacement. One of Hedrick & Struggles's senior partners, Gerald Roche, a lifelong friend and head of the company's New York office, called me one day, asking "if I could suggest anyone for the post," a classic way of finding out whether you yourself might be interested. His not so very subtle way of making that clear came when he asked, "Is it true you might be leaving Times Mirror?" I said that was indeed true, though I'd set no timetable. At which point he asked, rather urgently I thought, if he could set up a meeting between me and Bill Paley. I said of course he could, since I had never met the legendary man and figured, if nothing else, I would enjoy getting to know him.

Subsequently I met Paley in his posh, top-floor office of the CBS Building on Fifty-second Street, commonly known as Black Rock, because of its dark stone facade. We had several discussions about the top job, which had its attractions for a number of reasons. First and foremost, CBS had the reputation of being the classiest of the networks, committed to excellence in all its fields. It consistently topped the ratings in those years, without yielding to the growing temptation to capture audience share by lowering standards. For me, too, the transition from Times Mirror to CBS would have been quite smooth, since in my current post I had had considerable experience in television and the media. Like Times Mirror, CBS had in the preceding years branched out into allied communications fields by purchasing a number of magazines and book publishers.

I liked Paley, who struck me as very smart. I admired all he had done in building, almost from scratch, a communications empire that was not only big but seemingly still committed to quality. In the course of our first conversation it became clear to me that, as chairman, he was no figurehead: he was thoroughly versed on corporate organizations and how to lead them. I also found him urbane and gracious. But our initial meeting turned out to be less of a job interview than a sales pitch — from Paley to me, surprisingly. I didn't have to sell myself; obviously, Gerry had spoken highly of me, and Paley seemed intent on touting the manifold virtues of the job.

The job of president of CBS would indeed have been challenging, for the networks' ratings had gone over the previous few years from stable to negative, doubtless as a result of the encroach-

ing cable systems, which were offering ever larger and more di-
verse programming. But I suspected the job would also be reward-
ing. Still, there was a little red flag that kept appearing in my mind.
Paley and Stanton had been working together for years and, in my
book, should have developed between them a close and solid
working relationship based on trust and mutual admiration. The
fact was, they were at each other's throats. Stanton desperately
wanted the title of CEO, if only for a brief period, as a culmination of his career. Paley desperately wanted him out.

"Do you know," Paley said to me one day during our later
talks, "Frank Stanton's only one of two people in American business who rose to the top echelon via the personnel route. The
other one's Don Davis of Stanley Tool."

I wasn't quite sure what his point was, but I assumed he had
a rather lowly opinion of the personnel function of business, and
anyone who came out of it could scarcely aspire to a CEO's job.

Frank Stanton's office was right down the hall from Paley's,
but the distance between them, only a few yards by the tape measure, had grown almost infinite because of the tension. Knowing I
was seeing Paley, Stanton, whom I had never met, asked if we
could get together. He invited me to dinner in his executive suite,
where he probed me about the chairman's general frame of mind,
his thinking about the "Stanton situation," whether there was a
chance he might change his mind about the mandatory retirement age.

"Al," Stanton said, "Bill's really too old to handle the day-to-
day operations of CBS. Don't you think you could talk him into
retiring, so that I could take over?" And Paley in turn, knowing
that Stanton had called me in, reversed the role and began to
query me about his lame-duck president.

"I really think it's time I taught that guy a lesson," Paley said
to me one day. "He seems conveniently to forget that he was instrumental in putting through the retirement-at-sixty-five rule."

I found the whole thing petty, and feeling increasingly un-
comfortable and having no desire to act as buffer or go-between

between the two men, I bluntly told Stanton that, however much I sympathized with his dilemma, I felt it best that we not meet again.

A day or two later, after I was back in Los Angeles, Paley called. His tone sounded rather urgent. "After careful thought, and after consulting with a number of people about you, including key members of the CBS board, I'd like to offer you the job of president. It's yours for the taking, Al," he said. "There's no question in my mind you're our man. There's a board meeting in a few days, and I'd like very much to make the announcement at that meeting."

"I'm very flattered, Mr. Paley, and I want you to know I've already given your offer — which I sensed might be coming — considerable thought. But I've decided, however tempted, I must decline."

"You'd be making a terrible mistake," Paley said. "Being president of CBS is one of the plums of American business."

"I'm fully aware of that," I said, "and it's very possible I'm making the mistake of my life."

"Then you should reconsider," he said. "Sleep on it, and let's talk further."

I promised I would. Paley called a few days later. "Al," he said, "there's a board meeting in twenty minutes. Tell me if you'll take the job, or call me back in the next few minutes, and it's yours."

But I was afraid, even convinced, the arrangement wouldn't work. Paley was the heart and soul of CBS, even more so than the Chandlers were of Times Mirror. And as long as he was there, it would never truly be my show. However supportive on the surface, he would always be available to hear other CBS executives' complaints or concerns about what Casey had said and done. And in that battle — Paley versus Casey — there was no doubt who the winner would be.

"Mr. Paley," I said, "thank you. But we'd be in disagreement almost at once. I prefer your friendship to the assignment. Pick somebody else."

"But Al," Paley said, "you'll benefit enormously from my experience. Please reconsider."

"Thanks, Mr. Paley, but my mind is made up."

More or less at the same time, Edgar Bronfman, the Canadian billionaire who had bought MGM (Hollywood seems to run in the
Bronfman blood), was looking for someone to replace the outgoing MGM president, Bob O'Brien. Again, it was Hedrick &
Struggles who had been given the job of finding a new president,
and Gerry Roche, who seemed bound and determined to keep
me off the unemployment line, called O'Brien and extolled my
many virtues.

"He sounds great," O'Brien said. "Does he have any movie
experience?"

"Not per se," Roche said, "but lots of communications experience. And he's been living in LA for the past ten years, so he's
right at home out there. Meet with him. You'll see for yourself."

A day or two later, O'Brien called me and asked if I could fly
east to meet with him. We made an appointment for lunch at the
Stanhope Hotel, where for an hour O'Brien extolled the virtues
and perks of the movie business in general and MGM in particular. We met again at the MGM offices in midtown Manhattan,
where O'Brien filled me in on the finances and the specific projects and plans the company had on the drawing board. We went
over the existing corporate structure, and I laid out for him my
modus operandi, with only four people reporting to me. Did I
think that system would work in the movie business? he asked
during our third lunch at the Stanhope. I told him in my opinion
it would work in *any* business, assuming you had the right people
in each of the four positions.

In filling me in on the existing corporate structure, O'Brien
indicated — not emphasized — that Bronfman was not only the
owner of the company, but did involve himself often in the running of the business. How had he found working with Bronfman?

I wanted to know. No problem, O'Brien said. He's demanding, but he's great to work for. I didn't realize it then, but the preposition *for* was the key to the enterprise.

O'Brien arranged a lunch at New York's Brook Club, which was where Bronfman held most of his business meetings. I was staying at the Waldorf on Times Mirror business, and Franklin Murphy was there as well. Franklin of course knew of my plans to leave Times Mirror — though he was totally unaware of the reasons that had led to my decision — and had several times tried to change my mind. That day, in the fall of 1973, as I was preparing to meet Bronfman for lunch, Murphy made a final plea. My plan was to walk the four blocks from the Waldorf to the MGM offices, pick up O'Brien, and take the company car over to the Brook Club. Murphy insisted on walking with me to MGM.

"Al, I beg you to reconsider," he said. "You've really moved Times Mirror in the right direction. Everyone there likes and respects you. Please stay, Al," he finished as we reached the MGM offices, his hand tugging on my sleeve.

"Franklin," I said, "I am touched, and I truly appreciate your good wishes and goodwill. But as a fellow Irishman, you know that once we make up our mind it's impossible to change it."

During our ride over to the Brook Club, Bob O'Brien expounded once again the endless attractions of the movie business, stressing how exciting it was. I confessed that, although I'd been living in Los Angeles for many years, my only real contact with that enchanting world was my hour-long lunch with Lew Wasserman at the Universal cafeteria one day.

During lunch, Bronfman clearly was more than a trifle concerned about my lack of experience in movies, despite my Cinema 101 lunch at MCA ten years before. At one point he asked:

"Mr. Casey, how would you determine which movies to make if you were head of MGM? And who would you pick to play the leads?"

"Mr. Bronfman," I said, "let me answer that by telling you how I operate in general. And in the movie business I'd probably operate the same way." At which point I outlined for him, as I had for O'Brien, my basic management structure, with only four people reporting directly to me.

"That's very interesting," Bronfman said. "And from what I hear, you've made that system work very well. There is, however, one key point I should make clear from the start: I'll want to pick the pictures we'd do. And of course I'd also have a major say about who the stars should be."

It was all I could do to refrain from saying, "But Edgar, you don't want a president for MGM, you want a new doormat." In any event, from that moment on I knew there was no place for me in the Bronfman empire. The rest of the lunch proceeded without further incident, but I had the feeling that both Bronfman and O'Brien knew that I had decided then and there I was not their man.

The Lord indeed works in mysterious ways, and the next potential post on my lengthening list strikes me, as I look back, as bizarre and coincidental enough that I must impute at least a part to the Deity's desire.

When we acquired the *Dallas Times Herald* for Times Mirror, we had put Jim Aston, chairman of the Republic National Bank of Dallas, on the Times Mirror board, where he became one of my staunchest supporters. Jim was also a member of the board of American Airlines, which, although headquartered in New York, had deep roots in Dallas. Unbeknownst to me, American was looking for a new CEO, and the executive recruiter assigned the task of filling that post, Ward Howell, had apparently included my name on a fairly long list — roughly thirty I believe — of first-round candidates. Aston was a member of the American board's subcommittee working with Howell, and when he saw my name on the list he was aghast.

"Al Casey!" he said, taking a pencil and drawing a thick line through my name. "He can't be a candidate: he's the president of Times Mirror. I'm a board member of that company, too. I couldn't be part of stealing him away from Times Mirror. He's turned that company completely around. It just wouldn't be ethical. . . . Besides," he added, "I'm sure the headhunter's got the wrong guy. He probably meant Al's brother, *John* Casey, not Al. John's the airline man. Executive VP of Braniff. Good man. We should strike Al and add John to the list."

C. R. Smith, the founder and longtime chairman of American Airlines who had retired years before but been called back recently, was at that early search committee meeting. When he had returned to American, he had made clear his return was only provisional, until American could find a worthy successor. I doubt that C. R. had ever heard of me up to that point, and I had to be somewhere near the bottom of the headhunter's list as far as he was concerned. No airline experience, indeed! But what Aston had said intrigued him.

"Tell me more about this guy Casey," he said.

"I think he has the same sort of charisma and leadership ability you have, C. R.," Aston said.

"On a scale of one to ten?" C. R. asked.

"Outstanding," Aston replied.

"Would you call him?" C. R. said.

"C. R., I told you I couldn't do that. Besides, I'd be greatly surprised if he was even interested."

In fact, at that point Aston had no idea I had been talking to other parties or that I had made up my mind to leave Times Mirror.

"Would you talk to him if he called *you?*" C. R. insisted.

"Yes, sure," Aston said, still not convinced, still not sure he liked the way the conversation was turning.

When a mutual friend called and asked me to phone Jim Aston, I assumed Aston wanted to discuss some Times Mirror business. When I learned the real purpose of the call, I had to come clean with Aston and tell him I was indeed leaving Times Mirror.

"Why, Al?" he asked. "You're such a perfect fit for that job. You've even got the Chandlers talking to one another. No one else will ever be able to do that."

"I have my reasons, Jim, believe me."

He asked if I could fly down to Dallas, and I said I was already planning to visit brother John in the next few days.

"Fine," Aston said. "Call me as soon as you get in, and we'll set up a date."

During my stay, Aston filled me in on American's major problems, briefed me on the background of C. R. Smith — who, he indicated, would make the final choice — and asked if I would also agree to meet with Manly Fleischmann, a lawyer from Buffalo, New York, who was chairman of the American subcommittee board to find C. R.'s successor.

"Sure," I said, "I'd be happy to meet with Fleischmann, but only if I decide we should take this any further. I still think the man you want is my brother, John."

"I get the feeling it's Albert Vincent that C. R. wants. You should meet the man, Al. He's the heart and soul of this company."

"Look, Jim, let me think about it."

From the few facts I had learned from Aston about the airline's current ailments — starting with an unprecedented $48 million loss that year — I figured I had a lot of thinking to do before I made any decision.

Laurence Rockefeller, who among many other things was then the chairman of Eastern Airlines, was casting about for a new president for that company to replace the outgoing Sam Higginbottom. One day, shortly after my meeting with Aston in Dallas, Rockefeller, Jack Valenti, and C. R. Smith were sitting around Rockefeller's posh swimming pool in Florida discussing the fate of the world and the escalating problems of the nation's airlines. Smith, who had been secretary of commerce under Lyndon Johnson, had returned to American Airlines to deal with a double crisis there. On the one hand, the then chairman of American, George Spater, had just been found guilty of compromising himself, and his company, by yielding to the pressures of the Committee for the Re-election of the President and secretly contributing $55,000 of corporate funds to that dubious organization. Similar scandals involving other major American corporations were emerging almost daily, and I couldn't help but think at the time how relieved Franklin and Otis must be feeling because I had not yielded to Mr. X's pressures. On the other hand, American, in part because of the oil crisis, was suffering unprecedented losses. "Hemorrhaging," was the way C. R. put it.

"You're not alone, C. R.," Rockefeller said. "All airlines will be in deep trouble if the price of oil continues to rise this way."

I'm not sure whether Rockefeller knew that day that C. R. was also looking for a CEO, but I suspect not. In any case, at one point Rockefeller said to C. R.: "One of the people we're looking at for Eastern is Al Casey. He has no airline experience, but he's done everything. He's worked with a newspaper company — right now he's the president of Times Mirror in LA — he's acquired a lot of companies. But above all he seems to have a knack for putting good management teams together."

At which point Jack Valenti chimed in: "Al Casey? I went to Harvard Business School with him. The guy's a genius. He's a super executive. Doesn't matter that he has no experience in the airline business. When he went to Times Mirror he had no experience in the newspaper or communications business. And look what he did there, revitalized it completely." He went on and on, as Rockefeller took notes, which he turned over to his headhunter next day.

As for C. R. Smith, he didn't say a word. This was the second, if not third, time Albert Casey's name had been bandied about in his presence during the past few days. The next day he called Ward Howell.

"Get me some more information on this guy Casey," C. R. said. "It seems everyone in town is trying to hire him."

"You're sure you don't mean *John* Casey?" Howell asked.

"No, godammit, I mean Al Casey," C. R. growled. "Yes, yes, I know he has no airline experience. I don't give a damn. I want to meet with the man."

*   *   *

Next day Howell called me — I was at Palm Springs at the time, on a short vacation — and said that Mr. Smith would very much like to meet with me in Washington at my earliest convenience. Still insisting that I believed they had the wrong Casey, I accepted an appointment to meet a few days later with C. R. in D.C. (or was it with D. C. in C.R.?). It was early December, and the idea of giving up Palm Springs for the rigors of Washington winter, even for a day or two — especially with the forecasters predicting snow — was not wildly appealing. Two days later I checked in at the Madison Hotel, the same place where I had had my earth-shaking dialogue with Billy Graham three years earlier.

C. R. had set our appointment for seven o'clock the next morning at the hotel, and I was downstairs in the lobby several minutes early. It was snowing hard, a blizzard by Washington standards, and when seven thirty came and went with no C. R., I blamed the weather, wondering if it was even possible for cars to navigate that morning. But I had misjudged my man: a few minutes later, in he swept, covered from head to toe — all six foot three of him — with snow, including his hat, perched rakishly on his bald head. He had walked to the hotel from his apartment and mumbled an apology for being late. A laconic man, he was, I learned, much given to mumbling, which made it necessary for his listeners to pay close attention to his every word. We repaired to my room, where over coffee we had what I presumed to be a job interview. I say "presumed" because C. R. asked few if any penetrating questions. He did tell me that I had come highly recommended, that I apparently had made friends wherever I worked, that people spoke very highly of my light-handed touch and my management skills. He also wanted to know about my relationships with people in government, I assumed to make sure there would be no conflict-of-interest problem.

After a bit I interrupted: "Mr. Smith, I think you should know that I know nothing about the airline business."

"I'm well aware of that, Mr. Casey," he said.

"I think you should also know that I truly believe it's my brother, John, you should be talking to, not me. Flying's been

John's whole life. He knows everything there is to know about the business. He'd do a superb job for American." And I added, only half jokingly, "John's executive VP at Braniff, which as you know is one of your chief competitors. So by hiring John you'd be doing yourself a double service: getting a top man, and hurting a competitor."

"I am well acquainted with your brother John — a good man, but I want a nonairline man, Mr. Casey," C. R. said without a smile. "I want a financial person. I like what I've heard about you, and I like you. In fact, I'm going to recommend to my board that we hire you."

I later learned that, indeed, he had done a fair amount of research into my background and bona fides, including talking personally with Charles de Bretteville, chairman of the Bank of California, on whose board I had served.

Back in Palm Springs, I talked things over with Ellie, who advised that, for family harmony if nothing else, I discuss all this with John as soon as possible. Despite all its problems, American was a premier airline, and the job one of the real plums not only of the industry but of American business. John was as usual understanding, and greatly appreciative that I had filled him in.

"So are you going to take the job?" he asked.

"I'm going to make one last pitch for you," I said, "because I know you'd be a better man for the job. But if they still say no, then I'll probably consider it, yes."

I called C. R. and made a final plea for John. But, it seemed, the more I pleaded, the more they wanted me. The contrariness of human nature?

"For one last time," C. R. said, a note of exasperation in his voice, "I know John well. He's not my man."

"You realize you're giving me a helluva family problem," I said, knowing that despite all, John coveted the job for himself.

"That's your problem, not mine," C. R. said. "So, will you entertain the job or not?"

"All right," I said, sounding I'm sure like a man who has gone ten rounds and is about to lose on points, "I'll think it over."

After discussing it with Ellie at great length, I decided to accept C. R.'s offer. It was a huge challenge. For Ellie, it would mean uprooting once again, moving across the country, and resettling in a new home, a new environment. Although she had always done it with grace and good humor, and although now the children were grown up and leading independent lives, I knew it was harder for her than she would ever admit. As for me, I knew I was walking into the proverbial lion's den: not only was American staggering under unprecedented losses, but the whole industry was in real turmoil, starting with the oil crisis whose end no one could foresee, the stagnant economy that was curtailing airline passenger traffic, and the whole thrust toward airline deregulation that, I suspected, was bound to become law sometime in the fairly near future, adding further problems to an already beleaguered industry. But the greater the challenge, the greater the potential reward, I told myself.

I put in a call to C. R. and told him I would accept the job. He sounded more relieved than delighted and said that it was imperative I attend the next board meeting, to be introduced as the new CEO. The December meeting was only a few days off, but I readily agreed to go, since the company's problems were mounting daily and needed to be addressed, I knew, sooner rather than later.

Since American's board members came in from various parts of the country, it was customary for the CEO to host a cocktail and dinner the night before the meeting. During the December cocktail hour, C. R. introduced me warmly to the board members, then at one point drew me aside.

"One thing I should mention," he said. "A number of people have commented to me that they hope you're going to deal with the internal politics of the New York office."

"What kind of internal politics?" I asked.

"I think most of it has to do with the fact that, with the jobs of president and chairman open, everyone was running for office, maneuvering either to get the job for themselves or move into better posts if they didn't. Now that they know you're coming, that should solve itself. But if it doesn't, I'd like to give you a copy of a memo I wrote years ago, when I first came to the company. Remember, American was formed out of the merger of several small airlines, and the place was pulling itself apart with internal bickering. So I wrote a memo that went more or less like this: 'I do not want people in American criticizing people in American. We do have some sons of bitches around, but they are our sons of bitches. So long as they are on our payroll, we will support them. If you want to come in and knock someone in the company, you will be welcome. I will call in the person you are knocking, while you are here, and we will get to the bottom of the complaint.'"

I thanked him and said that his manner of dealing with office politics fit perfectly with mine, as did his dealing directly one-on-one. But if we were in complete agreement on that point, one potentially thorny problem remained to be resolved between us, which I had raised in our earlier conversations and on which C. R. had constantly equivocated. Although he had announced he was returning to American on an interim basis, he was now threatening to "stick around" for a few months, presumably to make sure the new president was doing his job properly. Since one of the reasons I had taken the job was to run my own show, the last thing I was going to countenance was having C. R. looking over my shoulder daily. Might as well have gone to work for Bill Paley or "I-pick-my-own-films" Bronfman. So in accepting, I had laid down one condition: that C. R. physically leave the company the day I arrived on board.

"Well, I don't know . . . ," C. R. had responded, obviously not pleased. "I could be of great help to you, you know. . . ."

But I stood firm, and he seemed to acquiesce. I knew that as long as C. R. was there I'd have no real authority. His roots in the company were just too deep. Texas roots. In fact, they went back more than forty years. In 1927 Temple Bowen, a prominent Fort Worth businessman, founded Texas Air Transport. Having secured certain mail contracts with the federal government, Texas Air Transport began serving Dallas and Forth Worth with two routes: one to Houston and Galveston, the other to Waco, Austin, and San Antonio. (Some of the old Texas Air Transport routes are still in American's schedule today, making it the operator of the state's longest continuous service.)

Two years after Texas Air Transport began, a new airline, Aviation Corporation, or Avco, was formed out of several small companies including Southern Transport and Colonial Airways. And the following year, in 1930, the company became American Airways. C. R. (for: Cyrus Rowland) Smith, a native Texan, had been an officer with Southern Transport and became head of American Airways, which in 1934 changed its name to American Airlines. Under C. R.'s firm hand, the airline grew into a major, national airline, but it still retained its Texas orientation. In 1940 the *Dallas Times Herald* ran a feature that noted: "It's a safe bet that no matter where you go on American's vast system, you'll hear the drawl of a Texan in the ranks of the employees." That was still true when I arrived, as it was true of a fair number of the board of directors. So loyalty — both of time and place — to C. R. ran deep in the company. Understandably. But that was all the more reason a new CEO would have to send him packing if he wanted to turn things around his own way. For to American's thirty-five thousand employees, C. R. was and would always be "the man," he who by his wisdom, calculated risk-taking, and ceaseless hard work had built American into the country's premier airline, the "crème de la crème" as one trade journal called, the one by which all other airlines were measured.

A pilot himself, though never professionally, C. R. was a tireless worker and a true Texas gambler. In 1938, when New York's closest airport, La Guardia, was built, most airlines preferred to remain where they were, in Newark, essentially to avoid incurring the considerable costs of moving. C. R., sensing both that the average passenger would prefer the airport closer to the Manhattan business district and that the first airline committing to La Guardia would probably be able to strike a better deal in airport lease fees, made the bold move. As he had predicted, he made a sweetheart deal for American. Other airlines followed later but paid higher rental fees and had to play catch-up to American's already well-established La Guardia operation.

After World War II, during which C. R. rose to the rank of major general as one of the key officers in the military Air Transport Command, he returned to American and, working with Douglas Aircraft, helped develop the four-motor DC-6, a long-range aircraft that he promptly put into service for American, ahead of his competitors. Anticipating a travel boom in the 1950s, he — against the advice of all the "experts" — ordered twenty-five of the larger, faster DC-7s, again ahead of the competition. And because he was there first, he negotiated a price of seven hundred thousand dollars less than the aircraft sold for subsequently.

C. R. was a visionary with guts, never afraid to take chances but making sure, before he placed his bets, that he had every scrap of knowledge there was to be had about a given effort. For years he used to spend his weekends flying on various American routes, simply to check out their efficiency, their courtesy, their on-time record, the temperature of the coffee. And when he got home he would sit down at his trusty typewriter and bang out memos on everything he had seen and observed. Most were no longer than a page, and I think it fair to say that anyone at American who ever received one of C. R.'s memos — even if it chastised or admonished — cherished and kept it.

I could go on. But one further story will give you a measure of the man. Jack Naish, the former president of Convair, an aircraft manufacturer, once said of C. R.: "He's one of the few businessmen left in America with whom you can close a $100 million deal on his word alone." His remark was based on the meeting he had had with C. R., who had studied the Convair 600 very carefully and decided it could meet American's present and future needs. If the price was right. C. R. requested a meeting with Naish, which went more or less like this:

C.R.: My guys tell me this 600 is a pretty good airplane.
NAISH: They're right.
C.R.: We want twenty-five of them. How much will it be?
NAISH: One hundred million dollars.
C.R.: Okay.
(*Exit C. R.*)

Need I say more about why, as long as C. R. was around, my authority would be somewhat less than minus one?

It was at the December dinner that C. R. planned to make the formal announcement about the new president. Near the end of the cocktail hour, I approached C. R., who was in deep conversation with one of his Texas board members, and asked to have a private word with him. I asked whether he was ready to make the *double* announcement, that is, regarding *my* arrival and *his* departure.

"Well, Al," he said, looking down like the bald eagle he was from his three-inch higher perch, "I honestly haven't made that decision yet. Given your lack of airline experience, the board won't go along with your demand. They simply want me to stick around and help you in any way I can."

"In that case, C. R., I won't be staying for dinner," I said. "You knew my conditions for taking the job, and apparently you're not ready to live up to them." With which I turned and left the room.

The next day C. R. called and apologized. "I understand your position, Al. You know I've put my heart and soul in this company for over forty years, and I'm sure you understand how hard it is sometimes to distance yourself from it."

We agreed that at the next board meeting in January I would be formally presented as the new president. And, as before, I joined the board for cocktails before dinner. Toward the end of the cocktail hour, C. R. came over to me and said, "Al, can we have a moment's conversation before dinner?" We repaired to a quiet corner of the room, where C. R., looking only slightly contrite, said:

"Al, I must tell you that I've told the board of directors about our conversations relative to my leaving, and while they all want you on board as our new president, they still insist I should stay on." Seeing the look on my face, he hastened to add: "Only briefly, only briefly, mind you."

"C. R.," I said, concealing my disappointment behind a broad smile, "I see you still haven't resolved this in your own mind. And until you do there's no point in my assuming the post." And again I left the room, forsaking what I knew was a first-rate corporate dinner of overcooked chicken and, hopefully, peas and rice. But I was sincere in my belief that I could not and would not operate with someone looking over my shoulder, however well intentioned.

Again C. R. called to apologize and told me that, now, absolutely, without qualification, he understood my position and was ready to abide by it. Yes, he had discussed it with the board, and yes, they, however reluctantly, had agreed that he would absent himself from the company premises the day I started. He gave me the time and date of the February board meeting, which I dutifully noted, at the same time wondering if it wouldn't be prudent to have dinner before arriving.

At cocktails before the February board meeting, I approached C. R. and asked if I could have a few words in private before dinner. This was beginning to sound like something in *Games People Play,* but I had to make sure there were no last-minutes glitches. My long experience with the Chandlers, and briefer but intense time with Bill Paley, had taught me that founders and family-owned companies have a dynamic all their own. In such situations you're dealing with a business, yes, but you're also dealing with an indefinable but undeniable something else: these companies are their children, their flesh and blood. And no matter how much their mind tells them how good and proper the move of succession they are making is, their heart tells them: at best the man's a foster father.

"I just wanted to make sure you haven't changed your mind," I opened.

"No," C. R. mumbled, "you win."

"It's not a question of winning," I countered. "It's simply that there's no way people will listen to me as long as you're around. If they disagree with anything I say or suggest, they'll come running to you." C. R. nodded in agreement and turned as if to leave, assuming that was all I had to say. "There's one other thing, C. R.," I added. "My conditions have changed. Now you have to leave the country."

"I *know* I have to leave the *company*," he said with a show of irritation, obviously mishearing me.

"No, C. R.," I repeated, "I said you have to leave the *country,* not just the company."

He stared at me as if I had gone mad, then slowly a look of recognition, and I must say almost new respect, came over him. He realized that by asking him to leave the country I would make it harder, if not impossible, for those executives who might want to second-guess me to get in touch with him.

I met with C. R. in his office the next morning before the board meeting. "Al, you are one tough SOB," he said. "Okay, I'll have the directors elect you, and then I'll call you in. I want you to give them a fiery speech about how you're going to lead this company back to greatness."

A few minutes later he returned. "I've told them your conditions, Al, and they all agree. So let's go in, and I'll give you a really rousing introduction."

I had expected that everyone in the room would be, if not standing at attention, at least paying attention at this historic moment. To my (slight) chagrin, when we arrived some board members were reading newspapers, others standing around talking. They certainly were not waiting with bated breath for the new savior to arrive.

"Gentlemen," C. R. said, "it's my great pleasure to formally present to you our new CEO, Albert Casey, who I'm convinced will bring American back to prominence."

Just as I was about to step forward and say a few words, C. R. went on: "I'd like to pass the baton to Al by telling a brief story some of you may have already heard. As you know, I was a major general in World War II, and at one point, at a base where I was stationed, a private walked by and failed to salute me. I called him over:

"'Soldier, you forgot to salute me. Do you know who I am?'

"'No, sir.'

"'Well, I'm General Smith, and I have two thousand aircraft under my command, twenty-two thousand men, and two thousand motorized vehicles, worth hundreds of millions of dollars.'

"'Well, General,' the private said, 'you sound like a very important person with a very impressive job, so please make sure you don't screw it up.'"

C. R. smiled at his little joke, which I'm sure everyone in the room had heard a dozen times, then turned to me and said:

"So, Al, don't screw it up."

With that rousing introduction, I began my official tenure with American Airlines.

Despite my tough stance with C. R. — and it's not easy banishing a legend, believe me — the following day he issued a memo to all employees, to be posted on "All Bulletin Boards." It read:

TO: The Men and Women of American Airlines
FROM: Chairman of the Board

I recommended Mr. Albert V. Casey to be President and Chief Executive Officer of American. Our Directors, most of whom have visited with him often, share my high opinion of him.

He has been elected by the Board. From this time he will be our Chief Executive. He will work hard at his job and he will work with you. Together, you can make American the Leading Airline again.

The question will arise: "What experience has he had in air transportation?" The answer is: "Very little airline experience; quite a lot of experience in other forms of transportation, railroad and Railway Express."

We were not looking for airline experience when we chose Mr. Casey; we were looking for a man with a record of accomplishment and success in business and financial management. Read Mr. Casey's biography and you will find that he qualifies.

We do run an airline, and a good one. But the airline is also a business organization. We want the airline operated well. We also want its operation to be profitable and successful. The business and financial experience Mr. Casey will bring to American will aid in reaching that objective.

Mr. Casey likes people, especially people with whom he will be associated. He likes also to travel, and he will be coming your way some time soon. Get acquainted with him; he will like you and you will like him.

I was touched by the sincerity and generosity of C. R.'s parting words as he entrusted his beloved child to this Irish Bostonian. As I read it I made myself a bet: I wagered fifty to one that he typed the memo on his own manual typewriter.

7

AMERICAN AIRLINES: THE FIRST YEAR

WHEN I ARRIVED AT AMERICAN AIRLINES in late February 1974, the company was in a crisis situation. The formerly high-flying airline — yes, pun intended — had ended 1973 with an unprecedented $48 million loss. Its cash position was dire, with only $55 million in cash and short-term investment capital, and current liabilities were well in excess of that. And it was carrying a long-term debt of almost $600 million.

In any business, the first order is to try and figure out what the problem is. Too often, in my experience, people offer solutions before they really understand the problem. Again, that appears simplistic, but I've often used a basic bit of arithmetic to make my point, and in my early days at American I used it again. With several key managers present, I wrote two numbers on a blackboard: a 4 on top and a 2 underneath. Then I drew a line under the 2 and asked people for the solution. One person said 6, another 2, another 8.

"No, ladies and gentlemen," I said, "you're all wrong. You're coming back with solutions without first defining the problem. Before you can give the solution to those two basic numbers on the blackboard, you first have to know whether there's a plus sign, a minus, a times, or a division sign in front of them. Once you know that, the solutions are simple. My job, our job, is to look at this company with a fine-toothed comb and identify its problems. We haven't got a helluva lot of time, but I have enormous confidence that we have the people, and the experience, to put American on top again."

I doubtless sounded more upbeat than I felt, given the financial crisis I had walked into. A major part of that crisis stemmed from the 1973 OPEC embargo, which had sent oil prices skyrocketing: the cost of jet fuel had almost tripled, from eleven cents a gallon to thirty. For American Airlines, a penny rise in the cost of fuel increased expenses by $12 million. So jet fuel alone had increased the company's operating costs, in only one year, by a staggering $129 million. Wages, too, had almost doubled in the preceding seven years. And yet the price of the average airline ticket over the previous decade had remained virtually flat: between 1963 and 1973 the cost of an airline ticket had risen only 4 percent, compared to the consumer price index in general, which had risen 45 percent. In addition, the dual bugbear of inflation and nagging recession was making Americans nervous and causing them to cancel or curtail their travel and vacation plans in droves.

It quickly became clear that many of American's problems were not of its own making, but the result of external factors over which we had little control. Many other airlines were beset with the same problems. I had to face up to the fact that some airlines were doing well despite the general upheaval industry-wide. Brother John's Braniff, for one, which was reporting record profits. Braniff had a uniform fleet of 727s, which was an enormous advantage, and its route structure was not as spread out as American's. Therefore, my second task was to focus on those factors we could control, both present and future. I say "second task" because my first, I decided, was to make my presence known, to meet and greet as many American employees as I could in the shortest time possible. I wanted it made clear that I would not be operating from some throne on high but would be down in the trenches from day one.

Thus it was that on February 20, 1974, my first day on the job, I was in the lobby of the Americana Hotel in Manhattan at six in the morning to greet the crew buses as they were going out to La Guardia and Kennedy airports. The Americana was owned by

American Airlines and served as accommodations for our flight personnel during their stays in New York. I lived at the hotel for several months, and during that entire time made it a ritual to greet both the morning and afternoon crews, starting with the six A.M. group. I'd stay on to greet the seven-thirty crews as well, then go to the office but try to be back to greet the five-thirty and six-thirty P.M. crews. It was not a matter of public relations — although there are people who, still, come up to me and say, "Mr. Casey, I remember meeting you in the lobby of the Americana Hotel," which shows there was a positive PR effect as well — but of learning as much as I could as quickly as I could from the people who knew what the company's fundamental, ongoing problems were.

Throughout my life, I've been a firm believer in communications. That's a term that can mean different things to different people. I'd seen countless CEOs to whom it meant, very simply, giving orders. To me it meant "two-way": I never did all the talking. I listened as well. Wherever I've worked, I've been a good, even avid, listener. People's ideas and suggestions were always welcome, not just in a crisis situation such as the one I was now facing, but in general.

After greeting the two sets of crews that first morning, I headed over to American headquarters at 633 Third Avenue. It was a cold, blustery late-winter morning, but the streets of New York were already alive at eight o'clock. People with upturned collars, swathed in heavy scarves, hanging on to their hats, were rushing to meet their destiny. Although I'd been headquartered on the West Coast for more than a decade, Times Mirror had had a New York office to which I'd repaired at least one week per month, so I had never really left New York. But in those years I'd felt like a visitor passing through. This morning I felt like a New Yorker again, and I liked the feeling, the energy, the diversity, the movement.

I took the elevator up to the seventh floor and walked down the corridor to C. R.'s old office, pausing to introduce myself to

the few people already in. On my new desk I found a note from
C. R.:

> Dear Al:
>
> Congratulations! From time to time I'm going to send you written
> suggestions with respect to how you can improve the operation of
> the airline.

Damn! I swore under my breath. The man's just not going to let
go, is he? I read on:

> The purpose of this first written suggestion is to tell you to pay
> no attention to all succeeding suggestions.
>
> Sincerely,
>
> C. R.

I chuckled out loud. Humor. The old guy was tough as nails
but had humor. Jesus! How important humor is in business. In the
world.

I sat down at the desk and pulled out the middle drawer,
which to my amazement was filled with crumpled paper: C. R.'s
wastebasket. I tried to open the left top: locked. Left bottom: ditto.
Right top: ditto. For God's sake, what in the hell did C. R. use this
desk for? Pulling on the last drawer, the bottom right, I discovered
a pull-up typewriter — surely the machine on which C. R. wrote
all his famous memos. I couldn't help laughing out loud. What the
hell! All I ever needed was a desktop anyway. Drawers are meant to
hold useless paper. Fact was, for the next four years, until we
moved, I never did open any of C. R.'s old desk drawers.

A week before, C. R. had written a number of other memos
evaluating American's key personnel. In one he noted that there
were too many vice presidents, adding, "ultimately this would
have to be remedied." On that score he was absolutely right, and
within a few months I had, in my way, remedied the problem. I
did, however, appreciate C. R.'s assessment of two men whom, I

knew, I'd have to count on completely, especially during my first few months. One was Don Lloyd-Jones, senior VP of operations; the other a young man named Robert Crandall. Of the former, C. R. wrote, "Excellent, competent officer. No need to worry about his qualifications." About the latter: "One of the brightest young financial men I've ever met. Formerly with TWA. Extremely competent."

Among his other recommendations was that I rehire Jack Mullins, who had been a key executive with American but left because he couldn't get along with my predecessor, George Spater. I'd check him out, but I wanted my own team.

During the next two weeks, C. R. continued to pepper me with advice. Just because I had banished him from the country did not mean he was not watching me from afar as he traveled from country to country. Barely a week after I started, I received one of his famous manual-typewriter letters, evaluating our competitors:

> I traveled on British Airways, TWA, and Pan American. In all cases the service was excellent, with perhaps BA a bit better than the others. But all are competitive. Alitalia was awful.

He also let me know what he thought of some of our key personnel abroad:

> I visited with the men in the London office; all are excellent; we are well represented there. I also visited with our representative in Rome; a good man. Dalgaard, London, is currently president, American Club London.

But the true measure of the man, I thought, and an insight into the degree to which even the smallest details mattered, was this paragraph:

> In Frankfurt Airport there is an excellent floor covering throughout the terminal; either a rubberoid or a plastic. Especially easy to walk on and much less expensive than carpet. You might like to ask PAA or TWA to get a sample for you; laydown tile.

And I was heartened by his report on my early performance, for I was sure that many of his former colleagues were reporting back to him, telling him how they thought things were going:

> From the limited reports I have had, you have made an excellent start. I was worried about the reaction to your limited airline experience. That has not come about with any strength. The usual reaction is that it may be time to have a business man.

Within a month of my arrival at American, by probing and listening to both the airline's executives and its operations people on all levels, I had come to some basic conclusions, perhaps not very original but key to my understanding the problems. I realized that, despite their similarities, no two airlines are alike. They are all influenced by their route structures, the nature and degree of their competition, their price structures, their load factors, their visibility and reliability (on-time record, quality of service, etc.). Why wasn't American profitable? In my early overview, I came up with the following "Airline Profit Equation," which was made up of four basic factors:

1. How much service, or capacity, we offer
2. How much of it we're able to sell
3. How much we sell it for
4. How much it costs us to provide the service

Checking back, I ascertained that over the previous five years American had increased the amount of service it *offered* by 38 percent. In principle good. But it had increased the amount of service it had *sold* by only 31 percent. Unequivocally bad. In short, from 1968 to 1973 we had failed to market our "product" as well as we had in the past. I also learned that during the same period total traffic growth in the forty-eight states had increased 27 percent while on the domestic routes served by American we had grown by only 19 percent.

I know how boring statistics can be, but if you're trying to figure out where you've gone wrong in a business, or what you must do to make it right, you often have to hack your way through a jungle of figures to get to the clearing. So bear with me: there is more.

American had always been a leader in first-class travel: that highly profitable area had eroded more than 30 percent over the previous five years, from 22 percent of our total business to only about 14 percent. A devastating decline, which affected both the top and bottom lines.

We also had a serious, ongoing problem with our city pairs ("city pairs" are simply the two key points: departure and destination). Of the fifty city pairs that had grown most rapidly over the past five years, American served only twenty-four. Of those we did serve, growth had been only 15 percent. Of the twenty-six we didn't, passenger traffic growth had been a whopping 25 percent, almost double. And looking at the top ten city pairs, I noted that we served only three. While some of the problems I uncovered in my first weeks at American I felt I could solve, the "city pair," or route problem, I knew was going to require a great deal of time and effort.

In any business, no matter what your experience or expertise — or lack thereof — I've always found it necessary to focus first on the areas of greatest expense. So I looked, almost immediately, into labor costs, which made up 44 percent of our total expenses, and was distressed to learn that during this same crucial five-year period, from 1968 to 1973, our productivity had not only *not* improved, it had declined. Which meant either that too many people were doing too little work, or that (maybe) the right number of people were doing the wrong things. In either case, we had a productivity problem.

Staying at the Americana Hotel those first few months also made me aware that we were in not only the airline business but the hotel business as well. In that, American had been copying, blindly as it turned out, TWA and Pan Am. What American had failed to take into account was that TWA's and Pan Am's hotels were overseas and served as what was called airline feed, providing

friendly lodging at those two airlines' destinations. American's hotels, by contrast, were a hodgepodge of both domestic and foreign, large and small, ranging from the 1,800-room Americana in
New York City to the 120-room Lodge in Rochester, New York;
from the Shoreham in Washington, D.C., to the Chosen in Seoul,
South Korea (where American didn't even fly!). There were vacation hotels in Hawaii, Mexico, and Puerto Rico, which meant we
were therefore also in the travel and leisure business. This might
have been fine if it was working, or if there was some logic behind
the hotel network or synergy with the parent company itself. In
all, we had twenty-one hotels, and they were losing the company
about $10 million a year. Twenty percent of our problem was right
there. More actually, because the drain on our personnel and resources was completely out of proportion to the rest of our operation. That, I have found, is almost always the case with a loss item
in your business: it causes problems disproportionate to its size. In
any event, within weeks of my arrival at American, I knew that
sooner or later we would have to dispose of the hotels. I hoped it
would be sooner.

In that my task had been made easier because I knew I
wouldn't have to fight the issue with the CEO of our hotel division, Carter Burgess. Burgess had resigned as soon as I arrived. Out
of pique, in fact. A member of the board of directors of American, Burgess had fully expected to be named president of American before my untimely, and unappreciated, arrival. He had a
distinguished career behind him, having served as an aide to General Eisenhower during World War II, and later as ambassador to
Argentina. And his background, unlike mine, included real airline
experience, Burgess having been CEO of TWA during the time
that airline was owned by Howard Hughes. So he had reason to be
especially unhappy with C. R.'s choice.

Burgess came to see me shortly after I had been appointed
and wasted no time getting to the point.

"Mr. Casey, I frankly don't understand why you were chosen
to run American instead of me. I was on the board, I was available,

and I had been in the business. And I must tell you that my fellow board members at Morgan Guaranty Trust, Ford Motor Company, and Smith Kline & French don't understand why you were chosen over me either. They would never understand why I would agree to serve under you."

"Mr. Burgess," I said, "I fully sympathize with your position. And you and your fellow board members may well prove to be right. But I'm going to do my damnedest to prove you — and them — wrong."

"Mr. Casey, I'm here to tender my resignation," Burgess said.

"I was aware of that," I said. "But I've got a lot to tackle here in a very short time, and I'd appreciate it if you'd stay on for at least a while. As an inducement, I'd like to offer you a bonus of twenty-five thousand dollars" — which in today's terms would be about seventy-five thousand dollars.

If I was going to sell the hotels, as I hoped, Burgess, who had been running them, could have been a great help in making sure we got proper value for each. But he had his mind made up, and he turned down the bonus. I was impressed by his stand, for I suspected he could have used the money. But his departure left me with one more problem to solve without the precious knowledge of the division's CEO to fill me in and back me up. So I had a gaping hole in the hotel area; but that was not the only personnel chasm that greeted me. Shortly before I arrived, C. R. Smith had summarily fired three-quarters of the marketing staff — twenty-three out of thirty people, to be exact — including the senior vice president, doubtless as a cost-saving measure. But the cost savings were minuscule when measured against the potential drop in sales, especially since one of my first tasks and goals was to increase sales dramatically, and for that we would need a top-notch, aggressive VP of marketing.

Even more serious was American's miscalculation, in the late sixties and early seventies, in having purchased over forty wide-body DC-10s and 747s in anticipation of a boom in air travel that never materialized. As a result, American cut back on its scheduled flights to try and fill the seats of its new wide-bodies, opening the door to its competitors on the same routes, whose more frequent flights lured away thousands upon thousands of American's customers. Which meant in turn a further decline in the wide-bodies' load factor, many of which in the early 1970s were flying at less than half their capacity. To compound the problem, it cost a helluva lot more to fly those planes than to fly the smaller aircraft our competitors were using. So, however painful and unpopular a move it might be, I made up my mind that we would have to sell some of our proud new 747s. Less than two months after I had assumed my post, we sold two of the wide-bodies for $16 million each to Flying Tigers (which converted them to freighters), thus generating some positive cash flow. One small step for American.

By late March, I had outlined a four-point program for turning American around, which I presented not only to the board but to the employees as well at a number of meetings around the country. In spite of my lack of experience in the airline business, I had soon figured out that airplanes are nothing more than flying manufacturing plants, whose basic product is a seat for a passenger traveling from point A to point B. This "product" cannot be stockpiled. It has no shelf life as a buffer against economic ups and downs; it is extremely perishable. If the seats available today are not sold today, they don't sit on the shelf for sale tomorrow or the next day. If a plane leaves the gate with empty seats, all the "manufacturing costs" to produce the seats on that plane are unrecoverable, and the revenue opportunity they represent is lost forever. Elementary, my dear Watson, you might say. And it is. But it's the image of those empty seats that gave me nightmares during my first weeks at American.

My four points were:

• *Offer more "product" and sell it at a profit* (easy to say, but oh so difficult to achieve). How could we do that? Our schedule makers and field organization had to work together to identify currently untapped or underdeveloped markets. More seats available, but especially more seats filled, would translate into increased revenue per plane mile. Freight, passenger, and charter business had to be found.

• *Increase our productivity and thereby reduce our costs.* Industry data had shown me that our labor costs were higher than those of our competitors. That meant focusing on the necessary and discontinuing the nonessential. It also meant challenging everything, and I asked American's employees to do so every day of their working lives. It also meant that everyone had to work a little harder. But I had always found that when people enjoyed what they were doing, when they were proud of their job and their company, hard work came easy. At that point, with the company mired in red ink, with the mass firings in the marketing department, with cutbacks in schedules, many employees were downright scared, and morale was shot. It was not just the bottom line that needed to be fixed, but company-wide morale. I promised American's thirty-five thousand employees that we intended to pay top wages to our best people, but that we could do so only if each carried his or her own weight.

• *Eliminate unprofitable operations and sell surplus aircraft.* I had already targeted our hotel business, and begun selling off aircraft. I knew we also had to analyze all our existing routes and make sure the planes being used on each one were the most efficient. "Fleet balance" became a buzzword,

• *Prevent our competitors from taking business that is rightfully ours.* We had to recapture at least some of the market share we had lost in recent years. That meant better service — in the air, on the ground, in our ticket offices, in every customer contact we had. And it meant more aggressive sales and marketing.

On this last point — aggressive sales and marketing — I knew we had a corporate hole you could have flown a 747 through with room to spare. Very simply, we had no marketing department, so exhorting our people to become aggressive was at this point an empty battle cry. A top priority was to find a senior vice president of marketing.

Given my lack of experience, I took counsel with a number of people I thought could help me understand the requirements of the job. As I generally do, I first looked inside the department, or what remained of it, to see if there were any obvious candidates. There were none. So I began to interview outside.

As a means of developing team spirit, I decided not to hire the person on my own but involve other top executives, notably Bob Crandall, the senior VP of finance, and Don Lloyd-Jones, operations senior vice president, and Gene Overbeck, senior vice president of administration. I would arrange to spend about an hour with each candidate, after which I would bring him to the office of Bob, Don, or Gene, depending on their availability, where the candidate would spend another half hour. I'd sit in on the last ten minutes or so of these follow-up interviews, which gave me the chance not only to get a further view of the candidates themselves but to become more familiar with the senior vice presidents as well.

Most of the candidates had considerable experience, but they all seemed to have one common failing: they wanted the job so badly they refused to be themselves and spent most of the time telling us things they thought we wanted to hear. Which I guess forces me to formulate, here and now, another of Casey's basic laws: never abdicate your real self, no matter what the situation. It will only do you harm, and maybe even do you in.

In any event, after several weeks of interviews, I found I could not work up great enthusiasm for any of the candidates. Each Monday morning, Bob, Don, Gene, and I would meet to discuss the people we had seen the previous week and look through the résumés of the upcoming candidates. After several of these Monday-morning meetings it became clear that both Crandall and Lloyd-Jones wanted the job themselves. Don was particularly open about this, for since he had already served as VP of finance, before Crandall, and was on the board of directors, he felt that adding marketing to his portfolio would greatly enhance his chances of succeeding me when I retired.

When I retired? Hold it, Casey, you've barely arrived and you're talking about retiring? I realize a footnote is in order, which for simplicity's sake I'll incorporate in the body of the text.

Back at that famous February board meeting, when C. R. and I finally saw eye to eye, I announced that it was my intent to remain as head of the company — if all went well and the board so desired — until I retired, which was eleven years away. That was my way of reassuring the board we *would* turn things around, for if I planned to be there all those years, it had to mean I was confident of making things work. But I also told them that well in advance of my retirement I intended to appoint a president and chief operating officer, to ensure a smooth transition. That statement did not go unnoticed by American's top executives.

As the weeks — and candidates — rolled by, the only marketing executive with airline experience who really impressed me was Charlie Bucks of Continental. But I was even more impressed by Bob Crandall's cogent and penetrating questions and comments, and I began to lean toward naming him to the post of senior VP, marketing. But before I made that all-important move, I decided to go outside the airline industry and interview a number of marketing executives of consumer products companies. Once again, I noticed, Crandall did the best job of trying to ascertain how their experience in consumer products might carry over into the sale of airplane tickets. He asked the best questions in greater depth than anyone else. He had an intensity about him I had rarely seen, and through his instinctive sense of logic he knew far more about marketing than the people he was interviewing. More and more, it became evident there was little or no parallel between consumer products marketing and the airline industry, so one day I called Crandall in and offered him the job. He damn near died — he had wanted the job but never dreamed it would happen. That decision did not sit very well with Don Lloyd-Jones. But if you're running a company, a division, a department, whatever, you've obviously always got to try and pick the best person for the job. Any time you compromise on that score, you're asking for trouble. And trouble is usually quick to surface.

With the all-important marketing position filled, I wanted to fill out a top management team that would function smoothly and efficiently. At the risk of repetition, I believe there are just four principal functions in managing any business: the function that makes the product or provides the service; the one that sells the product or service; the job of scorekeeper or accountant; and the people function. In Crandall we now had a preeminent marketing person; Lloyd-Jones, who had been with American since 1969, was as good an operations man as anyone in the business. I hired Bob Norris, a top-notch executive, to head up the finance department, thus bringing us up to full strength. It was, relatively speaking, a youth team: the average age of the four senior vice presidents was forty-five, but all were experienced airline managers. I felt now, for the first time since I had taken the post, reasonably confident that we could, and would, take this magnificent but ailing airline back into the wild blue yonder. Well, back into the black in any case.

If you're lucky in life, there are times of need when opportunities, however seemingly crazy, appear as if by magic. One morning only a week or so after I had arrived at American, I read in the *Wall Street Journal* that Republic National Bank of Dallas was offering to sell an oil company it owned, the Howard Corporation, to the highest bidder. Since Jim Aston, Republic's CEO, was on the American board, I donned my poker-player hat and decided to call him. Oil was fuel, and fuel was one of American's most desperate needs. I did a little checking on Howard and learned that it was the holder of proven oil-producing properties. I also learned that Republic "owned" Howard because Howard had defaulted on a loan back in the 1920s, and since then Republic had put many nonperforming oil loans in Howard and made it a property of its holding company and not of the bank. In recent years, the loans had come into their own. However, the Controller of Currency had determined that the Howard Corporation did not qualify as a "bank-line" business, and therefore forced Republic to divest it. I put in my call to Aston.

"Jim, I've just heard about your selling Howard," I began.

"That's correct, Al," he said. "You must have read today's *Wall Street Journal.*"

"Jim, you can't sell that company to just anyone," I said. "You first have to offer it to companies whose board you're on. You've got to give those companies that corporate opportunity."

There was a long pause on the other end. I was used to long pauses, so his didn't surprise me.

"Al," Aston said finally, "I've never heard of such a thing."

"Well, then, why don't you check with your general counsel and call me back."

While awaiting his call, I speculated further about the short- and long-term benefits of acquiring Howard, which could be an ideal fuel-price hedge for American. Given the OPEC embargo, and still soaring gas and jet fuel prices, there was no telling how high fuel costs would go in the next few years.

My secretary, Libby Scott, announced that Jim Aston was on the phone.

"Al," he said, "I've spoken to our general counsel and he doesn't know what you're talking about. And he seriously doubts you do either."

"Be that as it may," I said, "here's what I propose. Go ahead and open bids for Howard. And when you have your most favorable bid, come to me and we'll match it without knowing what it is, and improve it."

And that is exactly what happened. I matched the top bid, which was $63 million, then told Jim that in return for his "favor" I was going to offer him a unique "come-back-in."

"What's that, Al?" he asked, a bit suspiciously, I thought.

"After American has recovered its sixty-three-million-dollar investment, plus a ten percent return per annum for the period the purchase price was invested, we'll have the property evaluated. Then we'll pay an additional amount equal to one-half of the agreed-upon extra value."

"Go on," he said, clearly intrigued but still, I suspected, a trifle suspicious. I guessed, rightly it turned out, that my poker-playing reputation had preceded me.

"For example, if the property is valued at an additional ten million, say, then we'll pay you five million. That amount is the 'come-back-in.'"

"Well," he said, "that sounds fair."

"More than fair," I said. "Now, there *is* one more part of the deal, Jim."

"What's that, Al?"

"As you know, American has no cash and not much credit. So you'll have to help us arrange a sixty-three-million-dollar loan."

"On what security?" he asked.

"The oil property," I said. "You've just proved to me it's worth sixty-three million through open bidding, so you'll have Howard as your full collateral. Plus the 'come-back-in.'"

Aston had to admit there was a certain perverse logic in my offer, but he said we would have to clear the deal. A few days later he called me back, crestfallen. "No go, Al," he said, "the controller says absolutely not. If we lend you the money, and the loan goes bad, we're right back where we started: owning Howard. Sorry, Al."

"Give me a few days to see what I can do," I said.

"I can't give you very long," he said. "They're on my back about this."

"One week," I pleaded.

Next day, I made an appointment to meet with William Spencer, vice chairman of First National City Bank. Putting on all the Irish charm at my command, I laid out all the reasons why the deal made sense and got Spencer to agree to lend American up to one-half the required amount, roughly $31 million. With that in hand, I went back to Aston, who went back to the controller, who pondered for at least five minutes and came back with a resounding no.

For a moment I was tempted to say the hell with it, but I was being challenged, and I hate to give up when I'm still on my feet and breathing. So back I went to Bill Spencer, and within the hour had persuaded him to grant us the full amount of the purchase price: $63 million. I could impute that success to my charm, my good looks, or more rightly to my intelligence. Fairness compels me to admit that Spencer only granted my request after I agreed to jiggle up the interest rates a notch.

As it turned out, Spencer's faith — and good judgment — were well rewarded. The loan was not only paid off, it was paid off early.

Many years later, when we sold Howard, the valuation of the company above the purchase price plus the 10 percent was $22 million, so we paid Republic National Bank, as promised, an additional $11 million. We had our fuel hedge during the years we sorely needed it, and the bank made money. In business that's called win-win. I love win-wins; who doesn't? But in my experience they don't often happen without some special effort. They're great because not only have you done right by your own company, you've also done well for a colleague. And, after all, Jim was more than a colleague; he was a member of the American board.

In addition to forming the best management committee I could find, I also felt I should try to broaden the board of directors. I didn't want to pack the board — I knew from experience that a chairman who fills the board with his friends or cronies is more than likely to end up with a band of yes-men and -women, people who would tell him what he wanted to hear rather than speak their minds openly. At American I wanted all the good advice I could get, and one of the financial and business minds I most respected was Lew Wasserman, chairman of MCA. I knew Lew was famous for not accepting any board directorships for a number of reasons, starting with the fact that he was enormously wealthy and did not want to take on the financial exposure that board directorship implied. Nonetheless, I put in a call to him in LA. After he had congratulated me on my new post, I got straight to the point.

"Lew," I began, "I know you don't like to be on boards. But I remember when we burned that half-million-dollar note, you said that if I ever thought you could be of service to me, please call. Well, Lew, I'm calling to ask you to accept an appointment to the board of directors of American Airlines."

Dead silence. Finally, after about eighteen hours, I heard his voice arriving from somewhere beyond the farthest galaxy: "Al, when do you want me to come on?" He had made a promise, and he was not about to break it.

"How about right away?" I ventured.

"Okay, Al. When's the next board meeting?"

Lew Wasserman remained on the board of American Airlines for almost ten years. Brilliant and incisive, he had an extraordinary capacity for understanding the essence of a business situation, however far removed it might be from his personal experience. As opposed to some directors, who (understandably) were constantly concerned about immediate needs and short-term problems, Lew had the rare ability to see ahead and calculate the long-term implications of any move. He also gave wonderful counsel and advice on one of the most serious and worrisome problems facing American when I arrived, namely cash flow, and helped us improve our balance sheet year after year.

Lew was the oldest member of the board, and every time his age was about to disqualify him I would change the age limit. The age limit then was 68, so we first upped it to 70, then 72, just to keep him on the board. It also brought me closer personally to a man I had greatly admired, mostly from afar, when I worked in LA.

Years later, I was able to repay in small, but impressive, kind the many favors I owed Lew. One doesn't have many chances to play God in this life, and such opportunities, if they come along, should always be seized. Lew, his wife, Edie, and I were having dinner in New York one night at La Grenouille restaurant. Lew is pleasant and easygoing, but Edie, who has what I might call a strong personality, can sometimes be opinionated and contentious, so I always made an effort, not always successful, to avoid potentially controversial subjects when I was with her. She also exercised a strong influence over her husband. Let me give you an example.

My father and mother, John J. and Norine Doyle Casey, in the early 1950s in Arlington, Massachusetts.

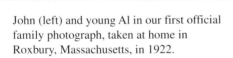

John (left) and young Al in our first official family photograph, taken at home in Roxbury, Massachusetts, in 1922.

The Casey home in Arlington. Beginning in 1933, part, and eventually all, of the house became the Bartlett School, which was founded and run by my mother.

Age nine, astride a pony on Irving Street in Arlington, Massachusetts.

With Ellie in Gloucester, Massachusetts, in March 1945, shortly after I had been commissioned second lieutenant and shortly before I got up my courage to propose to her.

In the early 1960s, at Times Mirror.

Norman Chandler, at a Times Mirror
board meeting in the mid-1960s.

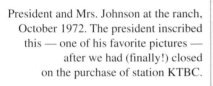

President and Mrs. Johnson at the ranch,
October 1972. The president inscribed
this — one of his favorite pictures —
after we had (finally!) closed
on the purchase of station KTBC.

Ellie at the Los Honores party in
Los Angeles in August 1973, shortly
before I left Times Mirror.

At my first board meeting as chairman of
American Airlines, held in Tulsa, Oklahoma,
in May 1974.

My brother, John, and I flanking C. R. Smith, the legendary founder and longtime chairman of
American Airlines, at a dinner for C. R. in Dallas, Texas, on April 15, 1975.

C. R. Smith, Ellie, and I at the same dinner honoring C. R.

Announcing the first SuperSaver fare in April 1977.

With Los Angeles county supervisor Kenneth Hahn and Mrs. Chandler, May 19, 1977.
It was Mrs. Chandler's birthday, and the ceremonies at the Dorothy Chandler Pavilion at
the Los Angeles Music Center were in honor of her cultural contribution to southern California.
As president of Times Mirror, I helped Mrs. Chandler by serving on the board for many
years thereafter.

Greeting President Jimmy Carter at the Shoreham Hotel in Washington, D.C., on the night
of Carter's inauguration, in January 1977. Is it possible the new president was mesmerized by
the well-turned ankle in the foreground?

Philosophizing (some call it pontificating) in my office at American Airlines in Dallas, Texas, March 1983.

With Ellie in Gloucester, Massachusetts, June 1983. To commemorate our thirty-eighth wedding anniversary, I brought Ellie back to the exact spot where I had proposed to her in 1945.

In my office at American Airlines in Dallas, Texas, shortly before my retirement in 1985.

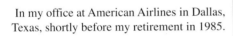

With Libby Scott at my American Airlines retirement party, February 1985.

With Ellie, talking to Justice Sandra Day O'Connor at a Washington reception in 1986 when I was postmaster general.

Official portrait as postmaster general, Washington, D.C., 1986.

The four Caseys—(clockwise from back right) John, Norine, Eva Marie, and A. C.—in my office in Washington, D.C.

With President and Mrs. Reagan, Ellie, and Libby Scott at the White House, July 1986.

Receiving the Benjamin Franklin Award, summer 1986.

With Chief Justice Warren Burger on the occasion of our dedicating a stamp honoring former Supreme Court Justice Hugo Black, summer 1986.

At my birthday party at the house on Kalorama Road in Washington, D.C., 1993. To my right is Pat Patterson and to my left Katharine Graham, chairwoman of the *Washington Post.*

With President Clinton, Washington, 1995. During our conversation he said, "Al, I made a major mistake in not keeping you on as the RTC chairman." He may have been joking or just being a good politician, but in fact I agreed with him.

June 1993, with Ben Bradlee (left) and Norman Mailer (right) after our famous—or infamous—debate at the fiftieth reunion.

A triple birthday celebration with Mary Evans, wife of Jim Evans, the retired chairman of Union Pacific Railroad, and my old friend Jim Burke on February 28, 1995. We all had the same birthday but not (quite!) the same age.

The Wassermans lived in California, on a lovely manorial estate. They had one of the largest, and poshest, swimming pools right outside their windows that I had ever seen. They were early risers — breakfast as I recall was at five thirty in the morning without fail. One morning Lew and Edie were at breakfast at the accustomed hour. Edie looked out the window and said: "Lew, do you realize the swimming pool runs the wrong way?"

"What do you mean, the wrong way?" Lew said. "It looks all right to me."

"No, no," Edie insisted, "it runs *along* the house. It should run *out* from the house."

"Maybe so, but there's not much we can do about it, is there?"

"What do you mean, there's not much we can do about it! Of course there is. We can *turn* it."

"*Turn* it!" Lew said. "It would be easier to turn the house than turn the swimming pool. And besides," he said, "look at all those old trees alongside the house. *They* can't be moved." Lew was sure he'd won that debate. He should've known better.

"Of course they can," Edie said.

And that was that. They brought in heavy earth-moving equipment, uprooted the trees, dug up the swimming pool, turned it ninety degrees, and replanted the trees. Like Edie said, easy as pie.

Anyway, that night in New York, over cocktails I picked what I thought was a bland enough subject as my opening remark: "So how are things at the Sherry Netherland?" Lew and Edie kept an apartment there, which they used whenever they came east.

"They're fine, Al, wonderful," said Lew. "It's a pleasure to be in New York."

"They're terrible. They're awful," Edie chimed in. "We've been staying at the Sherry Netherland for twelve, fifteen years. Everything was fine until Harry Helmsley bought the building across the street on Fifth Avenue next to the Plaza Hotel and put all those lights on its gilded roof. They leave the lights on *all* night, and I can't sleep."

"Why don't you put up blackout curtains?" I suggested.

"Why should I have to?" Edie countered, full of righteous indignation. "I don't think they have the right to have all those lights up there. It's just not right."

"Edie," I said, "if you had the power to do so, what time would you have those lights turned off?"

Eight or nine was a trifle early, we all agreed, and midnight was too late, so we finally all settled on eleven P.M., when pedestrian traffic had trickled to a minimum.

"All right, Edie," I said boldly. To myself, I thought, This time, Al, you've really done it; this time you're biting off more than you can chew, swallow, or digest. But I did have an idea; with a little luck, I might just pull it off. In any event, I announced grandly and, I hoped, convincingly: "Those lights will go out next Tuesday at eleven o'clock, and from then on they'll always go out at eleven."

"My God, Al, you think you can do *anything* in this world?" Lew said. "Who do you think you are, God?" I detected a bit of redundancy in his remarks, but magnanimously decided to let it pass.

"If Edie wants it done, then it shall be done," I said, sounding more and more like the Deity by the minute.

"I do want them out," Edie murmured, doubtless impressed by the presence of the all-powerful.

"All right," I said. "Remember: starting next Tuesday."

Next morning I called up my friend Doug Leigh, the man who had been hired by Harry Helmsley to light up the gilded tops of all the Helmsley properties. He was a lighting and signboard genius, the person responsible, or irresponsible, for the Camel cigarette sign in Times Square. I had done a favor or two for Leigh over the years and thought it was time to call in a chit.

"Doug," I said, "I'm going to ask you a small favor. You're wasting time and money, not to mention effort and maintenance, with all those lights on the Helmsley buildings, and I'd greatly appreciate it if you could turn them off at eleven o'clock starting next Tuesday."

I heard what I thought was a pregnant silence on the other end of the line and figured he was vacillating between hanging up and calling the medics.

"Al, have you lost your mind? What you're suggesting is totally absurd."

"Doug, do you remember when you sued a certain company for three million dollars, and I flew all the way from LA to testify on your behalf? As I recall, the judge ruled in your favor without the trial ever going to jury. Essentially on the basis of my deposition you were awarded three million dollars. For three million dollars you can't turn out the lights on the Helmsley buildings? Tell you what, I'll settle for the Helmsley building on Fifth Avenue across from the Sherry Netherland." Now that I was lowering my demands to a single property, he probably thought I was returning to the world of reason.

In any case, he said, noncommittally but not negatively either: "We'll see, we'll see."

The following Wednesday morning I had a phone call from Lew Wasserman. His voice was that of a disciple who thinks he's stumbled on the savior.

"Al," he began, "you'll never believe what happened last night."

"What's that, Lew?" I asked innocently.

"Edie and I were visiting old friends, having a wonderful time. And suddenly in the middle of the evening Edie looks at her watch and says 'Lew, we have to go.' 'Why do we have to go?' I said, 'The evening's still young.' 'No, we have to be back at the apartment before eleven. It's Tuesday night.' 'Oh,' I said, 'that Al thing about the lights. He was just pulling your leg,' I said. But she was insistent. 'If Al says the lights will go out, they'll go out,' she said firmly. So we went back to the Sherry Netherland, and Edie's sitting there by the window, looking, and, by God, at eleven o'clock sharp, out go the lights." There was a pause. "Al, was that a fluke?"

"Lew," I said, feeling despicably holy, "how long are you staying in New York?"

"Several more days."

"Call me before you leave."

A few days later Lew did indeed call back.

"Al," he said in hushed tones, "those lights are going out at eleven every night, just as you said. I have a message for you from Edie."

"What's that?" I asked.

"She says: 'Al, you *are* God Almighty!'"

It pays to do favors, especially for people you like and for causes you think are worthy, first because you're doing the right thing, and also because the favor might sometimes be returned. How many times in your life do you get to play God?

There are times, too, when you have to play Ogre. Or Enforcer. Unless the right term is Repo Man. In any event, in looking through the books and records of American Airlines, one long PAST DUE item caught my roving eye: the Democratic Party owed American over $500,000 dollars, for travel incurred during Hubert Humphrey's unsuccessful 1968 campaign. For a long time, corporations had been in the habit of forgiving the campaign debts of the losing party, largely because there was little or no money left in the till after the election. It was my strong feeling this was wrong, that both parties had been abusing the system.

Robert Strauss, the newly named head of the Democratic National Committee at the time, was a friend of mine, but that did not deter me from going after the money we were owed. It may have been a piddling sum in the context of our company's overall budget, but for me half a million dollars is enough to make me pick up the phone. I put in a call to Strauss.

"Bob, Al Casey."

"Al, how nice to hear from you. How is everything going in the new job?"

"Let's say it's enough to keep me busy. . . . Bob, I'm afraid this isn't a 'friendship' call."

"What is it, Al?"

"Your party owes us over half a million dollars. . . ."

"Oh, you mean from the 1968 campaign? Al, that's old history."

"Not for me it isn't. Unless the party pays us what it owes, we'll have to sue. And we'll have to name both you and your treasurer in the suit."

Strauss was a toughened warrior and was not much fazed by my threat. But his treasurer, Peter McCullough, who was also the CEO of Xerox, was so upset he promptly resigned, fearing the negative business repercussions of being involved in a political lawsuit.

I sent Gene Overbeck to Washington to meet with Strauss, armed with a letter confirming the amount owed. Gene's job was to get Strauss to sign that letter acknowledging the debt.

"I'll be happy to sign your letter," Strauss told Overbeck, "but it's pointless, since the DNC has no money and little prospect of raising any."

Over the next few weeks we continued to pressure the Democratic National Committee.

"Bob," I said in one phone call, "our stockholders know about this debt, which is becoming a public relations problem for us both."

"Al, maybe, just maybe, we could find a way to pay you twenty-five cents on the dollar."

"No way."

"How about fifty cents?"

"No, Bob. I want full payment. Besides, I think what you're suggesting is illegal."

I checked with Overbeck, and indeed learned that if we were to accept partial payment, we would be in violation of the Federal Aviation Act of 1958 outlawing rebates.

A few weeks later, Strauss called me and said he had a new treasurer, whom he wanted me to meet.

"Who is it, Bob?"

"His name's Edward Bennett Williams," he said evenly, doubtless hoping the name would strike dread in my heart. In fact, Williams was one of the most powerful and successful lawyers in the country, and I knew that, in our little business chess game, Strauss felt he had just made a masterful move.

"Sure, Bob, I'd be happy to meet with him. When and where?"

"Washington. You pick the day."

I flew down the following week and checked into the Madison Hotel. I was prepared to meet them at either the Democratic headquarters or Williams's office, but they preferred to come to the hotel. It was clear that the usually ebullient Mr. Strauss was going to let his treasurer do the talking. From the outset, I could tell Williams's time was precious, and he wasted none of it on amenities.

"Mr. Casey," he said, "you seem to have things a bit backward."

"Backward?"

"People don't sue me," he said imperiously. "I sue them."

"And very successfully, I understand," I said. "Mr. Williams, I'm not a lawyer, and I'm sure you can argue me under the table and give me sixteen legal reasons why I'll never get my money. But I'm also a stubborn cuss, and for me right is right."

I knew if I didn't cut him off, he'd give me a full legal education in fifteen minutes or less and hand me a diploma at the door.

"You'll never win, Mr. Casey, never. Besides, I'm sure you have better things to do than beat this old dead horse."

Right then and there, I decided to pursue. I should add — since Mr. Williams at one point insinuated that, as a Republican, I was perhaps playing politics — that politics never entered into it. If the Republicans had been the culprits, I would have done exactly the same thing.

Time went on, with the ball bouncing back and forth between New York and Washington, the Democrats hoping my problems at American, which were many, would distract me from this (in their eyes) minor matter. As time went on since my initial phone call, with no resolution in sight, I decided to tighten the screw one more notch. My patience had run out; I informed Bob Strauss that American was now formally instituting suit against the Democrats, not only for the amount due but for damages and interest. I noted that American's suit would not only attach the furniture and fixtures at the party's national headquarters in Washington, but attach all unpaid pledge cards as well. I knew Bob didn't give a damn about his tables and chairs, though there was an embarrassment factor in the threat, but the notion of having to reveal the names of delinquent donors had to give him pause. I was pretty sure that on that list would be a startling number of prominent entertainers and businessmen whose names had been used to induce pledges from others but who, having lent their good names, never anted up themselves.

"Al, you wouldn't do that," he said.

"Try me," I said.

"I need some time," he said. "I'll have to discuss this with a number of other people."

"We've already given you plenty of time, Bob."

"I know, Al. But you know how politics operates. Washington just doesn't move with the speed of light."

I laughed. "How about the speed of sound — the sound of their own voices?"

After several weeks had elapsed, with more talk but little progress, I called Strauss and said that I had just talked personally to Kay Graham, publisher of the *Washington Post*, and now planned to take a full-page ad in her paper detailing the whole story. By now an election was coming up, and the last thing the Democratic Party wanted or needed was an unsavory story in Washington's influential newspaper.

"Al, you're one tough negotiator," Strauss said when he called. "Before you run that ad, will you meet with me and my treasurer one more time?"

"Edward Bennett Williams? I've had my meeting with him."

"No, he never took the post," Strauss said. "This man's a lawyer too, a good guy from St. Louis you'll find reasonable."

Again I flew to Washington; again we jockeyed for almost an hour, but made no real progress. Finally I rose to my full six feet, trying to look even taller.

"Gentlemen," I said, "American can wait no longer. I'm afraid you give me no choice but to institute suit. And this time I mean it. We'll file papers tomorrow." I was still bluffing, but I sensed that Strauss was now concerned enough that he was ready to make a concrete proposal. Anything to keep those pledge cards out of my hands.

Almost two years had passed since my first phone call to Strauss — things do move slowly in Washington — and the Democrats had nominated Jimmy Carter, who, while a dark horse to many, seemed to have a real chance in the post-Watergate climate.

"Let's assume for a moment we recognize this debt," Strauss said. "And suppose we start to add interest to the debt as of September 1, 1976. Following a Carter win, we'll pay you the debt and interest."

"What if Carter loses?"

"He's going to win, Al."

"But what if he loses?" I insisted.

"Then you'll have to come and find me," Strauss said, and I only hoped he was kidding.

I knew it was the best deal I could doubtless strike, so I accepted his proposal. Fortunately for all concerned, Carter won and American received its money — over $700,000. But more important than the money was the principle involved, namely that American would vigorously protect its assets and revenues even if they seemed relatively small, for by now everybody in the airline business had become aware of my stubborn pursuit, and I'm sure many thought I was both mad or wasting my time.

Equally important for me was that Bob Strauss and I, despite all our differences and the protracted negotiations, remained good friends. I had not let friendship get in the way of doing what was right, and my worthy opponent, though I'm sure there were dozens of times over those two years when he wished I would go away, knew in his heart of hearts that my actions were entirely justified.

At various times in American's corporate history the roles of chairman and president had been filled by the same person; at others, the offices had been filled by two different people. C. R. Smith had simultaneously held both positions for several years, and upon occasion had elevated someone to the role of president, either to relieve himself of certain day-to-day duties or because he wanted to reward an especially deserving executive. Upon arriving at American I had been named president, with C. R. still holding the chairman's title, which was purely honorary.

At 633 Third, there were two contiguous offices on the executive floor, one for the chairman, the other for the president. In April, after the board elevated me from president to chairman, the adjoining presidential office remained conspicuously empty for several weeks. That darkened and cavernous entity didn't bother me in the least, but I began to realize as the weeks went by that it bothered some of my colleagues and was becoming an increasingly political issue. Who was Casey going to name president? Would he bring in someone from outside? Or perhaps promote from within, one of the current senior VPs. If I named an outsider — and I had considered that possibility because of my lack of airline experience — I stood to lose Lloyd-Jones or Crandall, both of whom I knew dreamed of running their own show one day. And if I named one of them, I risked losing the other.

I decided to take matters into my own hands. Literally. Ascertaining from utilities that the wall between the two offices was not sustaining, I had a sledgehammer brought up and with a few deft strokes broke a gaping hole through to the next office. At first the word at 633 was that the new guy Casey had lost it. Flipped. Then, as the symbolism of my move sank in, smiles replaced the worried frowns. For the moment at least I had solved the question of succession. Easy as snapping your fingers.

I only wish I could have snapped my fingers and willed American back to health, but I knew that task was going to be long and arduous. And there were many days, and nights, when I wondered if my lack of airline experience wasn't a detriment. On some matters, I would have loved to call brother John, if only to get technical advice or have him clarify some esoteric business curve that made no sense to my nonairline mind. But I knew I couldn't call John; our respective positions as head of competitive airlines forbade it. Whenever he and I got together, usually in Texas, we studiously avoided talking shop.

At American, we set to work: cutting costs, increasing fares on some busy routes — cross-country as well as to the Caribbean and Mexico — slashing prices on some night coach services (which resulted in a much higher volume of business on those flights). Over the next few months, we saw an almost 11 percent increase in revenues. We also reduced our available seat mile capacity by roughly 10 percent. In other words, we reduced some of our schedules — a calculated risk, since it could mean American passengers defecting to other carriers, but we chose our reductions with extreme care. The result, though, was just as we hoped: our passenger load factor — the percentage of seats sold versus seats available — increased in 1974 a solid 4.1 points, from 54 percent to 58.1 percent. Fuel costs still plagued us, as they plagued the whole industry. Although our fuel consumption decreased 15.5 percent that year because of our reduced schedules, fuel expenses still surged by $75.3 million, as the average cost per gallon rose 67.3 percent. Through attrition and reassignment, we managed to reduce our workforce by approximately two thousand people, without affecting morale. The net result of all this was that by early spring of 1975, reporting our 1974 performance, I could announce we had made a $68 million turnaround, from a $48 million loss in 1973 to a $20.5 million profit in 1974.

We weren't out of the woods yet, far from it, but we had made undeniable progress toward restoring American to its premier position. On page two of the 1974 annual report — the first in which my face appeared — I and all of American's senior executives were wearing broad smiles. And, for the first time in a long while, they were sincere.

8

THREE CRISES:
NEW YORK, SAINT THOMAS,
AND CASEY'S BRAIN

IN 1976, GOVERNOR HUGH CAREY of New York called me and asked if I could meet him at his New York City office in the MGM Building on the corner of the Avenue of the Americas and Fifty-third Street. He gave no clue about the purpose of our meeting. I was a registered Republican, and he, of course, was the leader of the Democratic Party in New York State. We met in his office in the late afternoon, and with him was David Burke, his administrator, who later went to ABC.

He started talking about New York's financial crisis. In a word, he said, the city was broke, which was news to me. For the previous eleven years we had lived in the Los Angeles area, and I was woefully ignorant of New York City's finances. "It's essential for corporations to be good community citizens," Carey said. "It's in their own best interest to contribute to the area in which they're located."

"I heartily agree," I added. And I started to relate the litany of my various community services to the city of Los Angeles. I could tell he was hardly listening, and after a few polite moments he interrupted to tell me about the new state law that had established an Emergency Financial Control Board.

He would be chairing the EFCB, which would also include the mayor of New York, Abe Beame, the controllers of both the state and the city, and three private citizens.

Then the governor came to the point. He wanted me to serve as one of the three private citizens. I strongly suspected my name had been put up by Felix Rohatyn, whom I had known from my Wall Street days. Rohatyn had agreed to head up MAC (Mutual Assistance Corporation), which was to issue bonds to make it possible for the city to pay its bills. Of course the method by which the bonds were to be collateralized was the paramount concern of all involved.

"We need a registered Republican to serve," said the governor. It was important to provide the perception that this was a bipartisan effort. I had always admired Felix Rohatyn and felt pressured to accept. But I was up to my ears — no, slightly above — in American Airlines' problems and didn't feel I could fairly assume this new responsibility.

I pleaded that in the great city of New York there surely had to be many better qualified, better known people for the job, people with fewer commitments and more free time.

"This is no time for American's new CEO to be diluting his efforts," I said.

Governor Carey ignored my plea and went on to explain that the other two private-sector members would be William Ellinghaus, president of New York Telephone, and David Margolis, president of Colt Industries. Both were admirable businessmen, well known, and close personal friends of the governor.

After several discussions with all concerned, and assurances that I was not expected to roll over and do as commanded, I accepted on the condition that I speak to the board of American and get its approval. I must say there was not exactly a burst of enthusiasm from the board, especially since the decision had union ramifications: the Transport Workers Union represented both the subway workers of New York City and the mechanics of American. But, having duly reflected and discussed it at length with my closest counselor, Ellie, I decided that I probably did owe it to my new hometown to give the job a shot. I reassured the board and told them I felt I could handle the New York assignment without in any way neglecting American, and the board gave its reluctant consent.

EFCB meetings were always held in the governor's New York

City office. Generally, about twenty people attended, including the seven board members. Also at the table was Jack Biegle, the head of the group that handled all the city unions' pension plans, and he had a good deal to say on all issues.

At our first meeting, Governor Carey focused on organizational matters. He explained that all the elected officials on the board were very busy and that from time to time they would be permitted to have substitutes. "But," he added, "this does not apply to Mssrs. Ellinghaus, Margolis, and Casey."

We three eyed one another. Because of the crowd, which included members of the press, there was silent agreement that we would revisit this issue with the governor at the end of the meeting.

Overall, the governor handled the meeting, the press, the union representatives, Big MAC (not McDonald's), and the board members admirably.

Following that first organizational meeting, we private-sector members met with the governor. We explained that he was the font of all power, and unless he was present the board could not speak with authority, nor could we be certain that he wouldn't reverse some decisions we might make in his absence. We added that we also expected the elected officials to attend all meetings; otherwise they would be demonstrating bad faith in the representations that had been made to us. Governor Carey understood our position and agreed that *all* members should be present at all times. And so it was.

Our next disagreement arose at the following meeting when Governor Carey explained that the elected official members did not have the time to chair various committees he was about to appoint; therefore, it was up to the private-sector members to fill these roles.

"Bill," he said to Ellinghaus, "as you head AT&T's largest company, you obviously understand organization better than the others here. I'd like you to take on the responsibility of reviewing the relationships and reporting responsibilities among and between the mayor's office, the city council, and the five boroughs."

"Excuse me, Governor, but that's a very large and extremely time-consuming assignment," Bill replied.

"Right," said Carey. Then he turned to Margolis and said, "Dave, you're considered to be a financial genius, and therefore I'd like you to head up a group of your own choosing to be responsible for the validity of all financial data presented to the EFCB. This should include all historical data, budgets, and forecasts of all kinds."

"Governor," Margolis said, "the scope of that assignment, as you've laid it out, borders on the impossible."

"True," said the governor, "but I know you can handle it." Just as I was congratulating myself for having escaped both those assignments, the governor turned to me, "Now Al, you will have a single subject matter, namely, reviewing and reporting to the EFCB regarding all contracts, especially for teachers, police, firemen, and subway employees. . . ."

"Is that all?" I replied, smiling. Then I said: "Governor, I think we should have another post-meeting conference."

Following that official meeting, we three and Governor Carey had a private meeting to redefine the plan: all three of us, we reminded him, were trying to carry out full-time corporate responsibilities as well as serve on the EFCB. The assignments he had wished on us would in our view be better performed by the EFCB staff, with each of us retaining the right to criticize, question, and accept or refuse the studies presented to the board as a whole. After considerable discussion, our proposal was adopted.

While all this drama was unfolding — and the city was indeed on the precipice of bankruptcy — the Republican administration in Washington, including the White House itself, seemed totally incapable of understanding our dilemma. In fact, the administration was looking at the situation in totally partisan terms. At one point in the middle of our crisis, President Ford addressed the Washington Press Club, castigating New York and the Democrats for their lack of fiscal responsibility. The next day, the *Daily News* headlined its story about his speech with "PRESIDENT SAYS, 'DROP DEAD NEW YORK!'"

I served on the EFCB for several months and contributed as much as I could. But, as I feared, the assignment proved in the long run too time-consuming. I don't mind sacrifice, I don't mind giving of my time if it's for a good cause. But there comes a point when, if a peripheral job is impinging on your principal responsibilities, you have to say no; and I finally, however reluctantly, resigned from the board. But by the time I did, the city's fiscal crisis, while far from over, was well on the road to being resolved.

Despite the many organizational and financial problems I had been dealing with during my early tenure at American, they were as nothing compared to real tragedy, which has the virtue of putting a great many things into proper focus.

On April 27, 1976, roughly two years into my tenure, one of our planes, a 727, went down at Harry S Truman Airport in Saint Thomas, the Virgin Islands. From the initial reports, the crash seemed to have been a result of pilot error. Coming in for the landing, the pilot had apparently changed his mind not once, which is bad enough, but twice. Making his approach, he realized he was "floating," that is, the plane's wheels were hovering above the runway, the prevailing trade wind keeping the plane as it were from touching down. The pilot realized he was going to overshoot the runway, so he gunned the engines in an effort to take the plane back up. But when you do that there's a thing called spool up: when you shove in the throttle it can take six to seven seconds — an eternity for a modern aircraft — for the jet turbine to build up enough pressure to accelerate the aircraft. So the pilot got impatient and throttled down, in other words, decided after all to land. As a result, he overshot the runway and crashed into a commercial complex, which included a gas station. There were thirty-eight known dead, and twenty-five to thirty injured, out of a total of ninety-two people on board. I was shaken and distraught as I read the reports streaming in. To make matters worse, the Saint Thomas hospital was by all reports woefully inadequate to handle the emergency situation.

I left my office and went down one floor to the operating center, which was in minute-to-minute touch with the crash scene. Don Lloyd-Jones was there, monitoring the situation.

"Don," I said, "I think you should get down to Saint Thomas as fast as possible. You should be coordinating things on the spot."

He shook his head. "You're wrong, Al. All my presence there would do would be to divert people from their duties."

I was furious but restrained myself. In crisis situations, Casey's Law says, restraint comes first. If restraint fails, then go to mode two.

"No, Don," I countered, "it's *you* who are wrong."

"Al," Don said, "I never go in these cases. Believe me, I'm more useful back here." He said it quietly, almost matter-of-factly, and I wondered how in the present situation he could be so self–controlled, so unemotional. In my brief experience, though I had found him always to be very detached, he was, as C. R. had said, very competent as well.

I turned and left the room, having decided that since Don wouldn't go, I would. The word *insubordination* crossed my mind, but on reflection, I knew Don actually felt he shouldn't go, that he sincerely felt not only that his presence would be mistaken for grandstanding, but that he could be more effective at the head-quarters operations center. He had to arrange for a company doctor to get down there, as well as bring in local doctors from neighboring islands. He had to check the passenger list against the list of people in Saint Thomas. He had to notify the next of kin and arrange for family members to be flown into the crash scene. He had to arrange for clergy of all denominations to be flown in to comfort the wounded and bereaved. In other words, he did have his hands full in New York.

I caught the first available plane for Saint Thomas. It was a scene of vast confusion, devastation, and despair. I spent my first night with the parents of children who had died, and children whose parents had died. I held the hand of a man who no longer had a face; just burnt skin. The next day I spent most of my time trying to comfort friends and relatives of victims. But mostly I marshaled aid. I spoke to people, incessantly it seemed, and did my best to comfort and calm. I spent three days there, with almost no sleep, dealing as best I could with pain and suffering and grief.

Air travel is the safest form of transportation we have, and safety the highest priority of all airlines. But, inevitably, there will be crashes, due to weather, mechanical failure, pilot error, and, alas, in today's world, terrorism. And when they happen, the magnitude of the tragedy is overwhelming.

I had spoken to Ellie several times on the phone from Saint Thomas, trying to reassure her, but she detected my true state of mind in my voice.

"Al," she said, "you sound terrible. You must get some rest."

"I'm here to take care of others," I said.

"But you must take care of yourself, too," she said.

Utterly exhausted and in a state of deep despair, I arrived back in New York on Saturday night. The next morning I woke up, if that is the proper term, unable to see or hear, unable to move. Ellie had tried to rouse me, to no avail. Devastated, she called our family doctor, Richard Rovit, at Saint Vincent's, who had me rushed to the hospital, where it was determined that I had suffered a stroke.

In the intensive care unit, I was monitored around the clock for the next four days. As time went on, I could hear something; then there was light and vague forms. Over and over I could hear the doctors but did not understand a word they were saying. Then I could faintly hear them asking me to move a leg, an arm, my fingers. I tried, but I couldn't. By Monday I could see again. By Thursday I had all my faculties back, except my throat. I could talk, but it was painful, and my vocal cords had lost their normal resonance. But that day I was back on my feet, walking. Not firmly, but walking.

The following Monday I went back to work. Aside from my voice, I felt okay. Ellie had argued that I should take another week or two of rest, but I said, "Nonsense, I feel fine." We compromised: for the first few days I'd go in but only for a couple of hours. Ellie finally relented, but since she (rightly) didn't trust me to keep my promise, she came to work with me and sat in the outer office till my two hours were up. At which point, like a good schoolmarm, she'd walk in, look at her watch, and say, "Time to go home, Al."

A week later, I was back full time, feeling my old self. Well, almost.

Although I was apparently, and quite miraculously, fully recovered, the doctors were concerned enough about my future that after I was discharged from the hospital they put me on a regular schedule of CAT scans. There was at the time only one CAT scan facility in New York, at New York University hospital, and I repaired there every six months to have a scan, usually at three in the morning, the only time available. The doctors were worried about possible permanent injury to my brain.

About a year later, Dr. Rovit, who besides being our family doctor was a neurosurgeon, called and asked me to come over to his office. He had, I knew, just received the most recent CAT scan, so I went over there with what is commonly called in novels "a sinking heart."

"Al, I'm afraid I have some bad news for you. Your latest CAT scan shows you have an aneurysm on the brain."

I wasn't sure what I had expected, but that sounded pretty bad. I'd heard the term before, but I wasn't sure what it meant or how dire it was in my case.

He explained the term in layman's language and said dealing with it would entail a delicate operation on the brain.

"Doctor," I said, "nobody's going to touch my brain until I've had several other opinions."

"Al," he said, "I've already gotten five, including my own. Three of the five — and I'm one of them — are absolutely certain of our findings."

I was told I'd have to have an angiogram, a wonderful procedure in which they cut your groin and insert a thin plastic tube up into your brain. Then they flush you with hot dye, which they monitor as it moves through your bloodstream, to see whether there is any leak or blockage. I had four angiograms in all, each more painful than the last. No anesthetic. I could look at the screen and see the dye coursing through my head. Even more painful than the angiograms was the news that, indeed, I did have an aneurysm. I was shocked, for till then I had preferred to pretend this was all a major medical error. But when you get bad news, never wonder why; instead, if given the chance, work as hard as you can to overcome it and put it behind you.

One of American Airlines' board members was my friend Francis "Hooks" Burr, head of the board of trustees of Massachusetts General Hospital in Boston. Hooks was a lawyer, not a doctor, but by his position at the hospital knew as much about medical practices as anyone. I told him my story and asked his advice.

"Al, don't have the operation," he said. "I know a lot about these operations. They're often fatal. They're scary, terrifying things. My advice is, quit your job, take Ellie, travel, play golf, and enjoy the rest of your life."

Tempting, but I decided I should do a little more exploring.

In my Times Mirror days we owned one of the leading American medical publishers, Mosby, so I decided to find out through my friends there who were the specialists and where the leading clinics were for treating aneurysms. It turned out there were two world-renowned clinics, one in Zurich, headed by a Hungarian surgeon, and another in London, Ontario, Canada, where a Dr. Charles Drake was in charge. With the help of Richard Rovit, I opted for Drake, both because Canada was closer and because I knew I would feel more comfortable in an English-speaking hospital. Dr. Rovit came up with me, as did a friend, William Morris, a senior partner at Salomon Brothers, and his wife Elizabeth, who knew that Ellie would need all the support she could get.

The doctors — and Ellie, who had paid close attention to

their briefings — tried to explain to me in detail what was involved in the operation.

"I really don't want to hear it," I kept saying. "If I'm here, it's because I've put my trust in you."

But they insisted. An aneurysm, I knew, was like a weak spot on a tire inner tube; when you had a blowout, it usually came from that "weak spot." If the aneurysm was on an artery, it was less of a problem. The surgeon puts a clip on the weakened area and leaves it in your head. If it's on a vein, he cuts out the vein because the vein will replace itself. My problem was right where an artery flowers into veins, so the surgeon had to take linen thread and wrap every one of those veins. It was a long and extremely delicate operation, over eleven and a half hours, but I came through it with — chalk this up to the business I was in — flying colors.

But somewhere in the back of my mind I could hear Murphy lamenting: "Okay, Casey: stroke, aneurysm on the brain. How unlucky can you get? Why don't you just give up!"

But in fact I knew how lucky I was. Pushing Murphy aside, I came to the conclusion that I was actually *lucky* to have had a stroke. Without it, the doctors would never have discovered my aneurysm — I sure as hell never knew I had it — and I might well have passed from this earth several years prematurely. "The hell with you, Murphy," I said. "What you don't understand, you negative nerd, is that I was *saved* by the stroke!"

Nonetheless, given all my medical problems I had to ask myself if I was in shape to handle as stressful a job as chairman of American Airlines. I also had to ask the doctors that question, and they assured me that unless *I* didn't feel up to it, I should go back to work. Again, Ellie made me ease my way back for the first few weeks, but soon I was back full time.

Given the experience, however, I told Ellie that she, too, should have a CAT scan, which she did. Happily there was no sign of any aneurysm. Yet when Ellie died in 1989, it turned out to have been from an aneurysm. I called Dr. Rovit to inform him of Ellie's passing and told him what the cause was. I heard him curse himself.

"I can't believe that," he said. "I'm the one who read her plates."

By this time it had been more than twelve years since I had had my operation, but the doctor asked if by chance I had kept Ellie's plates. I dug them out and sent them to him. He called a few days later to say he had reexamined the plates and could find no sign of any aneurysm. So he had shown them to several other eminent doctors, with the same result. Most people who die of aneurysms have had them all their life and never know it. Stress, strain, or age often causes them to burst, or in my case "leak."

To this day, my throat remains my only medical problem. It is partly constricted as a result of the stroke; I keep talking when there's no air behind my voice. But I look on that not as a handicap but a virtue: it forces me to talk more slowly, which is an asset in business as in life. Like C. R. Smith's habit of not enunciating clearly, my new "disability" tends to make people listen to me more closely.

Nineteen seventy-six was a momentous year for our country and our company. We celebrated our two-hundredth anniversary as a nation, and we saw an election that put a new president in the White House. In the history of the world there has been no other system that has enjoyed such peaceful transfers of power from one party to another over a period of two centuries.

For American, too, which was celebrating its fiftieth anniversary, it was a banner year. After the disappointing 1975, with the economy in the doldrums and fuel costs still volatile and unpredictable, we reported record earnings of $56 million in 1976 (against a loss of $28.5 million the year before). Our operating revenues were up 17.4 percent, topping $2 billion for the first time; our system's load factor was the highest since 1967; and for the third successive year we were recognized by frequent flyers as the number-one domestic airline. Luck also helped: our fuel prices were lower that year than the industry's in general, because of favorable contracts that would expire in August 1977, and also 1976 was a year of hiatus in labor negotiations. But more than luck was involved in the turnaround; there was an enormous amount of hard work by American's now highly motivated employees. For, from the uncertainty and dubious morale of 1974, our new management team had succeeded in instilling a sense of pride throughout the company, which translated into harder work and greater productivity. I have always been a firm believer that the harder you work the luckier you get.

As we came to the end of 1976, I felt that while most of our management team was operating efficiently and in close concert, one of the four, Bob Norris, was having increasing trouble fitting in. I had hired Bob out of the FEI, the Financial Executive Institute, where accounting theory and policy were analyzed and formulated for the profession. In a sense, I had hired him to replace me, since when I took over the company in February 1974, the one area where I felt completely comfortable was finance, and I had decided to fill that position myself until the rest of our executive committee was in place. To his credit, Bob was a crackerjack accountant, but he was a purist, a theoretician rather than a pragmatist, and in the fast-changing world of air transport, rigidity could not be the order of the day.

I had had several clashes with him over the preceding year, but despite our differences I had hoped he would adapt to this crazy industry of ours, where each day, it seemed, brought new challenges that demanded innovative, and usually immediate, solutions. But as the months rolled by, with Bob as recalcitrant as ever, I was fast coming to the conclusion that I would have to replace him. One week in late October I had a further clash with him in our weekly one-on-one meeting, over an important though not vital matter having to do with the reserves on the balance sheet. At the end of the meeting, slightly exasperated, I said to Bob:

"My friend, I'm tired of arguing this point. I'm flying out to California for the weekend, but when I get back on Monday morning I expect the matter to be done my way. Please have your report on my desk."

On Monday I asked Libby if Bob had delivered his report,

and she said that she had seen no sign of it. I called Bob in, and before I could open my mouth he said:

"Al, I didn't do as you asked. Nor do I intend to."

"Then I'm afraid, Bob, I have no choice but to ask you to leave. I'm the first to encourage honest disagreement, but this goes way beyond that."

"I expected that to be your reaction," he said, "and was fully prepared to be fired."

Bob, I repeat, was one of the best theoretical accountants I had ever met, but in business theory is often not enough. After he left American, Norris returned to the FEI, a place far better suited to his many talents.

Firing people is never easy. In fact, to my mind it's one of the hardest tasks a chief executive has to face. But failing to fire someone who is either ill-adapted to the post or not pulling his or her weight is even worse, because it negatively affects the company's productivity as well as morale. I have always felt that a leader should give a manager the benefit of the doubt, should go as far down the road as possible with him, but if it becomes clear things aren't working out, one should act sooner rather than later. The greatest sin is not acting at all.

9

THE GREAT MOVE

FOR SOME TIME I HAD QUESTIONED the wisdom of our maintaining corporate headquarters in New York City, especially in the light of the growing size and importance of our training centers in Dallas/Fort Worth: the Learning Center, whose principal function was to train flight attendants, and the Flight Academy, which had the dual purpose of training new pilots as well as putting experienced captains and first officers through their paces in the latest technology and equipment. It seemed to make good sense to me to locate our corporate headquarters in the same area; in a way, it was taking American back to its roots. But sentiments aside, I was convinced such a move would not only save the company money but also make us more efficient operationally, since Dallas/Fort Worth was already one of our key hubs.

But I was also acutely aware of the many personal and political problems such a decision would inevitably entail. My chief concern was the impact it would have on the roughly 1,200 people who worked at headquarters in New York City: assuming an average family of four, we would be disrupting the lives of over 5,000 people. My first instinct was to bring the matter up at one of our Monday-morning management meetings, but the more I thought, the more I refrained. No matter what internal security we might request or impose, the news would leak out sooner rather than later, with all the attendant pressures from press and politicians on me and the whole American board. After discussing it with Ellie at more length I'm sure than she needed or wanted, I decided that this was one problem I'd deal with largely if not completely myself. If there were negative repercussions within or outside the company, it would be Casey's fault, not American's. I'd need some help gathering statistics and putting numbers together, but by playing it close to the vest, I figured I could keep the potential backlash under control until a final decision had been made.

At the time, we were occupying 244,000 square feet at 633 Third Avenue, plus an additional 25,000 square feet a block down the street at 605, which housed our food service subsidiary, Sky Chefs, and the Americana Hotel headquarters staff. The lease at 605 was due to expire in mid 1979; at 633, we had to give notice before the end of that same year. We knew we were going to need additional space; we also knew the landlord was angling for a 15 percent increase for a new lease.

For years the Dallas/Fort Worth business community had been courting American, if only sporadically. C. R. had flirted with the idea; so had my predecessor, George Spater, who had actually commissioned a feasibility study in 1972. But then Spater, and the entire company, had been overwhelmed with far more pressing problems, which forced the idea onto the back burner.

Two senior American board members, Jim Aston and Amon Carter Jr., were both Texans. Periodically, they would raise the idea of "moving American back to where it belongs," and I would gently duck the issue, saying that we had some more urgent problems to deal with first, which they knew was true. That same notion was posed even more frequently by two other prominent Texas businessmen: Henry Stuart, who was chairman of the Dallas/Forth Worth airport, and Ernie Dean, its executive director. Given their positions, they had a vested interest in the move. During the previous four years, whenever they raised the matter, I'd inevitably respond:

"Gentlemen, you're wasting your breath. You know we're committed to New York. Why, even C. R. couldn't bring himself to make that move."

In the spring of 1978, however, American Airlines might not have been thinking of leaving New York, but Al Casey was. For many reasons, starting with deregulation; no matter how hard I'd fought it, I knew in my heart of hearts it was inevitable. There

were other reasons, too. Like survival. As we entered 1978 we
were out of money. We were out of the means to raise cash.
We were out of everything. I and the whole management team
knew we had to do something drastic. Deregulation would create
a whole new world in aviation, and everybody, including American, was cash short for the heavy expenditures we knew lay ahead.

In April, Stuart and Dean called and said we needed to meet
to discuss moving our southern central reservations office from its
current location at Amon Carter Field (an airport named after our
board member's father, an aviation pioneer and at one point
American's largest single stockholder) to the Dallas/Fort Worth
International Airport. That move was a no-brainer: the reservations center, one of our four largest, was then housed in a rundown, dilapidated old hangar at an airport that was closed down!
Having quickly settled that burning issue, Dean sprang his customary closing question.

"So, Al," he drawled, "when are y'all going to move the *rest*
of American to Dallas/Fort Worth?" As he uttered the classic
query, as if by rote, he snapped shut his briefcase and got to his
feet, clearly expecting the stock answer.

"That all depends, Ernie," I said, "on what your airport, and
the two cities that run it, have to offer."

"Are you *serious*, Al?" asked Stuart, who was also standing,
briefcase in hand.

"Have you ever known me not to be?" I asked.

Both men quickly sat back down again.

"Okay, let's talk," said Stuart.

Over the next hour, we structured the basics of a deal: we'd
move if the airport would build us a new headquarters and reservations center financed with tax-free airport bonds, then lease us
back the facilities at a rate sufficient to pay off the bonds. Before
our meeting that day I had run some rough estimates on the potential savings to American: by my calculations, on rent alone the
twenty-year savings would come to $200 million. Not to mention
productivity savings yet to be calculated.

Before we parted that day, we had an agreement in principle, subject to the dynamic duo from Texas being able to make the bond issue a reality.

As we shook hands, I said, "One thing, gentlemen. We must keep this confidential. If it leaks, there'll be hell to pay, I assure you."

"Does anyone here at headquarters know?" Dean asked.

"Hell, man, how could they?" I thundered in mock surprise. "I only shook hands with you on it two minutes ago!" Then, turning serious, I added: "I'm in an especially tricky situation, having served only two years ago on the governor's board to help *bring* business to New York, not remove it."

"We understand," Stuart said. "You know me well enough, Al, to count on my complete discretion."

In fact, I had known and admired Henry for many years. He was a highly successful real estate developer in the town of Addison, as well as the owner/operator of its private airport. He was also a good friend of Jim Aston, who for many years had been on both American's and Times Mirror's boards.

Within a month, Dean delivered a concrete proposal, which included $147 million in tax-free bond financing for our new headquarters. One giant step for American. But there were many more steps to be made before we came to a final decision.

At the June board meeting I presented the idea — stressing that it was only that — and got permission to conduct a full-scale feasibility study.

The next question: who was going to make it? Again, more out of discretion than desire, I decided to write it myself. Although I never really seriously considered any other alternative than Texas, for the form at least I looked into three other possible locations: Chicago, our second largest hub; Atlanta, where we planned a hub and where the quality of life was excellent; and Saint Louis, which had the virtue of being in the dead center of the country. If word got out, we could always say we were studying various alternatives, as the company had done many times in the past, but that we were still very much committed to New York.

At our Monday-morning meeting the following week I casually raised the subject and asked Tom Plaskett, whom Crandall had recruited from finance, to do some economic impact studies for a number of relocation sites. Start with Dallas/Fort Worth, I told him. What I didn't tell anyone was that I would make and write the rest of the study myself. By mid-July, in time for the next board meeting, I had completed a thirty-five-page study, setting forth the various pros and cons of the move. I ran off just enough copies for everyone, which I handed out at the start of the meeting, giving them an hour to read and digest it and asking them not to discuss it among themselves until we reconvened. There were other items on the agenda that day, but the move was the prime issue, and before we adjourned we had a consensus that American should move to Dallas/Fort Worth. Still hoping to maintain secrecy, at the end of the meeting I gathered up all twenty-five copies, twenty-three of which I burned. The other two I took with me.

I might just as well have saved myself the trouble. On August 2 the *Fort Worth Star-Telegram* broke the story that American was contemplating a move to Texas. Since the kitten was out of the bag, I flew the next day to Dallas and Fort Worth, meeting first with Mayor Robert Folsom of Dallas, then later with Fort Worth mayor Hugh Parmer, the members of the airport board, and Amon Carter Jr. I leveled with them all: barring circumstances I could not foresee, American would be moving its headquarters to the Dallas/Fort Worth area, an announcement that was greeted with the lay equivalent of loud hosannas. In early August, I was the local hero *numero uno*. But as I flew back to New York next day, I knew it was not exactly a ticker tape parade that would be awaiting me.

I walked into 633 early next morning. "Any messages?" I asked Libby with my broadest Irish grin.

"*Any messages!*" she said. "Only these," and she held up a stack about two inches thick.

"I mean, any of them *important?*"

"How about the top six," she said. "All from Mayor Koch. He urgently wants to meet with you."

"Wonder why?" I said. "Haven't talked to him in months."

Barely half an hour later the phone rang.

"It's the mayor," Libby said. "He sounds mad."

"Mr. Casey," the mayor began, "I hope the stories I've been hearing aren't true."

I was tempted to be flippant but fortunately refrained.

"Mr. Mayor, as with all news stories there's a particle of truth buried in a mountain of speculation," I said. But the mayor knew that the stories contained a good deal more than a particle. He asked if he could meet with me, and we set a date for the following week.

Koch showed up with Deputy Mayor Peter Solomon and half a dozen other city officials. I started by declaring that we were studying the possibility but that no final decision to move out of New York had been made. I hoped thus to defuse the collective anger I felt filling the room. I wanted to make this a friendly meeting, but I could not manage it alone. Unfortunately Koch had already told the press that I was a civic traitor, which did not sit very well with me, and added that I ought to be ashamed of myself. But at the meeting he was all affability and smiles. For five minutes.

Then, his real feelings obviously getting the upper hand, he said: "Mr. Casey, how can you, who accepted to serve on Governor Carey's emergency board, the goal of which was to help stabilize New York City, now turn your back on us?"

I answered that one had nothing to do with the other, and that as his job was to serve New York City, so mine was to look out for the best interests of American Airlines.

"Mr. Casey," he said, "we're here to let you know that we'll match any offer Dallas/Fort Worth comes up with."

I told him I greatly appreciated the city's offer. "I'm always ready to listen," I said, "but we should move quickly."

I sensed a certain desperation in the open offer. This was an election year, and the defection of American Airlines in the next few months could be seized upon by the political opposition as further proof that the mayor was incapable of keeping businesses in New York.

A few days later we met again, the New York City delegation swelled this time by local members of Congress. Clearly the pressure was on. In essence, the group offered American favorable rental terms, either in the World Trade Center or a prime midtown Manhattan office building.

I said that I would discuss the offer with my management team and take it as well to the board. But I sensed they wanted an immediate answer, which I was not prepared to give. They were insistent, and tempers were fragile.

"Maybe you actually *prefer* Texas," one member of the delegation said, as if the idea was tantamount to being banished to Siberia.

"Gentlemen, you must understand that my personal feelings have nothing to do with this decision. I'm a Bostonian. Boston's a lot closer to New York than to Dallas/Fort Worth. I went to work in New York straight out of college and was happy here for ten years. Then I came back to New York with REA in the 1960s, with offices only a few blocks from here. I love New York. More importantly, my wife loves New York. It's the most vibrant city in the world. It's the financial center of the world, and finances are my lifeblood. And as for culture, no other American city even comes close, and cultural life's very important to me. So let's not confuse personal feelings with a purely business decision."

It was a long declaration, but one I believed and hoped might have an effect. But from the steam rising from just behind Mayor Koch's ears, I could see that my eloquent pitch had failed. Miserably.

"Mr. Casey," the mayor said tightly, "it is my position that once a businessman has undertaken civic duties, as you have for New York, one is henceforth obligated to put the city's welfare above that of his corporation."

"Mr. Mayor," I responded, shaking my head, "I must respect-fully disagree with you on that point. When I took the job with the emergency board, I made it clear to all concerned that my prime responsibility was to American Airlines, and if ever I felt the board's demands in any way jeopardized that priority, I would have to resign. I believe any business leader would agree with me."

"In my view you're betraying this city, Mr. Casey, lock, stock, and barrel. Furthermore," he said, his voice rising, "if you persist and press forward with this plan to move American out of New York, we" — and he gestured to the assembled political throng — "have ways of seeing to it our constituents retaliate. Ways of hurt-ing your company."

Now, I have always taken poorly to intimidation, and that day was no exception. I could feel myself growing hot, and before my Irish temper got the upper hand I stood up and said:

"Gentlemen, this meeting is over. Thank you all for taking the time to come." And with a smile I most emphatically did not feel, I opened wide the conference room door. As the distin-guished delegation filed out, I could hear the mayor, clearly un-hinged, muttering under his breath. The only two words I could make out were "betrayal" and "treason." And then, loud and clear: "He ought to be *ashamed* of himself."

For the life of me, I couldn't figure out who hizzoner was re-ferring to.

We held off making a public announcement until November 15 — after the elections. But if that kind gesture on our part was appreciated, I failed to notice it. Koch went on the offensive again, singling me out for special opprobrium, comparing me to a CIA agent who had defected to the Russians. (As someone was quick to point out, that parallel went over big in Texas, where the Rus-sians were not viewed with particular affection.) The press also went to town. The usually staid *Business Week* accused me of mov-ing out of spite, because I personally had not become a big enough fish in New York and therefore decided to retreat and swim in a smaller pond.

I pointed out to the press that among other misconceptions was the notion we were abandoning New York. Even if we moved all 1,200 headquarters personnel to Texas, we'd still have more than 8,000 employees in New York. But the more I argued, the less the press listened. A couple of days later I opened the papers to read that the city's unions were threatening to boycott American. Worse yet, one of New York's major entertainment conglomerates, Warner Communications, stated publicly and unequivocally that it was ordering its several thousand employees not to fly American, its major carrier.

I was furious. In a sense, I understood to some degree the unions' position. But for a private company to take such a stance, I found downright silly. I put in a call to Warner's CEO, Steve Ross, and gave him a piece of my mind. I knew it wouldn't help, but it made me feel better. And somewhere, on some level, I suspected my message might seep into the deeper recesses of the man's brain. Maybe it did. A month or so later I was informed that there had been a Revocation of the Edict of New York: Warner informed its employees they were free to fly American if they so chose. Maybe because I had told the press, half jokingly, that despite Warner's position I still intended to show Warner Brothers films on our planes. Or, more likely, Steve Ross realized he had overreacted.

I suppose I should have been flattered rather than upset. The city had made no such protest when Eastern Airlines had moved to Miami. Or when Texaco and Shell and General Electric and Coca-Cola had abandoned the Big Apple. Even Mayor Koch seemed to have made peace, if not with me personally at least with American. Having won reelection, he was doubtless in a better frame of mind. In any event, he publicly stated that although he still thought the move a major mistake, he denounced the threatened boycott, reminding New Yorkers that American would still have a major presence in New York.

So that was the end of that.

Or so I thought. Murphy, who had been nagging me unmercifully over the previous six months, reminding me day and night that I had screwed up again, suddenly vanished into the New York night. Wanting to celebrate, I took Ellie out on the town.

Premature celebration.

In early December, Ray Hutchison, a lawyer and the Dallas/Fort Worth airport bond counsel, received a phone call from a close friend in Washington — what is known as a "usually reliable source" — who announced that he had it on good authority that the IRS was shortly going to rule that the $147 million Dallas/Fort Worth bond did not qualify for tax-free status. About the same time, I got a report that Deputy Mayor Solomon, speaking at a breakfast at the Harvard Club in New York, responded to a question about our move by declaring that it was "far from a foregone conclusion," adding that he had heard the IRS was about to rule against the upcoming bond issue.

It didn't take an Einstein to guess that the New York congressional delegation had set about sabotaging our deal. For if the rumor was true, the interest rate on the bond would have to increase — from 7 percent to roughly 10 percent — which would throw all our financial assumptions out the window at 633.

We immediately convened a meeting, where I announced the news and said it was time to counterattack. The only dissident among our generals was Lloyd-Jones, who had opposed the move from the start. It was time to bring on the impressive Texas trio: Majority Leader Jim Wright and Senators Tower and Bentsen. Working against the deadline of the Christmas recess, the three lobbied incessantly against the IRS ruling. Jim Wright had a Texas ace up his sleeve: he had taken part in drafting the original law that established tax-free financing for the nation's airports, and in mid-December he wrote a sharply worded letter to Secretary of the Treasury Michael Blumenthal protesting any such IRS ruling, adding that in any case it should not apply *retroactively*. On December 28, the IRS issued a notice that early the following year it would hold hearings to clarify the matter of tax-free bonds to finance airport facilities. Three months later the hearing took place, and it was held that nonoperational facilities, which included airline company headquarters, could *not* be financed by tax-free bonds.

That was the bad news. The good news was, by the time the ruling came down our bonds had already been issued and sold. American Airline's new headquarters at Dallas/Fort Worth was the last building of its kind to be financed by tax-free bonds.

We offered to move all 1,200 members of the New York headquarters staff. I had hoped that at least half, maybe as much as 60 percent, would accept. To our surprise and delight, more than 900 accepted. To ease the pain of moving, I mandated that everyone would have up to a year to decide if they wanted to move back to New York — at our expense.

One of our major problems on the personal level was home interest rates. Many of our employees had purchased homes in the New York area at interest rates far lower than those now prevailing. Home interest rates had soared in the previous decade. To encourage buying, Texas had put a ceiling of 10 percent on home mortgages, but this required banks to demand higher down payments than elsewhere in the nation. To solve the problem, I sent Tom Plaskett down to work out a blanket deal with the Texas banks, whereby American would buy certificates of deposit — $60 million worth — and the banks would provide our employees with mortgage money at 8.75 percent.

For the next several months we had special charter flights leaving New York for Dallas/Fort Worth every Friday night, returning on Sunday, to let people check out the area, look for a house, make up their minds. Once we made the move — staggered over a month — in the summer of 1979, we provided transportation back to the New York area every Friday evening, returning to Dallas/Fort Worth on Sunday, so our employees could conclude old business, visit old friends, or simply see a Broadway show. For years after, people would come up and thank me for dreaming up that wonderful Dallas/Fort Worth–New York "commuter" program, which, they said, had made the transition so much easier.

Inevitably, I responded that instituting the program had always struck me as so natural and normal that it hardly merited thanks.

10

DEREGULATION

EARLY IN 1979 I celebrated my fifth birthday with American and could look back with a certain fragile pride — "fragile" because I remembered that pride very often goeth before a fall — on the company's accomplishments during that difficult and volatile period. We had almost doubled our revenues, from $1.482 billion in 1973 to $2.736 billion in 1978, and had been highly profitable in four of those five years, the negative blip having come in 1975, when a combination of deepening recession and further escalating fuel costs had put us back in the red. But as noted, the following year, 1976, we had rebounded nicely, with traffic, revenues, and profits rising to record levels. Still, the one immutable fact I had learned about the airline business over the years was that it changed faster, and was subject to more unpredictable factors, than any business I knew. One new factor looming larger and larger on the horizon was the U.S. government, which in the fall of 1978 had passed the so-called deregulation bill. To understand the thrust on the part of Congress toward deregulation, a bit of background is in order.

Before World War II, when the DC-3 was the queen of the commercial skies, only 10 to 15 percent of the U.S. population had ever been in an airplane. By the end of the war, fully 25 percent of the nation had flown, many as a result of military leaves or changing assignments during wartime duty.

Under the impetus of improved technology, a more receptive public, and a stronger economy, commercial air travel really took off after World War II, as C. R. had so wisely foreseen. It was further spurred by the jet age. By 1971, 49 percent of Americans had flown at least once in their lives; today that figure has risen to over 65 percent. Major advances in aircraft have been achieved over the years. The improvements in size, technology, and speed have been obvious. Less apparent, however, have been the important productivity gains from increased seating capacity.

Consider the 2,500 nonstop air miles between Los Angeles and New York. With the four-engine DC-7 piston aircraft American flew on that route in the 1950s, we had 60 seats and generated 150,000 seat miles per trip. In 1959, American inaugurated the jet age domestically by introducing the 112-seat 707 in the Los Angeles to New York market. Overnight, the 707 cut three hours from the coast-to-coast trip; but, just as important, it increased total seat miles per flight to 280,000, 87 percent more than the DC-7. The 747 began flying the transcontinental route in 1970. It had 342 seats in those early days, yielding 855,000 seat miles per flight. That was a 200 percent increase over the 707 and nearly 500 percent better than the DC-7.

Since productivity improvements tend to flow directly to the bottom line, those advances had a lot of airline people smiling before the advent of deregulation. In fact, a major portion of the economic benefit was passed through in the form of increased wages. Much was also spent on faster and better computers, with American in the forefront of that major innovation with its SABRE system, which in the previous five years we had made a top priority.

When I arrived at American our computer system was in a shambles. Pre–Stone Age. One of our first goals was to bring it up to speed technically, then make it a key marketing tool. Crandall was no computer whiz, but once he assumed the marketing job he quickly understood the full importance, and potential, of SABRE, which under Spater had been allowed to fall far behind our competitors at Eastern, United, and Pan Am. Once he focuses on a problem, Crandall can be, and usually is, obsessive, and SABRE was no exception. Crandall's first airline job had been at TWA, where he was responsible for implementing the company's first computerized accounts receivable system. In the fall of 1974, he discovered — I have no idea how — that in our Tulsa warehouse there were two thousand cathode-ray tubes, sitting there gathering dust. Together with Max Hopper, chief of data processing, they salvaged them and set about installing SABRE with up-to-date equipment. We then hired away from TWA a man named Jim O'Neill, with whom Crandall had worked when he was there. Within two years we had one of the best systems in the business, making us more efficient with our customers but, almost as important, allowing us to be the first to offer our premier service to outside clients.

By May 1976 we installed our first SABRE unit in a travel agency, providing fast and efficient reservations information, replacing the cumbersome phone information system then in use. Before long, we had SABRE in several thousand travel agencies and hundreds of corporate travel departments. Our chief competitor, United, was so sure its Apollo system was superior to SABRE, it had refused our offer for a joint service to travel agents nationwide. I'm sure United is still ruing the day it allowed SABRE to get there first. SABRE didn't only book reservations; it kept track of fare changes, scheduled flight crews, gave pilots their flight plans almost instantaneously, kept track of airplane parts, and analyzed financial and performance data. In time, it also allowed passengers to book hotel reservations, car rentals, ask for special meals on our flights. In short, it made us overall vastly more efficient and customer oriented. But it was only in the late seventies and early eighties that SABRE came fully into its own: in the new era of deregulation, when fares changed at, it seemed, the speed of light, SABRE was equipped to handle more than ten thousand fare changes a day.

In fact, American Airlines' decision to invest heavily in SABRE in those early days was one of the best we ever made. By 1995, more than 40 percent of all airline bookings made in the United States were handled by SABRE, making it the largest domestic distributor of travel arrangements, far ahead of its competitors: Amadeus/System One, Galileo/Apollo, and Wordspan. But SABRE not only excels as a travel and reservation system: two decades after it began, about one-third of its revenues derive from consulting and other services. If SABRE had been independent in 1995, it would have reported record profits of $226 million on sales of $1.53 billion. That net margin of 14.8 percent compares with American Airlines' overall net margin of under 3 percent. Talk about children surpassing the parents!

But the real payout for AMR — the parent company of American Airlines and SABRE both — came in October 1996 when it took Sabre Group Holdings, Inc., public, selling 20.2 million shares — roughly 16 percent of the company — at $27 per share, or $545 million. That would place a value on the shares AMR continues to hold at $2.9 billion. From the proceeds of that sale, approximately $368 million was used to repay in part a debenture that SABRE had issued to American for $850,000, maturing on September 30, 2004. Another win–win situation: a nice windfall for American, a further strengthening of SABRE's dominant position in the marketplace.

In the old days, ours had been a much more stable and orderly business. If an airline wanted to change a fare, for instance, or introduce a new fare concept, it had to seek Civil Aeronautics Board permission at least a month in advance. And the CAB made sure that all airlines had plenty of time to adjust to the change and put the new fare into their reservations systems.

A good example is the so-called super saver fare, a discount package offering reductions of as much as 45 percent on coach tickets when certain restrictions regarding ticket purchase and length-of-stay requirements were met. American first proposed the fare on January 31, 1977. The CAB didn't approve it until March 15, and the first super saver passengers didn't travel until April 24. Today, in contrast, fares change almost daily. Furthermore, the great emphasis on competition has produced a staggering array of airfare permutations, as airlines resort more and more to market-by-market and even flight-by-flight pricing.

Competition has also had a big impact on airline routes. In

the old days, new routes were difficult to obtain, and dropping routes was almost unheard of. Under deregulation, there has been a massive reshaping of the airline route system as airlines have taken advantage of new rules.

Without government controls, airports were able to compete with other airports. To cover the costs of maintenance, administration, and services, airports charge landing fees and storage charges, or "tie down" fees. Deregulation enabled airports to make themselves attractive to new airline routes by reducing these fees.

Dramatic change has also come to the airline route map, now dotted with a series of hubs. In the days of regulation, the route system changed very little. The old system mandated by Congress in 1938 was designed to ensure service for everyone, and carriers were awarded stable route franchises as a means of making this social objective attainable. Deregulation was a social and political about-face from this forty-year commitment. The nation's policy emphasis suddenly shifted from service to competition, and route franchises, upon which all airline planning and aircraft purchases had been based, were abolished.

It may seem unfair and economically unfathomable, but it's simply a reflection of the fact that today's fares are dictated entirely by free-market forces, which can sometimes produce irrational and costly action. Whenever there's a fare war, the fare has to be matched. In the airline business (as in other commodity businesses), if you're significantly undersold by a major competitor, you're going to lose lots of business to the lower fare.

Under the former franchise system, which kept competition at reasonable levels, airlines had the ability to sustain nonstop or direct service on many routes. This was true even for marginal or unprofitable routes, because fares were structured in such a way that heavily traveled routes could help subsidize smaller ones. With deregulation, all that changed. Competition is more intense on large routes, and with fares also governed by competitive activity, it is no longer possible to cross-subsidize the leaner markets. As a result, the airlines are doing less nonstop flying between pairs of cities and more flying into and out of major connecting hubs, such as the ones American Airlines built in Dallas/Fort Worth and later in Chicago.

The hubs allow airlines to offer what they regard as a "unique product," the ability to provide convenient service several times a day to many different destinations, with the full range of reservations, ground, and in-flight services for which the major airlines are well known. In economic terms, hubs allow airlines to control traffic by funneling people through one central location and rerouting them to their final destinations.

Profitability, or rather the lack of it, is the most profoundly difficult problem facing the airline industry. The financial plight of the airlines should be a matter of serious concern for the entire nation. Without adequate profitability, an airline company simply cannot purchase the new aircraft necessary to keep the airline system up to date. If these airplanes go unpurchased, then the nation will have a less vital and less competitive aircraft manufacturing industry, which, in turn, will contribute further to our country's already serious balance-of-payments problem.

Airlines were once considered a quasi utility, wherein the industry accepted price control in return for route franchises. Deregulation, as I said, turned the industry into a commodity business, and as is always the case with commodities, oversupply spells trouble. Today, the vast majority of the traveling public views an airplane seat as a homogeneous unit and purchases on price alone. Deregulation is to blame.

Let me explain.

Although airplanes are hugely expensive machines, it is the cost of the personnel who fly and maintain them that can create financial havoc in the industry. The cost of a plane is amortized, but the cost of personnel is fixed for each flight, whether the plane is full or only a few seats have been sold. By inviting price cutting when it was not always possible, deregulation vastly complicated this formula, and many airlines — over a hundred, in fact — went out of business because they followed Murphy's Law.

Having experienced airline deregulation firsthand — in the trenches, I'm tempted to say, but the metaphor seems wrong for the airlines — I consider myself something of an expert on the subject. That is less a boast than a lament.

Most of us go into business feeling that we know the rules under which we are going to play. How they have changed over the years! And, of course, they will change again.

In life, we all have regulation forced upon us in one form or another. Its initial form is parental regulation. At the same time, there is school with its full set of regulations. Then we voluntarily accept regulation in the marital form. In a sense, governments are like people, and our society has gone through the same cycle as the individual.

At its birth, as our country was formed and developed, it evolved not only the necessary military and police organizations, but also road and canal networks. There also sprang up industry regulation where monopolistic or quasi-monopolistic opportunities existed or threatened. These regulations came to involve rail, motor, oil pipeline, and domestic water transportation under the Interstate Commerce Commission, civil aviation under the Civil Aeronautics Board, banking under the Federal Reserve System, communications under the Federal Communications Commission, and so forth. All of these boards are at the federal level and were established prior to World War II. In addition, there has always been a multitude of state and local regulations as well.

Beginning in the 1960s, the modus operandi of virtually all federal regulatory agencies was subject to increasing attack. By 1979–80, all had their authority challenged and changed, often drastically and, with few exceptions, in the direction of requiring increased reliance upon competitive forces.

While this type of government regulation was being relaxed, at least to a degree, new regulation arose in other forms. Generally these new forms did not deal with specific industries but cut across the entire business world. Examples are the Environmental Protection Agency and the Equal Employment Opportunity Commission. Thus there have been two conflicting trends during the past quarter century: one toward reducing the scope of regulation centering on certain industries (the so-called old-line regulatory agencies), and the other toward expanding regulation of the agencies that are free to roam in any direction.

In the airline industry, deregulation was undertaken in the name of getting government "off the back" of business. But it was justified in many other ways. Cries of "greater reliance upon competitive forces," "regulatory reform," and even complete deregulation, in some cases, became increasingly strident in the sixties and seventies.

In the broadest sense, deregulation created a restructuring of national priorities. Airline deregulation fundamentally changed, virtually overnight, a national transportation policy that sought to ensure easy, reasonable, reliable access to all sections of the nation.

Like most other industrialized nations, the United States had long appreciated the commercial, business, and social value of a national transportation network; witness the federal interstate waterways and highways programs. Airline regulation was designed to promote civil aviation through subsidy as well as to moderate competition through entry restriction and prohibition of rate competition. This was done on the theory that all, or nearly all, reasonable-sized communities were entitled to air service in order to speed up the development of the country. Thus, for example, only three airlines could serve the New York–Los Angeles route, and in return for this profitable quasi monopoly, each of the three was forced to serve unprofitable routes (for example, to Rochester, Providence, and Syracuse).

The full history of deregulation is very complicated, but a pivotal moment occurred when Stephen Breyer, the most recent appointee to the Supreme Court, wrote a paper while he was at Harvard's Kennedy School of Government. In his paper, Breyer argued that the public was forced to pay high airline fares by reason of governmental regulation. He brought this viewpoint to the attention of Senator Edward Kennedy of Massachusetts. Airline regulation at that time was under the control of the Senate Airline Committee, headed by Senator Howard Cannon of Nevada, who did not at all appreciate others trampling on his turf. So Senator Cannon stepped up the pace of the hearings he was conducting and proposed legislation. This, in turn, spurred Senator Kennedy to even greater efforts, and airline deregulation moved forward at a greatly accelerated pace, not because the need was urgent but essentially because each of the senators wanted the limelight.

Many of us in the industry spent endless hours talking to regulators, senators, and congressmen. We said that, as proposed, the change was simply a matter of economics: the big markets would get bigger, with lower prices and improved service, while the smaller markets would have high prices and less service, and many midsize cities would lose *all* jet service. The answer we received was that new operators would come into the small and midsize markets with new aircraft, lower prices, and improved service. We produced charts and graphs, cited demographics and geographics, to no avail. It was the old saying so prevalent in D.C.: "Don't confuse me with the facts. My mind is made up."

In the fall of 1977, I participated in a debate on the subject of deregulation, on a panel that included Senator Kennedy; M. Lamar Muse, president of Southwest Airlines; Edwin Colodny, president of Allegheny Airlines; and John Robson, former chairman of the Civil Aeronautics Board. Senator Kennedy and I, both natives and boosters of the fair state of Massachusetts, were about as far apart on the issue as two people can get. Kennedy talked in general, abstract terms — as politicians do once or twice in their lives — his words aimed more at the voters, I thought, than at the hard questions we were facing. "We want to take the heavy hand of the federal government out of economic regulation of the airline industry," he said. Sound familiar? Getting the government off people's backs has been one of the most effective vote-getting themes of the past twenty years. Today politicians are still spouting it as if they'd just made it up.

I responded by trying to explain that we weren't really

discussing deregulation at all but a substitute I viewed as wrong-headed and dangerous. "There has not been a society in the history of the world that has not had to regulate its transportation," I pointed out. "Over the past four decades we have used regulation to build a safe, convenient, coordinated, and totally integrated system second to none in the world." Which was true. But truth in the face of the prevailing storm — and there was a lot of warm air blowing forth that day — was but the proverbial straw in the wind. The irony, of course, was that I had spent my entire business life in an unregulated environment and firmly believed in the many virtues of competition. But with public utilities and transportation, I saw proper regulation as necessary for the common good.

Further congressional hearings on the deregulation issue were held. More and more congressmen became convinced that continued regulation no longer made any sense. The airline deregulation bill was then passed in the fall of 1978, when the crescendo of criticism against the industry reached an all-time high, principally because of the rising cost of fares.

When you look at the record of airline deregulation since 1979, 120 airlines have either filed for bankruptcy or ceased operations, and the trend has accelerated in recent years. Why? Deregulation.

Managements are now free to take risks and, if successful, enjoy the rewards of their accomplishments. But failure means they must suffer the consequences. This Darwinian struggle is not in any way unique to the airline business. Over the years, other industries undergoing dramatic structural change have gone through this same "natural selection" process.

What distinguishes the winners from the losers?

I believe the most common reasons for failure are overexpansion, underestimating the competition, and failure to reduce costs. Other reasons include overestimating demand, a deterioration of balance sheets, and pricing on an incremental cost basis.

Ironically, airlines were fortunate that they were deregulated while inflation was still in double digits. Today, corporate America is still trying to cope with the wrenching shift from the heady days of rapid inflation where mistakes were quickly buried with appreciating assets, and borrowing money was a way of life. Of course, there have been difficulties associated with greatly reduced inflation and, in some instances, actual disinflation. In the latter case, there is little room for error, and only the very best operators will produce consistent profit growth.

As American's CEO, I realized that the biggest threat to members of a newly deregulated industry was the entry of new low-cost producers into their markets. It matters not whether they are currently in the business or newly arrived. What counts is whether their costs are lower. Certainly, there will be a proliferation of new product/service combinations and the introduction of new technology. When you are in a commodity business, you cannot control price; therefore you must control costs. True, you may in some areas provide unique services or have geographical advantages, and you should exploit them fully, always protecting them by maintaining competitive costs. (Customer loyalty in the commodity business runs about as deep as the water in a Texas bayou after a three-year drought.)

I also sensed there would be even more overcapacity as new firms came in and existing firms expanded into new markets. In the airline industry, capacity grew by 8 percent a year in the two years after deregulation, compared to only 1 percent per year in the decade prior to deregulation. With the rapidly growing competition, price wars were waged, resulting in a decline in profits for all involved.

Industries experiencing deregulation must prepare for their most profitable markets to be the first attacked. Price competition will force them into dramatic expense-reduction programs. They must also be prepared for increased investment at a time when their profitability is being challenged.

Now, deregulation is not all bad; it does provide opportunities for gain. A company can broaden its product line and diversify its geographic exposure. However, a company must really know its costs. It must build up its marketing capabilities. It must reproduce low-cost operation in selected markets and/or product lines. In a deregulated industry, growth through acquisition is usually dangerous and expensive. A company must be especially careful of adding new capabilities through acquisition when it does not know the lines of supply and the marketplace.

Unfortunately, my brother John's company, Braniff, demonstrated all too well the potentially disastrous results of ignoring that verity. Even though John was the innocent victim of Braniff's misdeeds — or miscalculations — he was left holding the bag (to use an old Boston expression) and had to bear the consequences.

For years Braniff had been headed by the flamboyant Harding Lawrence, a man of high ambitions and lavish lifestyle, who had presided over the expansion of Braniff from a regional to a national and then international carrier. Braniff was already deeply in debt, suffering from the same problems besetting the entire industry, but without the balance sheet to ride out the postderegulation storms. In any case, Lawrence was convinced that Congress would soon see the error of its ways and reverse deregulation; therefore, he concluded, the smart strategy would be to "open" as many new routes — all of which were now up for grabs — as rapidly as possible, thereby "grandfathering" cities for Braniff before deregulation was rescinded. He sent John, who was then group vice president and vice chairman of the Braniff board, on the road to gain access to as many cities as possible: in one day, my tireless brother opened no fewer than fifteen cities. I've never figured out how he managed it logistically, but somehow he did. In a few short weeks, Braniff had dozens of new routes, not only within the United States but abroad: to Singapore, Hong Kong, Seoul, Amsterdam, London, Paris, Frankfurt. The only problem was, Lawrence had made a grave miscalculation: deregulation was here to stay, and he did not have the financial means, the aircraft, or the personnel to service the new routes Braniff had opened. For a time, he blustered and procrastinated, calling press conferences to denounce his enemies and proclaiming to one and all that the company was well on the way to solving its problems. But with Braniff's debts mounting, with the chaos and confusion at headquarters increasing daily, the bankers holding Braniff's debt summarily ousted Lawrence and put John in his place in January 1981.

John set about trying to save the situation, cutting routes and persuading Braniff's eleven thousand employees to take a 10 percent pay cut, setting the example by reducing his own $280,000 salary to zero. In an effort to strengthen the management team, in September John brought in Howard Putnam, who was then president of rival Southwest Airlines. But Putnam, who later claimed that he had been lured by John into joining Braniff under false pretenses — namely, that Braniff's problems were solvable — went behind my brother's back to several of the board members, including Perry Bass and Bob Stuart, and convinced them that he, not John, was the person to save the company. Feeling betrayed and thoroughly disgusted — and with no thanks from anyone on the Braniff board for his year-long pay drought — John resigned from the company in March 1982, a sadder but wiser man. He had worked faithfully and well for Braniff for fourteen years and deserved better.

I felt terrible for my older brother. Since my arrival at American, we had been arch business rivals but dear friends, as close as brothers can be. Thus a bad situation was made even worse when it was bruited about that Bob Crandall and I had played "dirty tricks," as the *New York Times* described it, on Braniff, to compound its cash-flow problems. On the basis of the rumors, the Civil Aeronautics Board conducted an investigation into the allegations that "we had withheld tickets issued by Braniff for travel agents and then put them through a clearinghouse," and concluded the allegations were completely unfounded.

I believe that in a tough business — and no business was tougher than the airlines in those years — you play as hard and competitively as you can. But I also believe even more strongly in ethics, that there is a line that you simply do not cross. I was angry at the rumor, which we suspected had been a conscious attempt to hurt or discredit American; I was even angrier at the implication that I was out to get my brother. What I did regret was a remark I had made a few years before, when a reporter asked how I felt being in direct competition with my own brother. I answered, trying to be facetious, that I'd "grind him into the dust," or words to that effect. I meant it as a joke. In retrospect it sounded far less funny.

The most common error committed by a newly deregulated business is that it keeps expecting things to settle down and everything to fall into place. This simply does not happen. The airlines by now have been deregulated for a full generation, but I expect confusion, even chaos, to prevail for many more years to come.

Essentially, the process of deregulation in any industry has three stages: first, agile opportunists versus entrenched bureaucrats; second, superior managements versus weak managements; and, third, superior managements with a rich resource base versus those without. The airline industry was slow to understand the new environment and identify its individual strengths. The industry is in the midst of the third phase right now, recognizing the need for a competitive cost structure and sophisticated marketing tools. This third phase poses a further threat as the market weakens and brilliance must be supplemented by financial staying power.

No matter what your business, Casey's Law says you can adapt to change as dramatic as deregulation. But if something is going to go right, you must take nothing for granted, watch expansion costs carefully, borrow when you can (do not wait until you need to), and watch your costs, watch your costs, watch your costs. Otherwise, as so many airlines sadly learned after deregulation, Murphy's Law will indeed prevail.

At the dawn of the 1980s, the other major challenge not only for American but for all domestic carriers was the fact that our fleets, much of which had come into service in the 1960s, were aging and fuel-inefficient, and needed to be replaced. For the immediate fleet replacement of American alone, more than $2 billion would be required. Even for an airline like ours, whose performance and balance sheet were far better than most, the question of where the money would come from was problematic, especially if my predictions for 1980 were close to the mark. In the 1979 annual report, I wrote: "With fuel costs soaring and the economy sagging, the outlook for 1980 is not bright." I was dead wrong: 1980 turned out to be not only "not bright," but downright dismal. American, after a string of profitable years, posted a startling net loss of $125 million. And while part of the reason included the tired old factors — higher fuel costs, decreased demand due to continuing recession — the real bugbear was deregulation. American had long been the dominant carrier on the major transcontinental routes linking the East and West Coasts. With the advent of "deregulation" — a term I found then, and still find, ill-conceived and inappropriate — new carriers began service on these routes and, in an effort to find significant market share, lowered prices below costs. The congressional proponents of deregulation patted one another on the back: "See, we were right!" But they were 100 percent wrong, as history would prove. Lower fares are dependent on lower costs and higher efficiency, and "deregulation" did nothing to lower airline costs. On the contrary, wasteful duplication of services soon became the order of the day, which meant lower load factors, therefore higher costs per passenger. Sooner or later — and being a gambling man, I wagered my money on "sooner" — these higher costs had to translate into higher fares. Because of my stand I was dubbed pro regulation, which could not have been further from the truth. I was and am a firm believer in competition, and my then five years as chairman of American had not changed that view.

How did "deregulation" come about? As noted, in my view, it was a political ploy aimed largely at getting publicity — and votes — for its cosponsors, Senators Howard Cannon and Edward Kennedy. The former wanted more and cheaper flights into Las Vegas, whose ability to grow and fleece was restricted by the limited air service to our nation's gaming capital; the latter still harbored presidential ambitions, and "deregulation-leading-to-lower-fares" was a high-profile issue. Voters loved the term, since its opposite, regulation, sounded like Washington interference to the average citizen, and even back then Washington was beginning to be viewed with indignation and suspicion. Washington was being blamed for the double-digit inflation that was plaguing people's lives, as it was bearing the brunt for the soaring prices at the local gas pump. But voters did like the bill's carrot: a promise that, if passed, the price of airline tickets would tumble. And they did, for a while, at least on the major transcontinental routes, because of wholesale price cutting, and for brief periods on some shorter routes as well. For a while there we were living in an era of a ticket to almost anywhere for under $100. But price cutters can operate only so long before going belly-up or raising their prices. And meanwhile, on the shorter routes, service was going to hell in a handbasket.

I was a staunch opponent of the Cannon/Kennedy bill, because I thought it bad for both American and America. I was more than once accused of trying to prevent the normal and inevitable evolution of the airline industry.

Senator Cannon later went so far as to nominate me for Dinosaur of the Year. That was fine with me: I've always been a firm believer that the world's honors should be shared as widely as possible.

11

TURBULENCE ALOFT:
PLEASE FASTEN YOUR SEAT BELTS

ROUGHLY HALFWAY THROUGH MY EXPECTED TENURE, I felt it was time to clarify our future management structure and end any possible company politics regarding my successor. As far as I was concerned, and the board concurred, Bob Crandall was the man to succeed me. I still had more than five years to go when, on July 16, 1980 — exactly a year after we had moved to Texas — we named him president and chief operating officer. I remained chairman and CEO, but now I had someone who could handle many of the day-to-day details of running the company, giving me more time to strategize and plan for our future, that is, spend more time leading and less managing. For in this new, "deregulated" climate, the future was anything but clear, and hard decisions had to be made faster and more decisively than ever before.

We still had not solved our productivity problem to my satisfaction, and most of that failing lay with the unions' refusal to cooperate in our efforts to extend some of our employees' hours to meet the new competition, or in times of financial stress to accept a temporary wage freeze. The latter move was not only agreed to but championed by our nonunion personnel when it was proposed in 1981. We proposed it then because our losses in 1980 — $125 million versus a 1979 profit of $87 million — were threatening our very existence. New entries in the airline business had as expected made inroads into our established routes, offering prices that were attractive to the customer but wholly impractical from a business point of view, and could not be maintained. In short order, we were, as I said, into the era of the $99 fares. We knew our new competitors were losing money on every ticket they sold. But now that we airlines were in the commodity business we had no choice but to match them.

The entrenched recession continued to plague all the airlines, as demand remained low. Dramatically higher fuel costs further drove up the cost of doing business, which on some less competitive routes resulted in higher fares, further depressing demand. American's fuel costs were rising more rapidly than its competitors': in 1980 we paid $50 million dollars more than we would have if we had been able to secure this vital commodity at the price paid by our principal competitor. In fact, our fuel costs in 1980 were $1.115 billion, up $313 million from 1979. Our price per gallon was not only above our main competitor's but well above the industry average as well, because of our obligation to purchase from high-cost producers. Years of government price and allocation controls, starting in 1973, had the effect of requiring airlines to purchase fuel from their historical suppliers. Thus our opportunities to seek competitive bids or to change suppliers were limited.

An even greater problem, with serious financial implications, faced us at the dawn of the decade. At the end of 1979, American was the not-so-proud owner of fifty-eight Boeing 707s, for many years the premier transcontinental airplane. But by the standards of the 1980s, they were aged warriors and, far worse, fuel guzzlers that each year ate further and further into our earnings. To ground them and put them up for sale, however, was going to mean a write-down of $57 million from book value, which several of our board members adamantly, and understandably, opposed. I made an eloquent plea to bite the bullet, pointing out that every day we waited was costing us hundreds of thousands of dollars.

"But, Al, a fifty-seven-million-dollar write-down, in a year like this . . . ," said one of the members.

In fact, 1980 had been the worst year in commercial aviation history, for all the reasons I have already mentioned. American had an operating loss of $86 million. Indeed, to take a further $57 million hit at this time could have had all sorts of negative repercussions, commencing with our bankers and stockholders. Once again, it was the indomitable Lew Wasserman who came to the rescue. Lew rose to his feet and made a brief but overwhelmingly convincing argument in favor of immediately selling the 707s.

"There is the short-term view, ladies and gentlemen," he said. "I would say that ostriches fall into that category, in fact are its chief proponents. And there is the long-term view. American is still the premier airline in this country. Refusing to take the action proposed by Mr. Casey, by management, is taking the first, sure step toward removing this company from that pinnacle. The choice is yours."

The decision was made to ground thirty-six of these outmoded aircraft by the end of the first quarter of 1981 and put them up for sale. The balance of the passenger craft, and all the 707 freighters, would be out of service by October.

The problem was not only the write-down; even more serious was how to replace the lost capacity, for the planes we wanted, 767s, were not yet available.

Sometimes, in the depths of night or the wee hours of the morning, I could actually *see* Murphy in my dreams, smiling gloatingly as he whispered over and over again: "Casey, you never should have taken this job in the first place. You're *never* going to solve all those damn problems!"

The next five years were more than a little like those moments all airline passengers are acquainted with, when the captain announces, "Please fasten your seat belts, we're expecting to encounter some turbulence up ahead."

The turbulence had begun for me in September 1980, shortly after the August board meeting, which was held in our temporary headquarters at Grand Prairie, where we were housed while the permanent new headquarters was being built.

I was back in my office after the board meeting when I began to feel severe chest pains. Some years earlier I had suffered two minor heart attacks, which I had shrugged off. In each of these two instances I had been back to normal within a day or two. The first was in 1968, when I was at Times Mirror. At home one morning, preparing to leave for work, I began to experience chest pains. I had never had a heart attack, but I knew enough from our Mosby medical texts to understand that I should take no chances. Ellie bundled me into the car and drove me down to the Good Samaritan Hospital in downtown Los Angeles, where I was under the care of the noted heart specialist Dr. George Griffith. The second occurred nine years later, when I was visiting my sister Norine at our old homestead in Arlington. Once again I was rushed to Symmes Medical Center, where I was diagnosed, treated, and sent home the next day. But this time, I could tell, the attack was more severe. Because of the earlier attacks, I always carried nitroglycerin tablets, and I quickly downed four. Libby Scott, whom I had alerted, hovered over me, looking far more worried than I. "Feel any better?" she asked.

"Not really," I said. "Better call the doctor."

Libby called Dr. Bob Wick, the company doctor, who arrived within a minute or two, took one look, and called the hospital. The ambulance screamed up in impressively short time, and the medics dashed up the stairs, burst into my office on the second floor, and quickly unfolded the carrier. They picked me up with surprising ease and grace and loaded me aboard.

"Where's the elevator?" one medic asked.

"Don't know," I said from my flat-on-my-back position. "I always use the stairs. Good for the heart, you know."

"Where's the elevator?" the same medic, who seemed to be in charge, asked Libby.

"I'm — I'm not sure. I always use the stairs, too."

"C'mon," the medic said to his buddies, "we've got to keep him flat, so let's find the elevator." He paused. "There *is* an elevator in this building, isn't there?"

"Oh, yes," I assured him.

So off we went through marketing . . . no elevator, through accounting . . . no elevator. As we raced through the aisles between the desks, people looked in surprise and dismay at the bizarre picture of their chairman being wheeled past them, in obvious distress.

"I'm sure this is hard on you, Mr. Casey," the chief medic said. "Suppose I just pull the sheet up and cover your head."

"If you do," I said, "I'll get up and put you in my place. For God's sake, man, if I'm covered with a sheet, everyone will think I'm dead."

We finally found the missing elevator and made it safely to the ambulance, which whisked me off to the hospital, where it was determined that the attack, while worse than the earlier one, was not so severe as we had feared or Murphy had hoped.

A week later I was back at my desk; slightly the worse the wear, no doubt, but in general feeling my old self.

In 1981 we moved back into the black, with operating earnings of $72 million, but the fourth quarter was a terrible downdraft, with an operating loss of $35 million. That quarter was a period fraught with problems and frustrations. Throughout the year, American had sought to persuade the unions representing the majority of its employees that different work rules were urgently needed to improve productivity and to enable us to compete more effectively in the new environment, but as the year drew to a close we knew that these efforts were going to be unsuccessful, at least in 1981. We were also still suffering from the lack of efficient two-engine aircraft to implement the "hub and spoke" operations to which we were committed. Very simply, we had come to the conclusion at the end of the 1970s that deregulation had made it impossible for us to subsidize the smaller, "leaner" markets that we had served in the past. But with two or more major hubs such as Dallas/Fort Worth and the one we had recently set up in Chicago, we had the ability to provide convenient service several times a day to many different destinations. In economic terms, hubs allowed airlines to control traffic by funneling customers through a central location and rerouting them to their final destination. In the long run, I was convinced the payoff would be substantial; for the moment, the benefits were still fragile.

Just as Murphy began to rear his head, to leer at all these ills, I hit him with a couple of positive blows to his scrawny body: in 1981 American recorded its first $4 billion sales year, and an article in *Fortune* magazine gave us the highest marks for quality in the business, citing our quality control and our impeccable service in everything from taking reservations — thank you, SABRE — to baggage handling.

As we entered the 1980s, I and our management team had set our principal goals for the five years to come: maintaining the high quality that was our trademark and a 5 percent operating margin. The temptation in trying times is to make some sacrifice in quality: cut here, pare there, nobody will really notice. But they will. And on that front we were doing fine. Early in 1982, *Air Transport World* magazine named us the airline of the year; and in March, by the widest margin ever, American was chosen the top domestic airline by members of the Airline Passengers Association. But on the matter of the elusive 5 percent operation margin, we were still struggling — no, flailing: in 1982 we had a razor-thin operating income of only $9 million, a pitiful 0.2 percent! On the positive side, we had at long last come to an agreement with the Transport Workers Union (TWU), which would give rise, for the first time in my tenure, to significant productivity gains. Breaking an old logjam, the new contract also enabled us to hire new employees at a lower pay scale than that of existing employees, thus making us for the first time competitive with the new airlines, who had been able to negotiate an overall lower wage schedule with the unions from the start. Some of our management team saw that breakthrough as "beating the unions," but both Crandall and I saw it as winning for everyone at American. We both gave and took. In return for the two-tier arrangement, we agreed to give up our right to furlough employees, as we had had to do in trying times, and offered the TWU the best job security terms in the industry. With that agreement in hand, which involved ten thousand employees, we worked out similar agreements with the pilots' and flight attendants' unions. As part of our package, we instituted that year our first profit-sharing deal. Looking back, negotiating those agreements with our union employees was the most important single event of 1982. It was the beginning of our improved productivity, our renewed collective pride, our sustained, unparalleled growth.

That year, we also began upgrading our fleet, taking delivery of our Boeing 767s and, in an innovative arrangement with McDonnell Douglas and Pratt & Whitney, purchasing twenty twin-jet Douglas Super 80s, one of the world's most fuel-efficient and technologically advanced commercial aircraft, which would be in service by the end of the second quarter of 1983.

Still, only two years into the eighties, I had to confess: Murphy was ahead of Casey, two to nothing. Nonetheless, I was bound and determined that before I retired, on schedule, I would send Murphy down for the count. I felt most of the elements of a turnaround were in place. The question was, how soon would it happen?

The answer was, in short, almost immediately. The next two years, 1983 and 1984, were banner years: earnings were great, and stockholders happy. We not only achieved but exceeded our long-standing 5 percent operating margin goal. Our operating income in 1983 was a comforting $281 million, or 5.9 percent, and the following year was American's best ever: not only did our sales top $5 billion but our operating income increased to $368 million. Even more important, in my mind, were the well-laid plans for the company's future, which included adding a third hub in Denver, increasing nonstop transcontinental flights, and expanding flights overseas. In addition, our cost-reduction efforts — essentially the two-tier pay level — had begun to bear fruit.

But as I wound down my term, I think the achievement of which I was most proud was the feeling — indeed, it was more than a feeling — that during my tenure we had improved the quality of life of American's now forty-seven thousand employees: in job security, the Quality of Work Life program, career development, employee assistance programs, job evaluation (and reevaluation), and profit sharing, we had created a company, and a climate, second to none. The management team, led by Bob Crandall, was superb; the employees were proud, informed, and dedicated. The partnership was not perfect — nothing is in this world — but as I moved into 1985, virtually eleven years to the day from my first board meeting where C. R. Smith introduced me with, I know, some misgivings, I felt I was leaving the company in good hands and in good shape. Bob Crandall had more than proved his mettle, and though our management styles differed, he was a man I had grown to admire greatly through the years. Only forty-nine, he had been with the company for twelve years, and he knew it inside and out. His intelligence, dedication, and vision would, I was certain, carry American through all the shoals and pitfalls of the next decade. And he had an uncommonly strong set of executives to help manage the company. In fact, one of the major business magazines, in commenting on my retirement from American, said, "You could take Casey's top management team and plunk it down in any business in America, and it would produce top results."

Deregulation was eight years behind us, and although many of its effects were still with us, we had weathered the "awful" 1980 and had emerged stronger than ever. We were now the second largest airline in the country, with perhaps the strongest balance sheet and the best morale in the business. Our pioneering policies — from job security to profit sharing to our frequent flyer program — had taken a shattered workforce and turned it into one filled with justifiable pride.

My only problem, the one I had utterly failed to solve during my eleven years at American, was this: I still didn't understand what made those one-hundred-fifty-ton jet monsters get off the ground.

During the last couple of weeks of February, as the official date of my retirement drew near, American threw no fewer than five farewell parties — "bashes" would be closer to the mark — from which I concluded that my esteemed fellow employees loved me more than I knew or that they were really delighted to see me go. Thinking positively, I opted for the former. Several local newspapers also saw fit to elicit some parting thoughts from me, doubtless in search of the wisdom that comes only with age. One of those who was most persistent about seeing me was Kathleen Stauder of the *Fort Worth Star-Telegram*, a journalist who was both charming and intelligent. I made an appointment with her for the twenty-fourth, thinking by then I would be such a lame duck that I'd have plenty of time on my hands. But of course when the day dawned I was still on a schedule that would make a workhorse weary, trying to tie up all manner of loose ends, when Libby announced: "Kathleen Stauder is here to see you."

After the usual amenities, she went right to the heart of the matter: my (rather strong) feelings about leaders and managers. A year or so before, I had given a speech in Fort Worth on the subject, and she had come up to me afterward wanting to know more, since, she said, she had never thought of management in those terms and wondered if I could elaborate. So I knew that would be on the top of her agenda. But I also knew, or suspected, that she would try to make me categorize various American executives, starting with my successor Bob Crandall, and I had no desire to fall into that trap.

"Mr. Casey," she said, "I'd like to follow up if I may on the matter of leaders and managers you talked about last year."

"Be happy to."

"Leaders, you said, are agents of change. They create an atmosphere of ferment, while managers have goals that are deeply embedded in the structure of the organization. Managers and leaders are both needed, one to maintain order, the other to effect change."

She had taken her notes well.

"Mr. Casey, which are you?"

"It's embarrassing to say, but I think I'm a much better leader than manager. A leader isn't interested in the in-basket — or the out-basket for that matter. He's not trying to build up market share in the Dallas-Chicago market. That's a manager's job. A leader's interested in new concepts, with a special awareness of the competition and trends in society, anticipating changes before they occur and taking steps to profit from them. At his or her best, a leader can change people's thinking — and behavior — raising their aspirations and values. I gave that speech last year to make our people think about the subject, try and get them to analyze themselves in terms of both categories — were they one or the other? — but also to a degree to get them riled up. A lot of people think they're both leaders and managers."

"Which is Bob Crandall?" she asked. I'd been expecting the question.

"I'm not going to answer that question, because if I say one thing Bob will probably say another, and the last thing I want during these final days of my tenure is a difference of opinion. On any subject."

"If I'm inferring rightly, you think he's a manager and he thinks he's a leader. Is that it?"

I never liked journalists — or anybody — putting words in my mouth, but I had a feeling Ms. Stauder wasn't going to let go till I pronounced myself.

"I think Bob Crandall believes he's both. Nobody can be both. This said, Bob comes closest to being both of anybody I know. He has an intensity, a focus, that I recognized almost from the first day I met him. And energy. If I had to limit myself to one quality a leader must possess, it would be energy. Some years back a Harvard professor — Abraham Zaleznik, he's the person to

credit for this whole concept of leaders and managers, not me —
researched hundreds of companies to determine the twenty most
common characteristics of leaders. The one attribute that came up
time and time again — far ahead of all the others — was energy,
just plain energy. If you're a leader, you never give up, you never
quit, you keep on working away at solving problems or finding
new or different ways to get the job done, to improve, to motivate
and encourage your fellow employees."

"You have fifty thousand employees here at American. How
does one man manage that many people?"

"I don't. I try to manage one — Bob Crandall," I said, and
couldn't suppress a laugh. For in a sense it was true, yet working
with — sometimes wrestling with — Bob Crandall over the past
eleven years had been sheer pleasure. We could fail to agree on a
subject, or argue tactics or strategies, but both of us knew not only
that we were on the same team but that, whatever our differences,
at the end of the day we wanted the same thing: the increased success of our company.

"But getting back to your question about managing fifty
thousand people, only a few divisions report to me: AA Training,
Sky Chefs, the oil and gas company, and, within the airline itself,
my usual four departments: finance, operations, marketing, and
law. The heads of those departments do the rest. One of the signs
that a leader's trying to be a manager is when you see too many
people reporting to him or her."

She glanced at her watch. "I hope I'm not taking too much
of your time," she said.

"I've all the time in the world," I said. Not true, but if you've
accepted to see someone, I think you should always make your
visitor feel as relaxed as possible.

"I, and I think a number of your business peers, have been
most impressed by the management team you've built up over the
years. Looking at the team you're leaving behind, what strikes me
especially is that you've surrounded yourself with executives
younger than yourself."

"A whole lot younger," I laughed.

"True," she said. "Crandall is forty-nine; Plaskett, your financial VP, is forty-one; Jack Pope, your treasurer, is thirty-six. Donald Carty, your controller, is thirty-eight.* Do you believe in hiring and promoting young people?"

"I try to hire people who are smart as hell and who strike me as committed. And energetic. And if they're young and hungry, so much the better. Young people are highly motivated. They'll work not only morning, noon, and night during the work week, but on the weekends, too. Get their spouses to pitch in, if it'll help get the job done. Highly motivated people don't get discouraged. Challenged, but never discouraged. But hiring youth poses two serious problems: one, you're often putting them in charge of older, more experienced employees, which can create a morale problem; and two, it's hard to keep very talented younger people. At one time we had eight or ten top managers, all under thirty-five. They look at each other and know there's only one top job. They make a reputation for themselves here and then move on. We've lost a lot of very good people over the past several years. It's as if we're running a college here, a training school for airline executives. I almost lost Crandall three different times. Big job offers from other major airlines. More money than I could offer him. . . ."

"So how did you keep him?"

"By giving him a bigger job. And he knew he had a real shot at the top job, at a company he truly loved."

She closed her notebook and put away her pen. "Thanks very much, Mr. Casey. Can I ask you one final question?"

"Please do."

"As a leader, what one piece of advice would you give to aspiring managers?"

"The basic, cardinal rule of management is to be certain that everybody who works for you understands exactly what it is you

---

*Plaskett went on to become head of Pan Am; Pope later became president of United Airlines; and Don Carty is today president of American Airlines, under Chairman Bob Crandall.

expect from them. That's really all there is to business management."

My God, I thought, thinking back to that afternoon on the Cape Cod beach forty years ago when a man named John Walsh had strolled into my life: you taught me that, John, and I'm forever grateful.

Two days later Ms. Stauder's article appeared, and I was pleased to see that, in contrast with some of the printed versions of interviews I had given in the past, which I frequently had difficulty recognizing or squaring with what I had said, hers was both straightforward and accurate.

I felt then, and I feel now, that understanding the differences between leaders and managers is basic to strengthening American business, to increasing productivity, to remaining competitive on a global scale. Leaders are risk-takers, entrepreneurs, constantly challenging conventional wisdom. They are instruments of change, defining future goals, hopefully raising standards, proposing new solutions. In the leader-manager alliance, leaders are the radicals — not politically but philosophically — managers are the conservatives, those who implement change. One is not more important than the other: they are two different elements of an equation, both of which are necessary to carry us forward into the next century.

In my farewell letter, on February 28, 1985 — my sixty-fifth birthday — I wrote:

> Just 11 years ago C. R. Smith and the other members of the board elected me chairman and president of American Airlines. My airline experience at that time was solely as a passenger. Of course, American was my preferred airline, and therefore I was determined to add to its great heritage.
>
> In 1974 the company was deeply troubled, struggling to cope with a variety of difficult problems. During my term there have been many changes both for the company and the air transportation industry — too many for me to even touch upon here. Suffice it to say that American is today a strong and aggressive competitor

in an industry in which the marketplace has become as demanding as any I have seen.

The time has come for me to step aside as chairman and chief executive officer effective March 1, 1985, although I shall continue as director of the company. Bob Crandall has served most ably as president and chief operating officer since July 1980, and now he will assume the added responsibilities. He is the most accomplished manager in the airline industry today, and I have every confidence that the company will continue to prosper under his leadership.

In the course of the rollicking retirement party that sent me on my way to whatever fields lay beyond American, I thought for a moment that I saw, lurking in the only dark corner of the ballroom, Murphy himself, shaking his head amid all the merriment and muttering (or so I swear I heard):

"Dammit, Casey, I was *sure* you couldn't pull it off."

12

THE BIG STAMP

RETIREMENT HAD NEVER BEEN A VIABLE OPTION for me. I don't pretend to speak for others who reach retirement age — we all have our own priorities, plans, and dreams — but at age sixty-five I felt I still had meaningful contributions to make. I planned to continue serving on a number of corporate boards, where I felt my experience could make itself felt. In addition to AMR, the corporate holding company of American Airlines, I was on the boards of the LTV Corporation, which was also based in Dallas; Times Mirror; Sears, Roebuck and AM International (formerly Addressograph-Multigraph), both in Chicago; and Colgate-Palmolive, which was headquartered in New York City. But I also wanted to hold a regular post, and somewhere on my priority list was teaching, probably in an MBA program. When someone asked me, shortly before I left American, whether I would ever consider teaching, I answered off-the-cuff, "No way! Not exciting enough." But the more I thought, the more the idea appealed to me. There was Harvard, my old stomping ground, and Stanford, since California was a place both Ellie and I knew well and were fond of. And then of course there was Dallas itself, where we had lived for the previous six years and put down meaningful roots. But before I could make any decisions I had to know where we would live in our post-American years. And as far as I was concerned that was Ellie's decision. Without a murmur or whimper, for almost forty years she had picked up stakes whenever and wherever my jobs had called me, and I was prepared this time to pull up stakes and move wherever she wanted to live.

Several months before my scheduled retirement I brought up the subject, which we had discussed a number of times earlier.

"Have you thought any more about where we should live after I leave American? I've said before, Ellie, and I say again, it's your decision. This time I'll follow you, wherever you'd like to go."

Ellie said she'd like to think it over for a few days. After reflecting for about a week, she sat me down one evening when I arrived home. "Al," she said, "I'm happy right here in Dallas. I like the people. I like the place. And I know you do, too. So why don't we stay here?"

And that was that.

Dallas would have been my first choice, too, but if Ellie had picked LA or New York, or Timbuktu for that matter, I would have respected her choice. But Dallas had a lot going for it. In addition to our many friends and business colleagues there, and our involvement in a number of Dallas cultural organizations, especially the symphony and the opera, it was geographically convenient, given the bicoastal location of my six boards.

Immediately following my formal retirement from American, I embarked upon an exotic vacation trip with Ellie. For Casey's Law also says that what you demand for yourself should also apply to others. Or — and note this well, since it may well be memorable — what's good for the goose is good for the gander. If my demand to C. R. Smith when I took the American job was that he remove his bodily self from the premises the day I arrived, then I in turn should do the same for Bob Crandall, I figured. I may not have been the legend C. R. was, but Crandall didn't need — or, I was sure, want — me even glancing over his shoulder. Knowing which, I had booked for Ellie and me a two-week safari in Kenya, starting March first, the day after my official retirement. And unlike C. R., I had no intention of bombarding Bob Crandall with memos, however well intentioned, from my

African retreat. It was his show to run now, and we planned our trip with that purpose in mind.

As soon as we got back, I took an office in a downtown Dallas skyscraper, with a splendid view of the city. My good and faithful secretary, Libby Scott, who had followed me in my peripatetic life since shortly after my arrival at Times Mirror, was as usual in charge of my business life, which, though considerably scaled back, still seemed to keep me on airplanes as much as I had been when I was at American. In the course of a single week in May, for example, after attending the board meeting of American Airlines in Dallas/Fort Worth, I headed for Maryland, where Mount Saint Mary's College had the misguided idea to award me an honorary doctorate; thence to Atlanta for the Sears, Roebuck annual meeting, and from there back to Maryland, for a National Flag Day award; on to LA for a Times Mirror board meeting, and the next day to New York for the AM International meeting. Without Libby, I would probably have been in all those cities on the wrong day or at the wrong time. Or both.

I was busy, and I hope helpful in my board activities, but I was also itchy. Thus, I was delighted when Texas governor Mark White called one day in early summer of 1985 and asked me to join a four-member advisory group of the Texas Economic Development Commission. The group's goal was to devise ways to attract new companies to the state, as well as persuade those already there to enlarge rather than move. When I moved American from New York to Dallas/Fort Worth in 1979, we had received the utmost cooperation from the entire Dallas business community. Our group's task now was to put together similar packages to convince business leaders across the country of the infinite attractions — well, finite but numerous — of our area. My work for the advisory group was stimulating and reminded me in many ways of my stint on New York governor Hugh Carey's committee to help save New York City ten years before.

However much I enjoyed my advisory roles, I also began to feel a bit like a senior sage, a shaman, an elder. I could almost feel my hair turning whiter by the minute. Truth was, I was itching to do something. But what? What could a man of my age — no matter how distinguished his business background — do in a climate that doted increasingly on youth? Rather than fret, I decided to figure out what, ideally, I'd like to do, then worry about how to implement the decision. Ellie and I discussed it at length: government service kept cropping up on my wish list, since I felt, sincerely and very profoundly, that life had been more than good to me, and I wanted in some way to repay the largesse. The other ideal job that kept reappearing on my mind screen was teaching. Passing on to the rising generation of very bright young people the fruit of my experience. The more Ellie and I talked, the more attractive the notion of teaching became.

Word to that effect apparently got out, for in September 1985 I got a call from Don Shields, president of Southern Methodist University, asking if the rumor was true. Southern Methodist University had, in the Edwin L. Cox School of Business, one of the best MBA programs in the country. When I admitted that I wanted to teach, Don offered me a job on the spot, throwing in the proposed title "distinguished professor" as an added incentive.

"I'm sure you'll want to think this over for a few days," he said. "It's too late for you to get involved in the current year, but I'd propose that you start next school year, which begins in September."

"Yes," I said, "I'd like to think it over. But not for as long as you suggest."

"Whatever time you need," he said.

"Fifteen seconds," I added, confusing him I'm sure.

"I beg your pardon?"

"I said I'd need fifteen seconds to make up my mind," I said. Pause. "There: I accept."

Pleased that my new, presumably orderly, life was now cast in academic stone, I began to work on the syllabuses of my courses. But as usual with me, the neat and tidy never seems to work.

On the morning of December 11, 1985, while I was studiously preparing one of my courses — for even though it was almost a year away, I'd been out of school for forty years and had a fair amount of boning up to do — Libby Scott told me I had a call from a William Moore, a hard-driving, highly respected head of a Dallas manufacturing firm, Recognition Equipment. I knew Moore not through business but because we both served on the board of trustees of a local school, Saint Mary's. I didn't know him well — more socially than professionally — but I liked and was impressed by him. I took the call.

"Al, I called simply to say that you may be receiving a call from a William Spartin," he said. "He's some kind of headhunter, who's been hired to look for a new postmaster general."

"But what's that have to do with me, Bill?"

"The way Spartin described it to me," Moore said, "they're looking for a smart, seasoned businessman to shake things up a bit at the postal service. I gave him two or three names, including yours."

"I have a commitment to SMU starting a year from now," I said, "so that would rule me out."

"Maybe not," Moore said. "They might prefer you short-term if you could do the job. Anyway, I wanted to let you know what I'd done. Why don't you at least hear Spartin out?"

I thanked Moore for his recommendation and went back to my syllabus, thinking that would be the end of that. But a couple of days later Spartin called.

"Mr. Casey," he began, "I wonder if you would consider serving your government in some important capacity."

The man must have been a pretty good fly fisher; that was a neat, careful cast, bound to elicit a positive response. Mr. Casey, do you believe in Mom and apple pie?

"I've thought seriously about government service since leaving American," I said, but before I could add a qualifier he cut in.

"Great! Because you have been highly recommended to me as a candidate to become our next postmaster general." He paused. "Following in the footsteps of Benjamin Franklin. As I'm sure you know, he was our first postmaster general."

"Excuse me, Mr. Spartin," I said, "don't I recall that someone was only recently named to that post? Maybe a year or so ago?"

"That's correct, sir. Paul Carlin. But I can tell you in complete confidence that the board of governors has apparently made up its mind to replace him. And your name is very high on our list for the job."

I explained my commitment to teach at the SMU School of Business, a commitment I took very seriously. But he would not be deterred.

"Would you at least *consider* it?" he insisted. "It's a great honor, you know. . . ."

"I don't give a damn about the honor," I said, which wasn't quite true. "The question is, could I have a meaningful effect on the postal service if I did take the job?" I realized I had already said more than I should have.

"In any event, Mr. Casey, would you at least agree to fly out and meet the chairmen of the board of governors?"

I told him I'd think it over, and this time I didn't mean for fifteen seconds.

I called Ellie and gave her the gist of my conversation with Mr. Spartin.

"I'd like to discuss it with you," I said.

"Al, what you're saying is, we'd have to move again, isn't that right?"

I averred we would but added that I hadn't taken the job yet; nor had it even been offered me. My call was simply to let Ellie know I might consider it, but I wouldn't have pursued it if I felt she was dead set against it. Still, I knew her well enough after forty years to anticipate, almost certainly, what her reaction would be.

One of the many things I loved about Ellie was that she never beat about the bush. That night we discussed the pros and cons of the job. Among the latter: moving to Washington, just after we'd decided once and for all to stay in Dallas; exposing myself to the inevitable criticism that anyone in a position of authority in Washington faces; dealing with perhaps the biggest bureaucracy in the country, encompassing a workforce of over three-quarters of a million people; coping with the several postal unions, which I knew had uniformly resisted change. Further, I would have to resign from the six corporate boards on which I was serving, and which I thoroughly enjoyed. Finally, and doubtless most important, given my commitment to SMU, if I took the job I could only serve for less than a year. I would be a lame duck before I started. On the plus side? Corny or not: serving my country. The challenge, which would be enormous — everybody has a post office story, and most are derogatory. The feeling that I could perhaps contribute something to improving the postal service's efficiency.

Ellie and I both agreed that the "cons" considerably outweighed the "pros." Acknowledging which, she looked at me and said: "Al, I feel you're intrigued. Why don't you at least go out and talk to the people?"

A few days later, in mid-December, Ellie and I flew out to LA, where a meeting had been set up by William Spartin with John McKean, chairman of the Postal Service board of governors, and the vice chairman, Peter Voss. McKean, who lived in San Francisco and had flown down for the meeting, met with me first, and we were joined an hour or so later by Voss, who arrived on crutches, having injured himself playing tennis. They gave me some essential background information about the problems facing the Postal Service, which included a bloated bureaucracy, the urgent need to pare payroll, and especially the necessity to automate in order to compete with the private sector companies, whose very existence no doubt derived from the U.S. Postal Service's presumed deficiencies.

Why were they firing Carlin? I needed to know. A sixteen-year postal veteran, Carlin was the first postmaster general who had come up through the ranks, breaking a long precedent when the job was filled by a political appointee. In fact, when Carlin was hired a little more than a year before, the Reagan White House had made a last-minute appeal to the board of governors to give the post to Ed Rollins, the high-profile former director of the Reagan-Bush campaign committee.

"Paul Carlin just couldn't make hard decisions," McKean said. "One of his goals was to reduce staff, and instead the postal workforce has *increased* more than five percent over the past year."

"Worse, he's been slow to automate," Voss added, shaking his head. "We've been pressing him for months to move ahead on that front, with no success. Key to the problem is the nine-digit zip," he explained, "and Carlin just can't make up his mind on purchasing the proper equipment."

"He delegates too much authority," McKean added. "We just don't get the feeling he's in command."

"He's so subservient," Voss chimed in, "that if the Reagan White House asked him to destroy the Post Office, I swear he would."

"What's more, the Postal Service is running at a sizable deficit. For the last fiscal year, which ended in September, we have a deficit of $251 million," McKean said.

"Which given our current mandate is wholly unacceptable," Voss chimed in.

The mandate to which he was referring was the effort, fifteen years before, to put the Post Office Department, a sprawling, gas-guzzling bureaucracy, onto a sound financial footing. Until 1970, the postmaster general had been a cabinet post, appointed by the White House, and the political appointee ran the show as he saw fit, the board of governors being pretty much a rubber stamp. Since most of the appointees had little business experience, nor were accountable financially, the Postal Service — the largest business organization in the country — was declining in service and efficiency.

In 1967, President Johnson had appointed a commission, headed by former chairman of AT&T Frederick Kappel, to ascertain what changes needed to be made to make the postal system more efficient. After two years of study, Kappel testified to Congress:

It is in my opinion academic to spend any time on any approach that does not substantially insulate the post office from politics, remove the postmaster general from the Cabinet, and free the department of the controls, lobbying pressures, and personnel practices that are now imposed upon it. . . . Each year the postal service slips further behind the rest of the economy in service, in efficiency, and in meeting its responsibility.

Lawrence O'Brien, who was then postmaster general, put it even more bluntly. Testifying that in his view the postal system was "in a race with catastrophe," he added: "The Post Office is the classic definition of an elephant — a mouse built to government specifications."

Johnson, in his final budget, recommended that Congress approve the Kappel commission recommendations, noting that the postal deficit for 1969 was expected to reach a staggering $1 billion. But Congress failed to act, and it was not until after a twelve-day mail strike in the spring of 1970 — the first in American history — that started in New York City and quickly spread to six hundred post offices across the country, that Congress finally moved. On August 6, 1970, Congress passed, and President Nixon signed, the Postal Reorganization Act, which was meant to turn the Postal Service into a self-supporting, government-owned, efficient organization. As part of that mandate, the board of governors — nine outside appointees plus the postmaster general and the deputy postmaster general — took a much more active part in overseeing the agency. I could tell by their concerns and probing questions that McKean and Voss, the latter perhaps more than the former, had their own priorities and intended to exercise their vested authority, far more, so it seemed to me, than the board of directors of a private company ever would have. I warned them that if I took the job, I intended not to be or act like a lame duck, despite the anticipated brevity of my tenure. Nor would I brook interference with my day-to-day operations. How often did the board of governors meet? Monthly. Fine. I would gladly and openly report to them monthly but was not about to take a job where, as CEO, I would have to report to them more often or clear my plans. They seemed to accept that, though I thought I detected reluctance on Voss's part.

Our discussions went on for several hours, during which I pressed both men to ascertain why they wanted me, given my self-imposed short tenure. Over lunch I asked why they didn't have a search committee looking for a long-term candidate. In essence, the answer was that they wanted Carlin out of the post and needed a replacement right away. Were they thinking of my tenure as a "holding action," therefore?

"You might put it that way," Voss said.

"Then you should count me out," I said. "I'll only come on board if I think — and you think — I can make a real contribution."

They asked me if I had any specific thoughts on the questions of paring payroll and automation particularly.

"On the former," I said, "I think there are ways of improving efficiency materially without firing scads of people. I don't want to be remembered as Casey the Ax." And I told them how I'd move people around, to more meaningful and productive jobs. And how I'd streamline the reporting process, which from a cursory glance struck me as cumbersome. As for automation, that would require closer study.

Ellie and I flew back to Dallas the next morning. Two days later, McKean called and formally offered me the job. He said he had spoken the day before to Representative William Ford, chairman of the post office and civil service committees, and informed him I was the board's choice. Since Senate confirmation was no longer required under the new postal regulation laws, the board of governors' decision was final. If I accepted, McKean said, a news release would be going out on Monday, January 6.

Over the year-end holiday, Ellie and I discussed again the pros and cons.

"It is a great honor," she said. "Not everyone gets to fill Ben Franklin's shoes."

"For me it boils down to whether in the course of only seven or eight months I can really be effective," I said.

"Knowing you," Ellie said, "the brevity will make you work even harder."

I called McKean and said that I'd take the post if the authority I had requested would be granted without qualification. He assured me it would and asked me to fly to Washington right after the New Year for a press conference.

On January 7, at the press conference, McKean introduced me, gave a brief résumé of my business background, then opened the field to questions. Some of the questions had to do with why Carlin was fired, and on that McKean remained purposefully vague, saying only that in the board's view Carlin had not dealt quickly or harshly enough with the postal bureaucracy. "If you believe that government bureaucracy can reorganize itself," he added, "then you clearly believe in monogenesis."

Asked what my toughest challenge would be, I said, "Convincing my wife to accept the Washington scene." The papers took me to task the next day for my flippant remark, but the fact was, I had simply told the truth. Furthermore, until I set foot on the postal ship, which everyone believed was foundering, I'd have been a fool to start making learned pronouncements or prognostications. McKean fielded most of the questions, which was fine with me, since I've never sought, nor ever desired, the limelight. And besides, he knew a helluva lot more about the Postal Service than I did. At least for the moment. But I couldn't resist answering a couple of questions, which couldn't have been better framed if I had my own straight man out there in the audience. Since I had made it clear my mandate would be short, the rumors had already been circulating that I was the board of governors' patsy, ready to be manipulated at will. "Stopgap Casey," as it were.

"How long do you intend to stay on the job, Mr. Casey?" one reporter asked.

"The primary goal of any chief executive is to arrange for his successor. So the answer to your question is: If I'm really good, six months. If I'm poor, nine months."

I thought I saw the reporter's mouth drop slightly, but he dutifully wrote down my response in his notebook.

"Doesn't it bother you to be a self-declared lame duck in this job?" another reporter asked.

"Isn't everybody in Washington a lame duck?" I countered. "The only problem is, some of them don't admit it."

Another probing question from a bespectacled gentleman near the rear: "Mr. Casey, could you tell us why you took this job?"

"Because I was unemployed," I said, trying hard to look dead serious. Then I added, "And also because I sincerely welcome this opportunity to serve my country."

My first day on the job, I discovered there were three consulting firms busily assessing the Postal Service, at considerable cost to the taxpayers. One by one I called them in and asked what precisely their mission was.

"We're attempting to determine what the role of the Postal Service is," said consultant number one.

I nodded and called for the second consultant. His reply, though worded slightly differently, came to the same thing. As did the third's. I asked Libby Scott to call in the persons in charge at each of the three consulting firms. When they were assembled, I said: "Gentlemen, in answer to your question: the role of the Postal Service is to deliver the mail. Now get your butts out of here. You're all terminated as of today."

Looking for other quick, obvious ways to save money, I discovered that former postmaster William Bolger, who had preceded Carlin, had the USPS purchase a private plane, essentially if not exclusively for his use. Knowing a fair amount about airplanes and what it cost to run them, and knowing that, however much I traveled during my tenure, I could do it far more inexpensively by taking commercial flights, I put the plane — a dandy Citation-2 — up for sale. It fetched $1.9 million, which went directly to the bottom line. But these two savings — the consultants and the private jet — were but drops in the enormous postal bucket.

It didn't take me long to ascertain that my real contribution would have to be in two areas: personnel and management structure. More than four-fifths of every Postal Service dollar, I learned, went for salaries — wages and benefits. And it was clear to me, almost immediately, that the agency's four levels of bureaucracy — Washington staff, regional staffs, district staffs, and individual postmasters around the country — were cumbersome at best. But I also had to bear in mind that the numbers I was dealing with here made American Airlines's look almost lilliputian. The postal service's 745,000 employees made it larger than the U.S. Army; its $27 billion in revenue made it five times the size of American Airlines. And in 1986 it would deliver roughly 145 billion pieces of mail.

One of my first moves was to assess Carlin's decision to increase the size of the agency's workforce — despite a mandate to trim jobs — by forty thousand during the previous year. That, I figured, might be a good place to start cutting costs. But the closer I looked the more credit I had to give Carlin: his decision to hire was an effort to cut down on the Post Office's considerable overtime expenses. And he had negotiated with the unions to hire new employees at costs considerably lower than earlier hires had been paid — no easy task, that, since the power of the postal unions was legendary. What he had done reminded me of the two-tier battle we had fought and won four years earlier at American Airlines. The upshot for the postal service was that despite the 6 percent increase in the workforce, overall personnel costs for the year were down substantially. Chalk one up for Carlin.

During my first week on the job I called in several key staff members, no more than two or three at a time, and asked them one simple question: "If you were named postmaster general for a day, what would you do to improve service and efficiency?"

Not surprisingly, the question took them so aback no one had a ready answer, but several came back over the next few days and weeks with some excellent, thoughtful suggestions, all of which we explored, many of which we implemented.

I also called in several top headquarters executives and asked them bluntly: "Do you consider yourself competent for the job you're doing?"

Surprisingly, several said they weren't sure. But all said they'd try their damnedest to show me they were, or improve if I pointed out their shortcomings. I told them I didn't think headquarters staff was working hard enough and said they should erase the notion of nine-to-five from their vocabularies. I added that if I lost confidence in them, they could never regain it.

I quickly ascertained that the deputy postmaster, Jackie Strange, was a highly competent, devoted executive. But both she and I had too many people reporting to us, and if I didn't do something fast, I knew I'd soon be drowning in minutiae. I also figured out, without too great a burnout of brain cells, that the people in charge of finance, operations, and public relations at headquarters were far from top caliber and told them so, giving them the choice either to resign or be reassigned. To fill their collective gaps, I called in my friend Jack Garrity, one of the best management consultants in the business, with a mandate to recommend methods to streamline our bulky boat. I told headquarters staff to look upon Garrity as my alter ego and cooperate with him fully.

By mid-March, six weeks into the job, I had determined, with the help of Jackie Strange and a close study of personnel files, who were generally considered the best, fairest, most hardworking executives in the agency, and I named them all to new key posts in the areas of systems development, management information and research technology, marketing, facilities, and supply. In keeping with my management principles, the only areas that reported to me directly were finance and planning, operations, general counsel, and chief postal inspector.

Looking back, I'm sure there are many who would accuse me of having acted too rashly and too precipitously in cleaning house at L'Enfant Plaza — USPS headquarters — but in fact when you're in a time/pressure situation, you generally move faster, and hopefully more efficiently, than when you seem to have all the time in the world. Just as Ellie had predicted.

I also quickly ascertained that I had walked into a goddamned hornet's nest. My timing couldn't have been worse. On the one hand, President Reagan himself, as well as his director of the office of management and budget, James Miller, were outspoken critics of the Postal Service, strongly suggesting that privatization might be the best solution. Early in my tenure, Miller wrote: "The Constitution . . . does not require the carriage of mail to be a monopoly, much less a government monopoly." On the other hand, the administration was making (very loud) noises about ending the time-honored Postal Service subsidies for nonprofit mail, to the tune of about $1 billion a year, an added burden the Postal Service could simply not endure. Plus Graham/Rudman — the balanced budget folk — handed me a mandate a month after I had stepped in the door to cut $51 million from our 1986 budget, stipulating that the monies be taken from postmasters' salaries. I declined, both because I felt such cuts would further undermine morale and because I thought the OMB had no right to tell us where we should slash. So I signed the paperwork and sent it back without specifying where we'd make the cuts, and — this being Washington — the OMB seemed satisfied.

By my third week on the job Ellie pointed out that I was again working twelve hours a day, seven days a week. Was that what I intended when I'd taken the post? I could only shrug and say, not proudly, that I had a lot to do in a very short time. Besides, I was asking everyone else to work harder and be more productive, so didn't I have to set the example? I could see by her look that she was thinking of that famous Reagan offhand remark to Jimmy Carter, a phrase so key to his political fortunes: "Now, there you go again. . . ."

One of the nice perks of the postmaster general job was a private dining room on the tenth floor of our building at L'Enfant Plaza,

with a lovely view over the Washington waterfront. *Perk* is probably the wrong word, because for me it was a useful, albeit pleasant
tool. It gave me a chance to meet every day with key executives
and, in the course of an hour or two, in a friendly, private environment, learn what they considered were the agency's most
pressing problems. In the course of these luncheon sessions I listened a lot and learned a lot in a relatively short time. Since my arrival, with McKean having publicly stated that I was there to clean
house, there had been an understandable nervousness among
headquarters staff. Rumors were circulating that I would be slashing the Washington staff by as much as 1,800 and reducing personnel overall by 140,000, or almost 20 percent. Stuff and
nonsense. But the published reports of those heady numbers didn't
make my job any easier. The postal unions were some of the most
powerful in the country, and they were, I sensed, dead set against
me. They knew they were going to outlast me, so all they needed
to do was batten down the hatches and wait for the Casey storm
to abate.

The board of governors was also nervous, wondering if they
had picked the wrong guy, but McKean, while in many ways a
martinet, sincerely wanted positive change, rapid improvement.
Voss, however, was proving to be a royal pain, constantly sticking
his nose into everything from operations to procurement. His pet
project was automation, and he kept pushing me to move ahead
and acquire the high-speed equipment capable of processing nine-
digit zip codes, which the agency had been considering for over a
year. There was even speculation that Voss had been instrumental
in having Carlin fired because he had been dragging his feet on the
zip-code processing equipment. The estimated cost of acquiring
the equipment, however, was a heady $250 million, and I didn't
feel comfortable about it for two reasons: first, I was not convinced it would be cost-effective, even assuming the unions didn't
rise up in arms (for, no question about it, the scanners would replace people); second, and far more important, one of the two
companies bidding for the installation was Dallas-based REI
(Recognition Equipment, Inc.), whose president was William

Moore, the man who had first recommended me for the job. So if the board insisted on moving ahead on the matter, I had determined to remove myself from the voting.

So insistent was Voss, so widespread his meddling, that I decided to put an end to him with another godlike move. If I could turn out the lights in mid-Manhattan, surely I could banish Voss to some distant shore. Knowing him to be an egotistical man, covetous of high and mighty titles, I nonchalantly asked him one day: "Peter, if you had your choice, what would you most like to do?"

I already knew the answer, but I let him fall into my diabolical trap.

"I've always wanted to be a U.S. ambassador," he said. "In fact, I happen to know the Nigerian post is open. Do you think you could help?"

"Let me try," I said, nodding sagely. I had a quid pro quo in mind that just might work.

I called John Whitehead, then deputy secretary of state under George Shultz, and asked if Vice Chairman Voss might be considered for the post of ambassador to Nigeria.

"Al," Whitehead replied stiffly, "why don't you stick to running the Post Office and Secretary Shultz will handle the ambassadorial appointments."

I had expected as much, so I called my old friend Don Regan, the White House chief-of-staff with whom I had lunched regularly since my arrival in D.C. I knew that Mrs. Reagan dearly wanted a stamp issued honoring the late Dr. Harvey Cushing of Boston, who had been very close to her father. Since it's customary to allow the postmaster general to designate one new stamp each year, Don had asked if I'd be willing to nominate Cushing. Don had had a falling out with Mrs. Reagan over a number of issues, but primarily she thought Regan worked the president too hard. He thought if he showed Mrs. Reagan that he had prevailed on me to grant her wish, the relationship might be improved. I hadn't acted on his request yet, but I could feel in my bones the time was drawing nigh.

"Don," I said, "it's an accepted practice for the White House to play a role in ambassadorial appointments. As I understand it, it's been a long time since it has used that prerogative. How about helping me send Vice Chairman Voss to Nigeria?"

I made no promise about the Cushing stamp, but I was sure Don had in mind that that was the quid of my quo.

A short time later I received a call from John Whitehead.

"Al," he said, "I think I see the fine Irish hand of Al Casey behind a call I just received from Don Regan. However, I did mention Mr. Voss to Secretary Shultz. To say he was less than enthusiastic would be a gross understatement. But he did forward the Voss nomination to the confirmation committee of the Senate for approval."

True to my nonword, I duly arranged for the Cushing stamp to be approved and quietly applauded myself for so quickly understanding how Washington works, and using it to good advantage. As I said before, you don't get many chances to play God. . . .

In April, our board of governors meeting was scheduled for Atlanta, and I was eager to see if any word had come down about the Voss appointment. Just as they were convening the meeting, I saw two postal inspectors approach Voss, whisper something to him, and saw a look of dismay come over his face. Without a word, he rose and followed the two inspectors from the room. The meeting progressed without him, but before the day was out word came down that he had been charged with a felony — something to do with falsifying his expense accounts — and had entered a guilty plea.

I suddenly realized my little godlike act was about to backfire. Me pushing a man charged with a felony to be our ambassador! Good work, Casey! Hurriedly, I called Don Regan, told him what had happened, and asked if he'd be good enough to call Secretary Shultz.

"Al," he said, "I have no intention of calling Secretary Shultz on the matter. You got yourself into this mess; now get yourself out of it."

I called John Whitehead and told him my story, but instead of reacting he transferred me to Secretary Shultz directly, who let me have it with both barrels. Served me right no doubt. I was beginning to learn how Washington worked, but not quite the way I had planned.

Voss, it turned out, was an even worse scoundrel than I thought. First, he was a petty scoundrel: the way he'd been cheating on his expense accounts was to buy a first-class ticket to all the board of governors meetings, plus a number of trips he claimed were Post Office related, then turn them in for reimbursement and ride economy class, pocketing the difference. That "difference," it turned out, came to a whopping $44,000 over the three years he had served on the board! In addition, he had collected $13,000 in fees from private contractors to do research the Postal Service had ample resources to undertake on its own. Both bad enough, but there was more. Far more. Voss, it turned out, had been badgering both my predecessor Carlin and me about committing to automation, and specifically to Recognition Equipment, because he had an arrangement with the public relations firm lobbying for Recognition, headed by John R. Gnau Jr., President Reagan's Ohio campaign manager in 1980, whereby Voss would share in the fee if Recognition got the nod. Some fee: 1 percent of the $250 million contract would have come to $2.5 million! Voss's share, apparently, would have been at least $625,000.

I was disgusted and revolted; I just couldn't believe people could so abuse the faith and public trust vested in them as had Voss. When it was suggested in some quarters that Voss might have connived to bring me on board in order to manipulate me, I retorted that I had loathed the man from the start, and (without telling why or how) had made a real Washington effort to get him out of my thinning hair.

Given all this, and our Dallas connection, I called Bill Moore and satisfied myself that he was completely clean. All he had done, he said, was aggressively try to get the business for REI, nothing more, nothing less. And indeed, later investigations gave Moore and REI a clean bill of health. Still, the whole episode left a foul taste in my mouth, and the bad publicity certainly didn't help our efforts at streamlining and improving the efficiency of the agency.

With the Voss scandal nipping at my heels like some stray mongrel, I made up my mind to move even faster than I had up till now. For weeks I had been studying the basic organizational structure of the USPS, taking counsel from a dozen top people I had learned to respect. There was no question in my mind that the public perception that we were overly bureaucratic was painfully accurate. Once again, I started at the top, at home, where far too many people were reporting to me. I created a new position, associate postmaster general. Together with the deputy postmaster general we formed the top management team. I elevated the marketing function to senior level and made it part of the new position's responsibility. As at Times Mirror and American Airlines, these two people, together with the general counsel and chief postal inspector, reported to me. But streamlining L'Enfant Plaza was only the first step. I still believed in the inverted pyramid, and in the winter of 1986 there was at least one bureaucratic level too many between the tip and the base: as things stood, our roughly 20,000 local post offices reported to 216 "management sectional centers," which reported to 42 district offices, which reported to 5 regional headquarters, which reported to Washington. The more I looked, the more we at headquarters were convinced that the district offices often impeded rather than speeded matters, and we took the hard decision to eliminate them. I appointed 5 regional postmasters and established 72 geographic divisions, all of whom reported to one of the 5 new postmasters. That way, questions or problems that had previously wended their way all the way to Washington for decisions could and would be dealt with at the regional level. To head the 72 divisions we picked and promoted the 72 best, most experienced, high-ranking postal employees we could find — based on their past records and performance review — thus sending a clear message to the entire postal establishment that merit and excellence were the order of the day. It caused some dislocation, obviously, but as I testified to Congress, my aim was not to fire people but move them about, make them more efficient. Our employees — all three-quarters of a million of them — had to understand that ours was a highly competitive business, and they had to be more responsive to their customers' needs. We needed to remain open for longer hours, we needed to improve our service, which meant both speedier and more accurate mail, and we needed to shorten those lines at our post offices. At various post offices around the country we instituted Saturday hours, and in several cities experimented with Sunday service as well. The response was immediate and positive everywhere. To help shorten lines, we installed 25,000 new stamp vending machines around the country. And to help speed the mail and relieve the weary feet of those who actually delivered it, we purchased 99,150 vans from Grumman, at Bethpage, Long Island, with the dual purpose of replacing the aging jeeplike trucks and putting thousands of mailmen and women, who had been making their rounds on foot, into the driver's seat. One innovation that provoked its share of jokes ("Think you're in England, mate?") but delighted the mail carriers was putting the steering wheel on the right, not the traditional left. That way, the mailmen and women could simply reach out the right window and stuff the mail in the boxes without having to get out of the truck and walk all the way around to the mailbox. But what attracted me the most, from a business viewpoint, was the fact that the truck bodies were all aluminum, therefore eight hundred pounds lighter than the existing equipment, therefore far more fuel efficient. Maybe it was my long experience battling rising fuel costs at American for over a decade, but the knowledge that we'd be saving tons of money on every truck every day pleased me especially. What was more, the new trucks, because of their aluminum bodies, were scheduled to last twenty-four years, three times longer than the life expectancy of our existing fleet.

The price tag was big — $1.1 billion — but it was spread over the six years it would take to deliver all the new vans. And if our calculations were correct — and we had every reason to believe they were — the overall savings to the Post Office would be $6 billion.

For my first two or three months on the job I had been largely spared the political spotlight of official Washington. To be sure, the press was watching me like the proverbial hawk — scarcely a day went by without an article in the press about the ongoing "problems" at L'Enfant Plaza and the major modifications and implementations being wrought by this upstart Casey. I paid scant attention to those pieces; I was, however, keeping my fingers crossed that I might avoid the time-wasting embarrassment of appearing before the House Post Office Committee or its subcommittee. Such periodic appearances were a Washington ritual, so it seemed. Every post-office goof — and with billions of pieces of mail distributed every day, how could there not be goofs? — was immediately brought to the pertinent representative's attention. When a sufficient quantity of gripes, real or imagined, had accumulated, it was the custom of the subcommittee to summon the postmaster general to appear and force him to listen to an hour or three — sometimes four — of complaints. Following which the representative would send his or her constituents copies of the *Congressional Record* showing that their complaints had been duly recorded, had in fact been brought to the attention of the postmaster general himself, no less. An acknowledged gripe equals a certain vote. So far I had sidestepped that bullet, and just as I was congratulating myself that it would be my successor's fate to play that martyr's role, I got a call from Mickey Leland, a congressman from my home state of Texas.

"Al," Leland began in his down-home drawl, "I'd like you to appear before my subcommittee next Thursday morning at ten thirty."

"I'm sorry, Mr. Chairman," I said, pretending to shuffle noisily through my agenda, "but I'm all tied up that morning. I couldn't make it before one thirty."

I hadn't learned much about Washington mores, but I had learned that after lunch is better than morning for hearings. And if you can *impinge* on the lunch hour, that's even better.

Leland was clearly miffed.

"Al," he said, "subcommittee hearings ought to take precedence over anything else in your schedule."

"I just can't do ten thirty," I said. "I truly wish I could." Then I added, "I have great admiration for you personally, and the highest respect for your committee."

The fact is, these hearings were lengthy, boring, and a burden not only to me but to my staff. But my words seemed to placate him, and he finally agreed to one thirty.

I immediately contacted Jack Garrity, who as usual was ready to serve in any capacity, and brought him up to date on our latest challenge.

"Jack," I said, "I want you to find as big a screen as you can lay your hands on, eight by ten at least, larger if it exists. Then dig up all the overhead projector plastic slides there are in the headquarters building. Stacks and stacks of them. And then find me the largest pointer in the country. Eight feet. Ten, if possible."

"I think I get the picture." Garrity laughed. "You can count on me."

Within hours, he appeared with all the equipment but only a two-inch pile of slides.

"More," I said, "we need more slides."

"There are a lot more in the basement," Jack said, "but they're all blank."

"Fetch them," I said. "Blank or full, they'll look just as threatening to the subcommittee."

At one P.M. on the appointed day, Jack and I set up the screen and projector in the hearing room, with my impressive stack of slides and two spare projector bulbs — indicating that ours would be a long session — on the table beside me. Jack, dressed in his best McKinsey suit, seated himself beside the screen, wielding his eight-foot pointer.

Shortly before one thirty, the members of the subcommittee

started drifting in. Most looked at the screen and projector with a combination of surprise and dismay. One congressman entered the room, glanced at the projector, turned heel, and left without a backward glance.

Congressman William H. Gray III from Pennsylvania motioned for me to come forward. He leaned over and said: "Mr. Casey, what's all this about?" nodding toward the screen and projector.

"Your chairman wants to make sure you all have the necessary background on the Postal Service, so I can then bring you up to date on recent developments."

"How long is this presentation going to take?" he asked, barely concealing a worried frown.

"About an hour and fifteen minutes," I said. I saw his frown deepen, so I added for good measure: "Assuming there are no questions or interruptions." A barely audible moan escaped his lips as I made my way back to my table.

Just then Chairman Leland arrived. He, too, saw the screen and projector and called me forward "Al, what's all this about?"

"Mr. Chairman," I said in a near whisper, "I'm well aware that you're fully informed on the background and structure of the Postal System, but we wanted to make sure your committee members were as well. . . ."

"Al," he said sternly, "how long is this going to take?"

"No longer than an hour and fifteen minutes, Mr. Chairman. If you can assure me there will be no interruptions or questions in the course of the presentation."

"Is there any way around this?" he asked anxiously, for he could hear his committee members stirring, talking among themselves about this unexpected turn of events. And the talk wasn't pro chairman. How could he have let this happen?

"Well, Mr. Chairman," I said, "perhaps you could open the meeting by saying a few nice things about the Post Office, and how we do our best to serve Congress and the public. Then I'll respond by paying you and your committee high compliments for all your good work. Then you adjourn the meeting."

"No way," Leland said. "Al, that's blackmail and you know it."

"Not at all," I said. "I was just trying to help, since I seem to hear your committee members asking you to do exactly what I've suggested." In fact, several of the members who had obviously overheard our discussion were not only urging Leland to agree but were waving their hands for emphasis.

Leland gave me one of the dirtiest looks I've ever had the pleasure of receiving, then hissed: "All right, Al. You win. But I guarantee I'll get you here another time."

And he did.

But meanwhile I signaled to Jack Garrity to begin dismantling our equipment. While he was busy folding camp, keeping an absolutely straight face, Congressman Leland opened the hearings by saying some of the nicest things that have ever been said about the Post Office. His ringing words were only outdone by my salutations and warm words about the diligence and intelligence of Chairman Leland and his entire committee.

The whole session lasted not my predicted hour and a half but exactly seven minutes, before Leland brought down the gavel and declared the session adjourned.

There were three other items on my agenda that I hoped to implement before I left for SMU. Our three basic mail services in essence promised one-day, two-day, and three-day delivery. A thorough study of all three classes showed that while our on-time performance for one-day and three-day deliveries was well over 90 percent, the two-day delivery was well below that mark. I strongly suggested dropping the two-day altogether, which amounted to 48.5 million pieces of mail a day. In recommending the move and trying to counter the built-in resistance I felt welling from some quarters ("Al, do you realize how hard it would be to put that into effect?"), I shrugged: "I say, don't raise the bridge, lower the river." But the brevity of my remaining term made it impossible to implement that plan; I therefore recommended it to my successor, Bob Tisch.

The second item, which I calculated would result in the greatest savings of all, was a proposal to standardize envelopes into three sizes, no more no less. The stationery and greeting card companies reacted as if I'd declared World War III and bombarded Congress with strongly worded protests, to good effect. A swing and a miss for Casey.

The third and final item was helping find a successor, someone in for the long haul, so that I could fire myself. I suggested two names, outstanding people from the business world, plus Jackie Strange, whose dedication to and knowledge of the entire postal system from top to bottom were impeccable.

At the same time, I personally wrote a several-page paper entitled "Observations Regarding the Postmaster General," in which I tried to pinpoint the characteristics necessary for the job. "The first thing that anybody in this job must have," I wrote, "is energy. You serve so many constituencies, you can't just delegate and walk away. You don't have to know every bit of the job — don't waste your time. What one learns by running a giant corporation is that you can't compromise. You can't bend to satisfy a particular union, a congressman, or governor. You've got to be able to hold your head high and explain to them, forthrightly and candidly, why you can't do special favors. So I guess right next to energy I'd have to put the quality of total integrity."

I was also delighted to report to the board of governors and Congress that, for the fiscal year during which I served, I predicted a profit for the Postal Service of between $400 and $425 million — a turnaround of about three-quarters of a billion dollars. I was credited in several quarters for that rapid shift from red to black, which I appreciated but felt was inappropriate or exaggerated. We had benefited from the economy in general that year, which had turned noninflationary, and from several labor practices put into effect before my arrival. Far more important in my view was that we had invested wisely and well in the future.

Before I took the job, I had been forewarned that I would doubtless encounter a stifling bureaucracy, a series of dead-end efforts, and a do-nothing atmosphere. But my abbreviated experience exposed me to a massive group of dedicated public servants who appreciated fully the magnitude of their responsibility — to keep the country in touch with itself. They were a great team and continue to improve to this day. The United States Postal Service, despite all its problems, is doubtless the best, and the least expensive, in the world. My hope was that my efforts would help keep it there.

Although he was not one of my recommended replacements, Bob Tisch, who was president of Loews Corporation, was named to succeed me at the August board of governors meeting. He was a man with considerable business experience, and at sixty he would, I was certain, have the energy and dedication essential to the job. I wished him — and his eight hundred thousand employees! — godspeed.

After the self-imposed hectic pace of Washington, or at least of the Postal Service — twelve-hour days seven days a week for eight months nonstop — I was looking forward to the more peaceful, slower-paced life of Dallas and academe. And I knew that Ellie was even happier at the prospect than I.

13

ACADEME AND THE FIRST REPUBLICBANK

It was the best of times, it was the worst of times, it was the age of wisdom, it was the age of foolishness. . . .

— Charles Dickens

T EACHING TURNED OUT TO BE EVERYTHING I had hoped it would be.

The students were bright and eager; I felt renewed and rejuvenated by my twice weekly contact with them. Remembering my own MBA years, I focused on case studies, using actual companies and actual problems. Figuring a good place to start was at home, I included in my case studies American Airlines, about which I still remembered a thing or two, and the problems that had plagued the airline industry over the past several decades. To make the course interesting and high profile, I planned to bring in the CEO of the company under scrutiny, both to talk to the students and evaluate their proposed solutions to the problems under study. It would be great for the students and without question great for the CEOs too. Making contact with inquisitive, motivated young people might stimulate the corporate synapses more than they realized. Bob Crandall didn't know it yet, but he was first on my academic hit list, which eventually included Colgate, Sears, Times Mirror, Addressograph-Multigraph, and the Bank of California, among others.

Although I'd had a reputation during my business career for

being jovial — Mr. Nice Guy — and very much a people person, I had also never been afraid to be tough. In my first year at American I fired half a dozen vice presidents, and abruptly terminated several management consulting firms at both American and the Post Office. Some CEOs who have a reputation for being tough find it difficult, even impossible, to fire people. I understand but respectfully disagree. Keeping on employees who are not pulling their weight, or who aren't up to their jobs, is patently unfair to those people who are producing 100 percent. And unfair to the company you're running. I believe in giving both leaders and managers a fair chance, but if after a reasonable period they aren't living up to expectations — I've always believed two years is the fair, maybe the outside, limit — they should go.

In the same sense, I expected my students to perform: I demanded that they be present at all classes, that they come prepared, that they all participate in class discussions.

In a course I gave in the summer of 1987, Business Policy I, I focused on five actual cases:

> Polaroid v. Kodak
> The Chain Saw Case, 1974
> Air Products and Chemicals
> General Cinema
> People Express Airlines

The problems we dealt with had been confronted in reality by the companies, and all included "hard" numbers issues and "soft" people issues. Human nature is such that each of us tends to focus on one or the other, but I strongly felt the most successful managers are those who are able to balance both. In fact, I urged the students to try and put the greater emphasis on the issue to which they were not naturally drawn.

From day one, classes were lively, interesting, sometimes combative, but always productive. I suspect the ultimate test of teaching is: are you learning as much as your students? And in my case, at age sixty-seven, the answer was a resounding yes.

In keeping with my business experience and principles, I also made myself available for one-on-one meetings every Wednesday to answer any questions or clarify problems that had perhaps not been made clear, and in those meetings, as had been true throughout my business life, I got to know and understand the students better.

The first professor of business administration, I told my classes, was Moses' father-in-law. In Exodus, chapter 18, verses 13 through 27, the Bible says that Moses sat in judgment of people from morning to night, and even with that effort and those hours he was unable to handle the job. Moses' father-in-law advised him he would "surely wear away, both thou, and this people . . . thou art not able to perform it thyself alone." He went on to say that Moses should develop a structure and "place such over them, to be rulers of thousands, and rulers of hundreds, rulers of fifties, and rulers of tens . . . then thou shalt be able to endure, and all this people shall also go to their place in peace."

I always reminded my classes that if we are to learn from the past, from our mistakes, we must ask: why did this happen, and how can we be sure it won't happen again?

Teaching is a lot different from running a corporation, but in some ways just as challenging. The new challenges and perspectives my young students presented me every semester helped to keep my spirit young and my mind alert.

When you're teaching, you really have to work at it; you can't just prattle about your experiences. You've got to have a cohesive plan or program, decide exactly what lesson or point you want to get across.

There were always a few groans and rolling eyes when students first looked over my syllabus at the beginning of the semester. My courses weren't easy and required a lot of effort and time to complete both individual and group projects, as well as papers and other shorter assignments. But most of my students rose to the challenge. For example, I met an increasing number of students intent on being good managers and executives but who questioned what they viewed as business driven only by the profit motive. They felt too many businesses were willing to reach their goals by any means possible. Many were also deeply concerned that businesses make positive strides toward environmental and social goals.

"Good," I told them. "I'm glad to see that you had parents, like my mother, who instilled a sense of social responsibility in their children."

I made a point of keeping in touch with students who impressed me, and I talked them into going on pro bono boards whenever and wherever possible.

I also tried to pass on to my students what I learned during my forty-year career: they have all had a firsthand course in Casey's Law.

One student called up some time back and said, "Mr. Casey, I would love to take advantage of the network you've developed through the years. Could you send me a list, especially of your closest friends!"

Most of them, however, are very decent and highly motivated. "You've got to work at whatever you're doing," I tell them. "You get out what you put in."

It's true for the teacher too.

The other plus of academe was that it gave Ellie and me more time to socialize, relax, and travel.

I had always enjoyed golf, though I never was able to play as much as I would have liked. Occasionally, I had played in the pro-ams associated with many of the PGA tournaments. One of the magazines we had acquired while I was still at Times Mirror was *Golf.* The Hall of Famer Jack Nicklaus was a contributing editor, and thus I got to know him and play in some of his pro-am tournaments.

One year *Golf* gave an award to Nicklaus, who received us in his Lost Tree Clubhouse in southern Florida. Though only four people were in the room, he insisted on reading his entire speech, which took twenty minutes. We were trying to figure whether to flee or hit him over the head with one of his clubs, the speech was so boring. In all fairness, Nicklaus did evolve; he's a much different person now, much more gracious and charming. He has even developed a sense of humor.

"I used to be a real pain in the ass, didn't I?" he once said to me.

"Jack, we all change for the better," I replied. "That is, if we make the effort."

Some years later, when I was at American Airlines, I played in Jack's Memorial Tournament in Ohio. Dean Witter was the tournament sponsor, and Phil Purcell, Dean Witter's CEO, asked if I wanted to join the fun. Purcell's company was owned by Sears, and I was a Sears board member at the time, but I'm positive that connection had nothing to do with the invitation. It certainly couldn't have been the quality of my golf. In any event, I usually accepted such invitations with pleasure and alacrity, mostly for the pure fun of it. But there were other reasons for me to participate: I met many old business friends and made a number of new ones. And I always learned something playing golf. It's a little like poker: you see people in moments of satisfaction and pleasure, and you see how people handle losing and winning. You can tell a lot about a person's leadership qualities in such situations.

Playing in Jack's tournament was primarily pleasure. I'm always amazed at how often people lose sight of such a basic reason for doing something. There is a very important distinction between taking your responsibilities seriously and taking yourself *too* seriously. I have always taken my responsibilities to heart, but I have tried to think of what I was doing as a form of play. There are rules, but they are not secret rules; they are simply the rules that ought to govern us all in our relationships, business or personal. The most important one, of course, is to play fair. Too many people in business, even the vast majority who treat others well, forget that first word. And often the second.

Poor Jack Nicklaus could forget this sometimes, even though his profession was to play a game. He had wanted to recreate the feeling of the Masters in Augusta as much as possible with his golf tournament in Muirfield, Ohio. The professionals played

Thursday, Friday, Saturday, Sunday, and then the pro-am was held on Monday. It was primarily advertisers and business associates who competed in the pro-am. Some of the pros played, but not many.

In the spring of 1980 I was playing along in the pro-am, on about the twelfth or thirteenth hole, when I was summoned to the phone. I was the high handicapper on the team, the D player, but I had banged in a couple of pretty decent putts. The team never used a drive or approach shot of mine, so no one would notice when I went to take the call.

"Your daughter's on the phone" was the message from the clubhouse. "She wants to talk to you." Before I left home she had developed conjunctivitis, and she was suffering terribly. So I left the course and called her, then spoke to her doctor. By that time, there seemed no point in my going out to play golf anymore.

"What the hell," I said to myself. "I'll go to the shower and be the first one at the bar."

Later Jack came in and said, "Al, we just got the final results. Congratulations. Your foursome won the tournament."

"Get out of here!" I replied.

"It's true, you won," he repeated.

"That's great, Jack," I said. "What's the prize?"

He was upset that I didn't know, because he had personally selected the prize.

"We already told you what the prize was," he said, slightly ir-ritated. "A reproduction of the MacGregor clubs I used in the 1960s, when I racked up a great string of victories."

"That's very nice," I said. "Will they make them for my length?"

"Al, you're not supposed to *use* them!"

At the pro-am dinner that night Jack poked good-natured fun at me.

"Casey didn't even play the last six holes, he didn't even know what the prize was, and then he wanted to *use* these things," Jack said as he presented me with my MacGregors.

I wonder what Jack would think today if he knew I have those clubs proudly on public display. In my garage.

*   *   *

After resigning as postmaster general, I had resumed my place on most of the boards from which I had been obliged to resign when I took the job. I enjoyed the give-and-take of board meetings. It also gave me a chance to renew old, often cherished, friendships.

But even in my relative ivory tower, I felt, as we moved into 1988, a growing malaise not only in Texas but throughout the country. Bad times in the commercial real estate market, coupled with falling oil prices, were the twin seeds that were eventually to grow into what became known as the savings and loan crisis.

To understand the financial debacle that descended, like the proverbial plague of locusts, on the United States in the early 1990s, it is essential to understand the background out of which the crisis, which truly threatened to plunge the country into a new depression, evolved. All of us have very short memories, which I understand some psychiatrists say is our way of surviving and keeping our sanity by blocking out unpleasantries. But the truth is, the savings and loan crisis could well have precipitated a depression even worse than that of the 1930s, if that's imaginable.

During the Depression, banks — both commercial banks and the so-called thrifts — had failed by the hundreds, millions of Americans had lost their hard-earned savings, millions more were out of work. The country was on the brink of ruin. To try and deal with the mounting crisis, Congress passed historic legislation to reform the banking system. The problem was to restore people's faith, and essential to that was providing deposit insurance for American depositors. The goal was to insure liquidity, stability, and hopefully prosperity. No one wanted to go through the financial panic of the 1930s again. And as we know, the banking system slowly began to recover, though it was a slow and painful process for more than a decade. Then, for about twenty years after World War II, the country enjoyed a period of unparalleled prosperity. Prices and interest rates remained stable. Under the protection of banking regulation, banks and thrifts prospered. And as we Americans flocked to buy new homes in the suburbs in the 1950s

and 1960s, it was the thrift institutions — the savings and loans —
that underwrote our way of life. These community-based institutions had a dual function: to lend money for home mortgages and
take in deposits for people's savings. As long as rates remained stable, the spread between the interest taken in on mortgages and the
interest paid on deposits kept these institutions profitable.

But in the late 1960s a new period of transition began: the financing of the Vietnam War, together with funding the various
ambitious and costly programs of the Great Society, fueled the
fires of inflation. Adding to the inflationary pressures was the
emergence of OPEC in 1973 as a world political force. Dictating
oil prices, which spiraled upward month after month, the oil-
producing countries soon had the so-called developed countries
not only on the defensive but on their knees. Inflation burned a
hole in American pockets and American hopes. And where inflation went, interest rates soon followed, till at the end of the 1970s
rates had reached an astonishing 20 percent. There were other unsettling forces at work: as the 1970s drew to a close, competition
in financial services began to heat up. There was more innovation,
more ambition, more drive to create new investment sources. And
computer technology opened up new investment opportunities.
With interest rates so high, people felt the urgent need to seek
higher returns than they had been receiving from their traditional
sources of savings.

One of the more attractive alternatives was the money market mutual funds, which were able to avoid the restrictions of
Depression-era government regulations and offer higher interest
rates on deposits than the thrifts. So throughout the 1970s and into
the 1980s money flowed from the thrifts — still hamstrung with
outmoded regulations on what they could pay out to depositors
and how they could invest their depositors' money — into the
mutual funds. Under increasing pressure because their decades-
long profitability was fast becoming fond memory, the thrifts, not
surprisingly, began pressuring Congress for deregulation. All they
wanted, they said, was to level the playing field, give them a fair

chance to compete in the new financial environment. In 1980 Congress passed a law lifting the former restrictions on the savings and loan banks: the old ceilings on loans, and the interest limits paid on deposits, were phased out, and thrifts were allowed to move into more complex and speculative investments. The bill also raised the ceiling on deposit insurance from forty thousand dollars to one hundred thousand dollars.

Then, in 1982, Congress passed another bill, the Garn–Saint Germain Depository Insurance Act. This legislation allowed thrifts to make unsecured loans, and also allowed them for the first time to invest significantly in commercial real estate. Coupled with this was a relaxation on the restrictions concerning who could own a thrift. In Texas, California, Florida, and several other states, there was a sudden chartering frenzy, as speculators realized that owning a thrift was like owning their own mint without having to risk their personal resources.

Unfortunately, Congress's two bills were also a double-barreled shotgun aimed directly at the American taxpayer. For the growth, speculation, investment, and risk were being financed, leveraged, and paid for by the taxpayer, in the form of deposit insurance. In other words, deposit insurance, which had once been part of the careful framework of banking regulation, now was part of a new deregulatory environment in which risk and speculation were a way of life. It was now possible to speculate heavily — and there is a bit of the gambler in all of us, I strongly suspect — using vast sums of insured deposits. Many investors, relying on the safety net of deposit insurance, began making increasingly risky investments. Many thrift owners were completely honest, driven to speculate in areas they would have shunned years before only to satisfy the increasing demands of their customers. They may in many instances have invested foolishly but in no way broke the law. Others, however, seizing the opportunities offered to them by their own Congress, went on a wild spending spree in the 1980s. There were among them outright thieves and swindlers, whose only goal was to get rich quick, the depositor be damned. The wreckage they left in their wake — in broken institutions, broken faith, and broken hope — was far more devastating than any financial crisis since the Great Depression.

Unfortunately, many innocent people were swept up in the chaos that followed the engulfing wave of bankruptcies and lawsuits. Many banks had elected directors — especially women — without properly or adequately educating them about their responsibilities and their potential personal liability in case the banks on whose boards they served ever ran into trouble. In this environment, people suddenly found themselves guilty of illegal acts for having done "what everyone else did for decades." Some who had sold their property years before now found themselves owners again as the notes were defaulted on — and then they were held responsible for the actions of the defaulters.

But as bad as the situation was, it does not end here; it gets worse.

In 1986, Congress passed another well-intentioned bill — the Tax Reform Act of 1986 — the goal of which was to streamline tax rates and eliminate tax shelters. While the goals were doubtless worthy, no one in Congress quite foresaw the consequences, especially in the real estate market. But the overnight elimination of incentives for real estate investment had an immediate, negative effect in that key area of American business. Investors quickly withdrew their money from commercial real estate, leaving the financing burden, and the empty office buildings, to the thrifts. At about the same time, the oil boom of the 1970s, which had driven prices ever higher and led both thrifts and banks to invest heavily in oil, collapsed. The banks and thrifts had made loans anticipating ever increasing prices for a barrel of oil. In other words, repayment of their loans was based not on increased oil production but on price inflation. This dual collapse — the commercial real estate market and oil — led to the crash, in a very short period of time, of hundreds of overextended thrifts, especially in Texas but also in other parts of the country.

There was another, equally serious problem. While Congress had raised the thrifts' deposit insurance guarantee to one hundred thousand dollars, it had failed to require proportionate increases in the insurance premiums, so that the bankers' and thrifts' privately supported insurance funds could boost their reserves to protect themselves from the added risks of deregulation. By the mid-1980s, the thrifts' insurance fund was dead broke, and no amount of smoke and mirrors could conceal it. By 1985, privately supported, state-regulated insurance funds had gone belly-up in Texas and Ohio. If the problem was not addressed quickly, there was a clear potential for a run on thrifts and banks as well. And yet for another four years, no one in government wanted to face up to the problem, doubtless hoping that by some cyclical miracle it would go away. But by 1989 it was impossible to ignore the crisis any longer. There was panic in the air that year — you could almost feel it. Since 1980, almost 500 thrifts had been closed — 205 in 1988 alone — which gives some idea of the geometric progression of the problem. The thrifts' losses were staggering. And there was no insurance money to pay off the depositors. In an effort to stem the tide and keep the public from panicking, many insolvent thrifts were kept open, which only added to the mounting losses. Congress began debating how much the taxpayers would have to ante up to bail out the thrifts, and many in government and the financial community were predicting the demise of the entire thrift industry. To make matters worse, the budget deficit, which had been a nagging problem for years, was at an all-time high: for the Congress, it was the proverbial rock and hard place.

To his credit, President Bush, shortly after he took office, did face up to the crisis, and in 1989 Congress pushed through landmark legislation overhauling the thrift regulatory structure and creating the Resolution Trust Corporation, whose basic mandate was to handle the crisis and restore the trust placed in deposit insurance. Pragmatically, its job was to close down failed thrifts, sell their assets at the best possible price, and pursue and punish the wrongdoers who had contributed to the mess. Very simply, the RTC was a rescue operation aimed at saving the financial lives of the taxpayers and depositors. In fulfilling that function, it became a corporate takeover machine — taking over bankrupt thrifts and preparing them for sale. It also became a diversified retail operation, selling everything from half-finished developments to art collections. It had also become a law firm, since part of its cleanup operation was ferreting out and prosecuting civil cases against savings and loan operators who had abused their authority. Finally, and most diplomatically delicate, it was forced to become a distributor of congressional "gifts." To fund the RTC, Congress, after a great deal of wrangling, authorized $30 billion, with the crazy stipulation, which to this day I fail to comprehend, that it all be spent in sixty days! As a result, fewer dams and post offices and the like would be built in every congressional district, while funds were diverted to pay off the depositors of failed and ailing thrifts. Thus, almost immediately after it started in business, the RTC was also a political football, subjected to daily pressure from various members of Congress seeking funds from sold-off assets to spread among their constituents. In short, there was no precedent in American history for what the RTC had been asked to do. According to Washington pundits, anyone who took the job as the RTC administrator had to be "part politician, part tycoon, and part crazy." I figure I fit at least one-third of that job description.

How did I become the head of the RTC? Even my eleven years in the volatile and constantly challenging airline business had not prepared me for the financial, not to mention political, demands of that job. I can't say for sure, but I suspect my ascension to that precarious post began on April 9, 1988. It was a Saturday morning. I was at home in Dallas when I received a phone call from Washington. It was Alan Greenspan, then as now head of the Federal Reserve Board.

"Mr. Casey," he said, "as you doubtless know, we have a terrible problem with the First RepublicBank down there."

"I'm aware it's had problems," I said, "but I'm not sure I know the full extent, or the details. In any event, I'm not even on the board of the bank. Wouldn't you be better off talking to some of the board members, who can fill you in, I'm sure?"

"That's not why I'm calling, Mr. Casey. I have all the details I need."

There was another of those long pauses I'd gotten used to in my career, so I knew something unexpected was coming. But I had no idea what.

"Mr. Casey," he said, "I want you to move in and take over First RepublicBank."

"I'm not qualified to do that, Mr. Greenspan. Banking isn't my expertise."

"Mr. Casey, I wouldn't be calling if the situation wasn't desperate. First Republic's near failure. But our concern goes deeper than that: First Republic serves as clearinghouse for fifteen hundred other banks in the Southwest. We're afraid its checks might not be accepted."

"The domino effect."

"Exactly," Greenspan said. "It could be devastating."

I was just finishing my second year of teaching at the business school at SMU, was enjoying myself mightily, and had no desire to get involved in what was obviously a messy, probably inextricable, banking situation. For First Republic, a commercial bank, had been badly hurt in the past several years by the exponential expansion of the S&Ls in the Dallas/Fort Worth area, which had moved aggressively, and often dangerously, into both commercial and home mortgages, putting the squeeze on banks like First Republic. From 1984 to 1986 real estate loans had increased by 50 percent, to a peak of $30 billion. After the price of oil plunged in 1986 from twenty-eight dollars a barrel to ten dollars, housing prices dropped like lead: 35–40 percent in Houston, 20 percent in Dallas. Many people who had put only 10 percent down to buy their homes simply upped and walked. In Dallas, the building vacancy rate that year was 33 percent; in Austin, 38 percent.

In an effort to deal with their mounting losses, First Republic merged on June 6, 1987, with First National. Both were major Texas banks. It was a case of two $500 dogs becoming a $1,000 cat. In any event, the new "cat" on the block was faced with all the same problems as before, only greater. I didn't need to know any more of the unpleasant details to decline, politely I trusted, Washington's request.

"I really don't think I bring sufficient experience to the table to be helpful," I said.

"Mr. Casey, various people with whom I've consulted convince me otherwise. We don't need a banking expert here. We need a man with solid business experience. Would you agree to talk with Bill Seidman and Robert Clarke?"

Seidman was chairman of the Federal Deposit Insurance Corporation and Clarke the Controller of the Currency. Big guns. Clearly big problem. Bigger no doubt than I had realized. But I had learned from long experience that, at this stage of my life at least, I should try to avoid walking into swamps I know are over my head.

"I really appreciate the compliment, but my answer is still no." And with that I hung up and went about my day, feeling slightly guilty but nonetheless relieved that I had not yielded.

The next morning the phone rang. Before I picked it up I knew who it was. Greenspan: the man who wouldn't take no for an answer.

"Mr. Casey, we've had further discussions here, and they've only reinforced our belief that you *must* take this on. Sir, it's your patriotic duty." He went on to explain that unless immediate action was taken, there could well be a run on the area's banks. And he concluded: "We've got to make an announcement, and make it soon, to prevent that. Clarke is on a plane to Dallas. Would you please meet with him as soon as he arrives?"

Realizing the situation was far graver than I had imagined, I agreed to meet that night with Clarke and three others: Gerry Fronterhouse, chairman and CEO of First Republic; Jim Berry, who was the former chairman, had served on the board of directors of the bank, and was an officer and board member of the bank's holding company; and H. R. (Bum) Bright, one of the bank's largest shareholders and a board member.

Gerry picked me up at about eight P.M. and drove me over to Bum Bright's house on Lakeside, where for almost two hours we went over the most pressing problems and explored various possible strategies. The deteriorating real estate loans, coupled with a run on the bank by commercial depositors, had resulted in a $1.5 billion loss for the first quarter. And things weren't looking much brighter for the second quarter. Everyone there pressed me to take on the chairmanship of the bank immediately; they wanted to announce my appointment at nine the next morning. Sensing that the penny I was already in for was probably going to turn into a very heavy pound, I nonetheless said I would have to sleep on it. However, I agreed to reconvene with each of them for half an hour the following morning, starting at seven o'clock. I wanted time to think through the commitments that I would ask them to make.

The next morning, after meeting with the last of the four, Bum Bright, I authorized them to announce that the board would elect me the following day as chairman. I then met with various officers and directors, many of whom seemed less concerned about the dreadful state of the bank — among other things, it was overdrawn at the Federal Reserve — than their own personal liability. The more I learned, the more the term *chaotic* kept flashing through my mind. Thank you, Mr. Greenspan!

> *Mind playlet, starring the two Als, Greenspan and Casey:*
> CASEY: You're out of your skull, Casey!
> GREENSPAN: You're doing a great deed for your country.
> CASEY: Railroads, okay. Newspapers, okay. Airlines, well
> . . . okay. Post Office, okay. Dying banks: no way.
> GREENSPAN: You'll be proud you agreed to take this on!
> Your country will be forever grateful!

I went home, took a deep breath, sat down, and began to write on a yellow legal pad what I saw as the bank's biggest problems and the major work to be undertaken:

- management in disarray, many resignations
- settling working arrangements with FDIC
- working to hold major accounts
- restructuring programs, lawyers and investment bankers

- outside directors' insurance coming up for renewal in early June
- interviewing for a new CEO

Almost immediately, I put together a sixty-person task force of fifteen teams, first to determine the precise current status of things, and second to map out Republic's future strategy. The most pressing task was preparing the bank for sale. Every Saturday we held uninterrupted department meetings — they could go on as long as questions and suggestions flowed — among the various managers. Every Sunday I worked as well with the individual department heads. And once a week I met with the entire headquarters staff, about six hundred people, to update them and answer questions. The number and size of the problems were overwhelming, but I made up my mind that the only way to solve them — *possibly* solve them — was to use openness, communication, accountability, and humor. In a crisis situation, reinstilling confidence in a staff whose morale is shot is the first order of business. Ask any army general. If this new chairman was working his tail off twelve hours a day, seven days a week, there had to be *some* hope, no?

About three weeks into the job I woke up at six one morning and said to Ellie: "What was all this I've always heard about bankers' hours?"

She laughed and said I'd better get a move on, I was already late. "And what was all this I heard about taking it easier in your retirement years?" she added.

I asked for, and received, resignations from six of the board members: the current CEO Gerry Fronterhouse; Jim Berry; Bum Bright; vice chairman Jim Keay; Joe Musolino; and David Florence, the son of a legendary earlier president of the bank. I immediately reappointed Musolino to the bank's presidency, and reassigned another key officer, Jim Erwin, as vice president since I desperately needed a couple of people familiar with the inner workings and with the personnel of the bank, bridges to past management and actions.

At one point I had eighty-five FDIC examiners in First Republic's Dallas bank, and another forty in the Houston bank, all assessing the liquidation value, to determine whether it should be reorganized or liquidated.

But I had another plan, which I felt would work and have the great virtue of keeping the bank locally owned. Working with Drexel Burnham, and Sears, Roebuck subsidiaries Dean Witter and Coldwell Banker Real Estate, we would divide the ailing bank into two components: a "new" First Republic, which would hold all the good assets, and a "workout bank," which would hold the loans that had already gone bad as well as those that were labeled "dubious." Part of the equity of these two entities would be held by the FDIC, part sold to investors. Drexel and Dean Witter would act as co-underwriters of the proposed $1 billion offering to the public, and Coldwell Banker would manage the distressed assets. Why would the public want to buy shares in a bank that was in the process of reorganization? Because we'd offer bonds with very attractive interest rates — in the 11 to 12 percent range — because the FDIC would be standing behind it, and because even with the bad and dubious loans, First Republic still had a formidable array of performing assets — more than $25 billion in all. It was my and my colleagues' opinion that the public offering would be fully, perhaps overly, subscribed.

On June 9, 1988, I submitted my plan to the FDIC, which provided for the creation of a workout bank to assume First Republic's bad credits: the FDIC would hold 75 percent of the stock of the institution, while the remaining 25 percent would be sold to outside investors. The FDIC at first set a deadline of June 15 for us to find bidders, then extended the deadline to June 30 because by June 15 ours was the only bid it had received. Seidman and the FDIC approached several other major banks, including Wells Fargo and Citibank, but after doing due diligence none was interested. Meanwhile, North Carolina National Bank, now Nations Bank, had for some time been indicating an interest but had not come up with a concrete proposal. Unbeknownst to me, NCNB finally sat down with Seidman and worked out a deal in late July, and I was sorely distressed. To consummate the deal, the FDIC had to provide NCNB with a "dowry" of $4 billion — the biggest rescue in history. The infusion of FDIC cash wiped out First Republic's current debts and bad loans and provided enough capital for it to begin anew. For its money, NCNB gained control of a $26.8 billion array of assets, and overnight doubled its size. The cost of the deal plunged the FDIC into the red for the first time; the $4 billion bailout check far surpassed the $2 billion to $3 billion the FDIC was earning annually from insurance fees it was charging its member banks.

I thought then, and I still believe today, that my alternative plan was both workable and economically far preferable. Among other things, an out-of-state bank had different priorities than an independent Texas bank. But Bill Seidman, the head of the FDIC, obviously thought otherwise. Part of the problem, I suspect, is that Drexel Burnham and its flamboyant junk-bond "king," Michael Milken, were coming under increasing scrutiny in the press in those days, and the FDIC doubtless wanted no part of a plan in which Drexel Burnham or Milken was involved. Still, as far as we or anyone knew, Milken, however controversial, was both astute and intelligent, and the risk he and Drexel Burnham were taking seemed fully justified. Be that as it may, the crisis had been averted, and confidence restored, at least for the moment. Seidman called me and thanked me profusely for "my contribution." During those wild few weeks, I learned more than I ever wanted to know about our banking system. I'm glad I have all that behind me, I thought as I returned to my normal routine and began preparing my notes for the fall semester. Little did I know that my banking career had barely begun.

In late November 1989, Ellie and I flew to Nassau to attend a board meeting of Memorex Telex. After the meeting, we closed with a ceremonial dinner, which was wonderfully festive. Ellie, who knew most of the board members and their wives, was having an especially good time. She was always interested in other people, their plans, their hopes, their children, and she had spent a good deal of the evening getting updates on her friends' lives.

After dessert, she noticed our good friend Bob Strauss slipping away.

"Bob can't leave without saying good-bye," she said to me. With which she got up, walked quickly across the room, and kissed him good-bye in the doorway. Then she turned and called back to me:

"Al, I'm going upstairs to get a sweater."

Evenings were chilly, even in Nassau, at this time of year, and she knew after coffee we'd stroll over to the casino.

When after fifteen minutes, she still hadn't come down, I went up to our room and banged on the door.

"Ellie," I shouted, "the door's locked. Open up."

There was no answer, so I went down to the desk and got a key. I opened the door to find Ellie on the floor, unmoving. I called the doctor, then tried mouth-to-mouth resuscitation for a very long time — even after the doctor arrived — to no avail. Despite all our efforts, there was not even the faintest sign of a pulse. Later, it was determined, as I noted earlier, she had died of a brain aneurysm, similar to the one that had necessitated my operation.

An American Airlines volunteer cockpit and cabin crew flew to Nassau, then to Boston, where Ellie was interred in her family plot in Holyhood Cemetery, in Brookline, Massachusetts. The ceremony preceding her burial was held at Saint Theresa's Church in West Roxbury. The church was filled to overflowing with family and friends. During the service, I delivered, with great difficulty, these words in memory of Ellie:

Ellie enjoyed being everybody's friend. In fact, that attribute — friendship — came easily to her, for she was truly interested in everyone she met: What were their hopes, their ambitions? How were their children? Each of you may be certain that she held you most dear and that she highly valued your friendship. Each of you is a jewel in her crown, for she certainly was a queen — my queen, my wife.

We loved each other very much. Ellie certainly did everything possible for this itinerant workman who couldn't hold a job, or his health. I should be the one out there — would to God I were. . . .

Please learn from her untimely passing one important lesson: every day tell your loved ones of your appreciation and affection for them.

That was the hardest day of my life. Those words were the most difficult, and the most heartfelt, I had ever spoken.

For fifteen months after Ellie's passing, I felt not only totally bereft but devoid of any desire to re-enter the social scene. A seemingly endless parade of well-wishing widows called, with a succession of casseroles and sympathies, all of whom I thanked profusely and gently sent packing. My daughter Judy moved in with me and was a great and constant source of good cheer and comfort.

One very good friend of Ellie's was Pat Patterson, whose home, known locally as Pink House, was a Dallas showplace. Pat had often made her home available for social receptions and various charities, including several with which Ellie had been involved. Pat was very helpful and supportive to me during those difficult months, and when finally I did begin to reappear socially, it was often at some function at Pink House. One thing leading to another — which seems to happen in life, I've noticed — Pat and I were increasingly attracted to each other. For decades I'd practiced one of my famous dictums — look forward, not back — and after a year and a half of ignoring that "law," I decided it was high time to start practicing it again.

14

THE RESOLUTION TRUST CORPORATION

WANTED: Tough manager to take over a stifling bureaucracy and make the best of a no-win
situation. Applicant should be a quick decision
maker able to streamline cluttered operation.
Comparatively low pay and benefits. Send résumés to the Resolution Trust Corporation.

— *Dallas Morning News*
September 19, 1991

ONE DAY IN MID-SEPTEMBER 1991, I received a phone call
in my Dallas office at SMU, where the new semester had
just begun. Libby Scott took the call, then buzzed me,
rather insistently I thought.

"It's the deputy secretary of the treasury, John Robson," she
said. "He sounds excited."

"Good morning, John," I said. "How're things in our nation's
capital?"

"Fine, Al, fine. Let me get straight to the point. We've
reached a decision in the RTC post."

"Who's the lucky fellow?" I had read in the newspaper that
the search committee had drawn up a list of two hundred candidates, then narrowed it down to fifty, then to six. What I didn't
know — no one had thought to tell me — was that my name had
recently been added to the short list.

"Al, we want *you* to head it up. But we don't have the

authority to appoint you, since there's a search committee. So we'd like you to meet with the search committee. And with Treasury Secretary Brady."

"Wait a minute, wait a minute. You're going too fast, John. Besides, you know I'm not a banker."

"Al, we all remember what you did at Republic. Anyway, this job needs an astute businessman, not a banker."

"From the little I know," I said, "it sounds like it needs a master juggler. Is someone running it now?"

"Bill Seidman," he said. "As head of the FDIC, he's acting CEO. But he'll step down as soon as the new man is named."

From my experience with the First RepublicBank, I had some firsthand knowledge about the kinds of problems facing the RTC. But I also knew taking on such a job would be willfully walking into the lion's den. How many failed thrifts were there to date? How many more would there be in the next couple of years? What kind of support would I get from Congress? from the administration? from the oversight committee? What kind of staffing would I have? Would Congress continue to fund us as time went on, for it was clear to me that this was no "quickie"; this might take years to solve. The numbers at stake were staggering: in the hundreds of billions. And what if I failed?

That last question probably helped me make up my mind, for suddenly I realized that was a Murphy question. Think positively, Al: You like being involved in big problems, you like big dollar numbers (my inner voice responding: Okay, but *that* big?), you like working with a lot of people. And let's face it, you like the idea of government service, giving back to your country something of what it gave you. May sound corny, but that's how I felt. There was another factor in my decision: with Ellie's death, my priorities had changed. Our priority had been to travel and enjoy, spend more time together. Now my goal was to keep busy. Taking on the RTC job would more than fulfill that goal, I was sure.

In short, I agreed to meet with the search committee. I stressed that if I did say yes, my goal would be to put the RTC out of business and, as it had been at the Postal Service, put myself out of a job.

"Do you have any idea what your timetable might be, Mr. Casey?" one of the committee members asked.

"We're dealing with huge numbers — over four hundred billion dollars as you know — and a diversity of assets that is mind-boggling. But in answer to your question, I would like to see the RTC closed down by the end of 1996."

"And in that time frame, Mr. Casey," said another, "what percentage of those assets do you think you can 'rescue,' if that's the proper term?"

I answered that it would be foolhardy for me to hazard a guess until I had a better grasp of the situation, but I averred that, in the abstract, I wanted to get as close to 100 percent as possible.

Before my tenure officially began on October 15, I was a consultant for two weeks. During the interim Bill Seidman explained the setup to me, ran me through the roster of key posts and personnel, and gave me his evaluation of the various department heads. While it was helpful, I saw immediately that we were woefully understaffed, had no infrastructure, and had an agenda whose first item was to deal with the 262 failed thrifts with an asset value of $104 billion that comprised our priority list. *Daunting* was the word that kept crossing my mind those first two weeks.

Before he left, Seidman asked me to do him one favor. I'm always a trifle leery of last-minute favors requested by outgoing executives.

"In order to get my four assistants to leave their secure positions with the FDIC," he said, "I gave them, when they went over to the RTC, very generous early-out provisions in the event they were let go. Al, I'd really like you to guarantee the early-out provision for them. The money for it is already in the proposed legislation that will be coming up on the next funding bill."

"That sounds reasonable," I said.

"The early-out provision is very important to me," he went on. "Senator Terry Sanford will propose that it be included in the funding bill."

I called Senator Sanford and requested an early appointment. When we met, he confirmed that he had agreed to put the early-out provision in the funding bill. "I support Seidman," he said, and I left his office satisfied that there would be no problem.

As it turned out, there was. Which leads me to propound another deathless law: even after you've satisfied yourself that you've made the right decision, assume there's a chance, however slight, you haven't put the matter, any matter, wholly to rest. Amen.

A short while after I took the job, David Cooke, one of Seidman's men who had a position at the RTC roughly equivalent to a corporate executive vice president, left early. Unbeknownst to me, by the terms of the legislation, the burden of the early-out was not on the RTC but on the FDIC. Understandably, the people at the FDIC were extremely upset, since the cost of Cooke's early-out was in the neighborhood of $1.5 million, a figure that would put a serious dent in their budget. The General Accounting Office made the FDIC book the early-out cost at the time Cooke resigned. There was a big stink in the newspapers, and someone called Seidman to ask him about it.

"Yeah, I'm upset, too," Seidman said. "I don't know why Casey ever sponsored the early-out provision. I certainly would never have approved such a request."

I was livid and put in a call to Seidman. "Bill," I said, "you seem to have a short memory. *You* asked me to support your 'early out' provision. Don't you remember asking me to go over and see Terry Sanford?"

There was one of those wonderful pauses on the other end, but this time shorter than most. "Oh, Al," Seidman said, and I could almost see him shaking his head, "you just don't understand how things work in this town. You'll get used to Washington."

"Bill, that's disgraceful. You're not the friend I thought you were. And you're not the man I thought you were."

I hung up, vowing to never talk to him again. And I never have.

On October 1, 1991, I rented a suite in the Jefferson Hotel (later made famous by President Clinton's former political strategist,

Richard Morris), with a six-month lease. Toward the end of the year I prevailed upon Pat Patterson to join me in Washington.

The assignment appeared to have a relatively long life, at least a couple of years, I estimated, since it seemed certain at that point that Bush would be reelected in 1992. We therefore decided to rent a house, and Pat, through the kind auspices of Toni Hatfield, Senator Mark Hatfield's wife, found a lovely place on Kalorama Road, with ample space for entertaining. It also had several bedrooms, which meant we could receive friends as well as our children — her children, Patty and Caroline, as well as Judy and Peter — and their families. Pat made Kalorama Road a virtual replica of Pink House, bringing north her French antiques, Aubusson rugs, and King Charles spaniels.

We entertained extensively. Before many weeks had gone by, Pat became one of the capital's leading hostesses. In Washington, where a great deal of business is transacted after hours — at a quiet corner over cocktails or at dinner — entertaining is one of the most efficient ways of getting the job done. We also entertained many members of the RTC staff, which helped cement good relations and offered us a chance, outside the always hectic office, to discuss quietly and soberly many of the burning issues we had to confront, and hopefully solve, in the coming weeks and months. And then the Texans: we had so many Texas guests that before long Kalorama Road became known as the Texas embassy.

My old friend Governor Hugh Carey, under whom I had served when I lived in New York City, reciprocated by making our humble abode his second home whenever he was in Washington. In fact, his (always pleasant) visits were so frequent that he ended up leaving a complete wardrobe in the closet of his room. Whenever he was in residence, Pat would always check with him to see if he planned to join us for family meals. A true friend, he even took care of the dogs when we were traveling.

One of our most memorable, and unusual, receptions during that period was a Sunday-afternoon football party. No, it was not Al Casey playing touch football with Teddy Kennedy; it was the Washington Redskins playing the Kansas City Chiefs at Kansas

City. The honored guest was Jack Kent Cooke, the owner of the Redskins, who had long ago forgiven me for my Teleprompter *mano a mano* with him. We had a star-studded Washington guest list, which included Alan Greenspan, the Vernon Jordans, Andrea Mitchell, and a dozen politicians and businesspeople who, whatever their differences professionally, were united in their devotion to the Redskins. We had set up half a dozen television sets in various parts of the house, with the largest screen in the living room. We looked forward to a rousing, animated party. Jack and his wife Marlena arrived shortly before the game began, strode into the living room, and seated themselves in front of the big screen. As soon as the game began, Jack's concentration on the events in Kansas City became total, and woe to anyone who broke the silence — even if it was to cheer — or otherwise interfered with his concentration. It quickly became apparent that Jack was convinced that if his concentration wavered for even an instant, the Redskins would be in immediate trouble. Therefore, having ascertained that the living room was to be a place of deadly silence for the next three hours, the guests, one by one and two by two, quietly tiptoed out of the room to watch the game on other, less rigorous screens. (P.S. The Redskins lost.)

As time went on, the RTC became more and more demanding of my time and energy, and many were the evenings when I had to call Pat either to postpone or cancel dinner. Never was my bad news greeted with a word of reproach. There were, too, days of real accomplishment when I would arrive at Kalorama Road in a state of exhilaration, and we would celebrate; other times, when nothing seemed to go right and Murphy was in full charge, I would arrive home exhausted, wondering (for a moment) if it was all worth it, at which times Pat would cheer me up and ready me for the next day's combat. Without her, I doubt seriously I could have coped with the rigors of that job — easily the most demanding of my business career — and for that unstinting support I am eternally grateful.

*   *   *

During the first week in October I met with the RTC executives and told them to start meeting once a week one-on-one with the key people who reported to them. I also attended a large staff meeting of RTC officials, which, I learned, was held every month.

At the end of my first meeting I made an announcement in the form of a suggestion: "Ladies and gentlemen," I said, "I recommend that we henceforth hold these regular large staff meetings once a year. Maybe around Christmastime."

I couldn't tell from their reaction whether or not they were amused. But for the most part I was impressed, after meeting each for an hour myself, with the top RTC staff, and said so publicly.

Someone from the press asked me, during that initial period, what my first priority was.

"I'm trying to learn to speak RTC," I said.

"I beg your pardon?"

"You know, the government jargon. I need to learn it so I can talk to the public."

Not all Washington was like Bill Seidman. Justice Sandra Day O'Connor, whom I had met during my stint as postmaster general, asked if she could host a reception for my swearing-in ceremony. Flattered, I said I'd be delighted. She arranged for the swearing-in to take place in the Supreme Court Building, and she hosted a reception preceding the ceremony for about four hundred people.

Several of the other Supreme Court justices came to the reception. I arrived early, bringing my daughter, Judy, with me. When we arrived, Sandra Day was wearing a lovely dress, but not her robes.

"Justice O'Connor," I said, assuming my most serious expression, "I really appreciate what you're doing for me today. But I note you're not wearing your official robe. I don't think the swearing in will be official unless you're suitably garbed."

"Really?" she said, looking nonplussed. And with that she

disappeared, to reappear minutes later in her full judicial robes. In the pictures taken after the ceremony, she looked wonderfully impressive.

During the latter half of the 1980s, as the savings and loan problem was building to a crisis, the media, for whatever reasons, had paid little attention to it. Smoke, I guess, is of far less interest than a fire, especially if the fire's out of control. But by the time I arrived, the RTC, now at the center of a firestorm, was not only being examined by the press, it was being overly scrutinized, as if it were the culprit in the scandal it was trying to correct. Very often a reporter would focus on one event, narrow down the facts selectively, get quotes from some (often vocal) critics, and accuse the RTC of one thing or another: of being bloated, of being understaffed, of being inept, of favoritism in the disposition of assets. It was none of these things, with the possible exception that when I arrived there were some staff members who I found were nonproducers, and I set about downsizing at once. But, in some areas, we also had to staff up, for we were dealing at that point with over seven hundred failed thrifts, whose combined assets totaled over $400 billion. To provide some perspective, that number exceeds the combined asset value of two of our largest corporations, Citibank and General Motors. What was more, the diversity of our "product" — what we were selling off, everything from completely unoccupied office buildings to half-finished golf courses — would have sent most CEOs to bed with a serious case of "bad product mix."

The first congressional funding in 1989 of $30 billion was used primarily to pay off the insured depositors. We needed additional funding to deal with the second part of the crisis, selling off the assets to save the taxpayers from bearing the burden. And Congress, always wary of funding and not entirely happy with the way the RTC was operating, refused to authorize any further money. In Congress's view, the RTC had been moving too slowly, and in that it was not all wrong. "Fast action" was the order of the day, but I knew that if we moved too quickly, it would look like a fire sale, sending asset values plunging, whereas I saw my mandate to recuperate as much of those assets as possible: as I said to Congress, 100 percent was my personal goal, though no one believed it attainable. Maybe I didn't wholly believe it myself. In any event, part of the problem was that initially the RTC had been selling assets piecemeal — a plot of land here, an office building there, a golf course to a local entrepreneur. Piecemeal posed a triple problem: it would probably take forever, you had difficulty knowing whether you were getting a fair price, and there was a fair chance that various assets would be subject to political pressure. Voters were calling their congressman and asking for various favors.

"Mr. Congressman, I want to buy my mortgage. Can you help me?"

"Ms Congresswoman, there's a golf course down the road that I know the RTC is selling off. I'd like to buy it. Can I count on you to help us local folks?"

In addition to all the other dangers in proceeding piecemeal was the undeniable fact that it would not have been cost-effective. It was almost as expensive to sell a single building or mortgage as it would be to sell a half-billion-dollar package. So I could foresee that, with Congress already reluctant to fund us further, the spigot would be turned off completely unless we produced impressive, tangible results.

Early in 1992, having decided to make the CEO a congressionally approved position, Congress passed a separate set of laws for new funding and set up new conditions for the CEO. Under the new law, I took over on February 1, 1992.

My first job was to constitute a new executive committee, parallel to those I had instituted at Times Mirror and American Airlines. I wanted a decentralized, lean, more customer-responsive, and more flexible organization, and I wanted to allow more decisions to be made at field level, where people knew what the values and economic conditions were.

Bill Roelle, formerly with the FDIC, was the CFO and chief accounting officer. Lamar Kelly, also from the FDIC, was in charge of disposing of assets, roughly the corporate equivalent of a marketing director. Gerald Jacobs was already on board as general counsel when I arrived, but had to be let go within a year because of a relationship with the governor of Arizona; he was replaced by Rick Aboussie. Rick was much more an administrator than an adviser, because he had to set up departments throughout the country whose job was to determine whether there was cause to sue the directors and officers of the failed banks. If we agreed there was a case, it was his job, in conjunction with the local counsel, to work up a budget, assess the expected recovery and time period and what the cost would be to the RTC. The fourth executive was David Greer, whose job was to manage the corporate wastebasket: purchasing, auditing, ethics, personnel, and public relations.

Every Monday morning I met with all four executives, organizing our agenda, assessing the previous week's progress, and focusing on problems that had surfaced. Roelle had the additional job, and it was a major one, of taking over the savings and loans identified as insolvent by the Office of Thrift Supervision, putting management into them, and setting up books of accounting for each. The RTC would then administer the assets — the deposits and collateral that its banks had claim to — and pay the insured depositors. The same procedure applied to the commercial banks, except that it was the Controller of the Currency that determined their insolvency and the FDIC took them over for resolution. So we had two parallel structures, one for commercial banks and one for the thrifts.

At the rate and the manner in which the RTC had been disposing of assets until now, it would never have unburdened itself of the $400 billion of mortgages, assets, and securities in a hundred years. So we hit on a new approach: securitization. Simply put, securitization is the packaging, or "pooling," of loans and the issuing of securities against them as collateral, typically bonds, which can then be traded like any other bond. Groups of loans are aggregated into pass-through securities, for example, mortgage pass-throughs.

Investors purchase the securities backed by these mortgages. The transformation of these pools into standardized securities enables issuers to deal in volumes large enough to bypass intermediaries. The price of the securities issued is, of course, dependent directly on the financial strength of the collateral, but in general the attraction to the investor is an above-average rate of return. When we first propounded the idea, many people were skeptical. But as time went on, and despite the complexities involved in packaging various assets that did not always make a magic fit, we recovered monies far faster, and far more efficiently, than we ever would have by continuing to sell piecemeal.

In 1992 the RTC had a lot of land in its inventory, and there was considerable pressure on us to get rid of it as quickly as possible. But that, too, would have meant selling it at giveaway prices, which I refused to do unless all other efforts had failed. So we structured a new "land fund" designed to raise the value of the land assets. The fund was structured like a joint venture, with private sector managers who were incentivized to get the best possible price for each land asset, with the RTC retaining a partnership interest in future profits. The initial response to this proposed program by the large Wall Street underwriters was less than enthusiastic, but after it was announced bidders came by the hundreds if not thousands. Even Wall Street took note and applauded. I think the high point for me was when the Pentagon called and inquired about the program, wondering whether the concept could be extended to manage its outdated military bases.

From all this, one may conclude that we at the RTC were able to operate with a completely free hand. Not so. We had to contend with Congress, whose continued funding was necessary for us to operate. There were in addition a congressionally appointed oversight committee and, of course, the press. As for the oversight committee, it included Secretary of the Treasury Nick Brady, Deputy Secretary John Robson, and Alan Greenspan, still chairman of the Federal Reserve Board, all of whom were complaining that I didn't consult with them enough. Which was absolutely true. The reason I didn't was that it became apparent very early on that they disapproved of virtually everything I was doing. To clear the air, I called a meeting of the board.

"Gentlemen, I've called this meeting to ask you one simple question: why did you hire me?"

They looked at one another as if to say, Now that's an odd question. Then one of them piped up: "Why, to sell off the failed thrifts' assets. . . ."

"At the maximum prices possible," said another.

"Do any of you gentlemen understand how *stressful* this job is? I mean just *doing* it?"

The collective mumbling that ensued I took to be affirmation.

"I can work with people, but I don't like to be supervised. I like to run my own show. I assume you hired me because you thought I might get the job done. I'll take full responsibility for it. But I cannot and will not be second-guessed. If that's the way you want it, then get rid of me. Now."

They gave me a full vote of confidence, and from that day on I won't say that things got easier — that wasn't the nature of the RTC — but our plans and programs moved ahead much more quickly and smoothly.

Casey's Law says that when you have a nagging problem like my oversight board, don't let it linger, don't let it fester. Confront it, fully prepared to back up your threats if they don't succeed. Hell, I didn't want to leave the RTC, but if I was forced to try and run it with watchdogs snapping at my heels, chances were I wouldn't succeed, and it might be better to cut bait right away. I had gambled that the board would back down as soon as confronted, and I was right.

Even though I had "solved" the oversight committee problem, never a day went by, as I remember, that I didn't offend or upset someone. People wanted favors, and I'm not a favor dispenser. Because of my securitization approach to solving the problem, I was accused of favoring the rich and powerful. Because I was thwarting people from picking up their local piece of land or office building, I was accused of discriminating against the little guy. I suppose I was, during my time at the RTC, one of the most disliked people in Washington. Hell, I didn't care. I'd gone into the job with my eyes open.

One day, I ran into then vice president Dan Quayle, who congratulated me, in a backhanded way, for what we were doing and had already done. "Al," he said, "you are bringing this country together. You have become a common hate object. Congress hates you, the White House hates you, the bankers don't like you, and your employees don't like you."

"Thank you, Mr. Vice President," I said. "What you say is probably true. But I want you to know I didn't take the job to be liked. I took it so I could get rid of it."

During my first weeks on the job, I learned something new — I'm a firm believer that the learning process never ends. In Washington, if you want to do something, just barrel ahead and do it. The worst possible course of action is to ask for permission. If you do, stagnation ensues. But if you go ahead without asking, you have to be damn well prepared to defend your move or moves.

When I took over, there was pretty thin support for the RTC on all fronts: the people didn't like it, fearing it would somehow reach into their pockets in the form of added taxes; Congress didn't like it, because it was a political embarrassment and potential bombshell; the press lit into it because it was such an easy target. But when Representative Sam Johnson of my home state of Texas went after us in late November, I felt I had been hit below the belt, and I struck back in an op-ed piece in the *Dallas Morning News*:

S&L BAILOUT FUNDS ARE VITAL

The saying "Everything is bigger in Texas" unfortunately is true with respect to the S&L debacle and cleanup effort in the Lone Star State. While in no way a reflection on most Texans, this fact has resulted in frustration over S&L failures and in anger over the operations of the Resolution Trust Corp., which is charged with cleaning up an enormous financial mess.

Texans have seen more S&L wheeling and dealing, more S&L insolvencies and more of the Resolution Trust Corp. than they ever want to see. So I am not surprised that Rep. Sam Johnson has struck a nerve with his constituents when he complains about the Resolution Trust Corp. In Texas, the Resolution Trust Corp. is a lightning rod for fury over the S&L fiasco.

Yet, if we are to help Texas regain financial health and protect depositors, we must not confuse the Resolution Trust Corp. with the problems that preceded it. This is like blaming the fireman for the fire. The Resolution Trust Corp. has an especially large fire to put out, more so in Texas than anywhere else.

I take seriously all constructive criticism. But Mr. Johnson's criticisms take the buckshot approach, without firm reliance on facts. Let's look closely at the record before deciding that we should stop funding to protect depositors.

Has the Resolution Trust Corp. hurt Texans? No. Texas leads the nation in S&L failures, causing the Resolution Trust Corp. to funnel more money and resources here. With the lion's share of losses nationwide — a whopping $24 billion, or nearly one-third of the loss money spent thus far — the 137 failed thrifts in Texas command our attention. The "go-go" mentality and dangerous speculative ventures of a few wayward Texans caused the state to suffer, and left taxpayers with a big tab for cleaning up Texas. By closing or selling 130 insolvent thrifts, and protecting nearly three million depositor accounts worth $37 billion, the Resolution Trust Corp. prevented further disaster from striking Texans.

Is the Resolution Trust Corp. depressing the Texas economy? No. It is moving to finish its job and get out, like a Texas Ranger who restores justice and leaves town. Contrary to Mr. Johnson's portrayal, the Resolution Trust Corp. has sold Texas assets at a fast clip; we are ahead of schedule for 1991, having achieved asset sales and collections of $11.8 billion by Sept. 30. Since 1989, we have disposed of nearly $29 billion in assets from Texas institutions. Most of our overvalued real estate is in Texas, but we are selling Texas real estate assets at an average of $130 million per month. We intend to avoid dumping, which would depress the fragile Texas marketplace and lessen our recovery rate for taxpayers. Nationwide, recoveries now are about 96 percent of book value for all asset sales.

Is the Resolution Trust Corp. spending too much on lawyers' fees? No. The Resolution Trust Corp. was directed by law to contract with private-sector professionals. We retain lawyers to work on nearly 100,000 pending legal matters, more than half of which are inherited from failed S&L estates. We carefully evaluate a failed S&L's caseload to determine if a suit is worth pursuing, and we keep expenses to a minimum. If we must chase down a crook or resolve a bankruptcy to clear an asset for sale, we hire the appropriate professionals to help recover taxpayers' money. The agency was mandated to build a partnership with the private sector — lawyers, real estate brokers, appraisers, and scores of other Texans are involved.

Taxpayers do deserve a break, but Mr. Johnson knows that a delay in funding the S&L cleanup simply raises the price, adding about $4 million a day to the taxpayers' burden. Taxpayers are better off if we finish the job and move on. Contrary to Mr. Johnson's complaints about mismanagement, the Resolution Trust Corp. is meeting its enormous challenge. We have closed or sold 583 insolvent thrifts nationwide — about one every business day. Asset sales and collections now exceed $200 billion, or about $344 million every business day. This is not the time to stop and debate whether to continue funding to protect depositors.

Congress was right to fund the Resolution Trust Corp. through April 1, and next year it should provide the remaining $55 billion to complete the task. Funding is needed because the number of failed S&Ls has nearly doubled since 1989. Sam Johnson was not in Congress when our lawmakers decided to deal with the S&L debacle. At that time, despite the fact that the bulk of S&L failures were in Texas, our representatives acted as statesmen and voted for depositor protection. Now that most depositors of failed Texas institutions have their money, it is not the time to be parochial and withdraw support for depositors in other states.

Of all our detractors, though, the press was the most relentless. I'm a great admirer of the fourth estate, and a fervent believer in absolute freedom of speech. But there were times when I was appalled at the lack of responsibility on the part of the media. Thousands of people throughout the country were working day and night to avert a financial disaster, and there were times when all the press was interested in was a sixty-seven-cent item in our working budget.

Let me explain.

One day, on February 18, 1993, to be precise, as I drove into the basement garage of the RTC building, I noticed Sam Donaldson, the ABC-TV commentator, standing beside my parking space. As I pulled in and opened my door, TV floodlights suddenly switched on and Sam began talking.

"For heaven's sake, Sam, what are you doing here in the garage?" I said. "Why don't you come up to my office?"

"We were pretty sure you wouldn't let us in," Sam said.

"What nonsense!" I said. "Of course I'll let you in."

When Donaldson and I reached my office and were comfortably seated, he began asking questions about newspaper reports that the RTC had paid sixty-seven cents per photocopy for some material.

I nodded, having read the newspaper reports on the matter, and decided this was a good opportunity to set the record straight. The reports, taken badly out of context, related to the Home Federal Savings Bank in San Diego, California. With $12 billion in assets, Home Fed was the largest institution handled by the RTC. In February 1992, the Office of Thrift Supervision and the RTC initiated discussions about resolving Home Fed's problems without putting it under the aegis of the RTC, via a program developed jointly by the OTS and RTC called the Accelerated Resolution Program (ARP) (oh, these acronyms!). The point of ARP was to speed up the process of selling assets before there was any deterioration of value. Our plan was to market Home Fed's deposit franchise and asset base simultaneously, which meant that we had to do extensive due diligence on all Home Fed's assets, both to inform potential investors and to give the RTC the full information it needed to evaluate bids and issue the standard representations and warranties. Given the size and complexity of Home Fed's asset base, we had to hire several due diligence firms, as well as a due diligence manager to oversee and coordinate the various contractors. Through a competitive process, Price Waterhouse was chosen as the "management continuity contractor," whose primary role was supervision. But included in the contract, estimated at $5 million, were costs of photocopying, and by reason of the conditions imposed, we did run consistently over budget.

At the time Price Waterhouse was selected, no one at the RTC or Price Waterhouse knew that there was an outstanding federal grand jury subpoena for all Home Fed's documents. While we had some experience with Justice Department subpoenas in the past, we had never before been required to produce anything like this volume of documents under subpoena: the Home Fed subpoena applied to substantially all the books and records of the institution. To avoid having to produce original documents such as promissory notes, mortgages, certificates of deposit, loan agreements, and the like — which would have slowed down the asset sale for months if not years — the U.S. attorney agreed to accept photocopies. But for photocopies to meet the technical requirements of the federal rules of evidence, certain extraordinary measures were required in the copying process. The documents had to be protected against loss or damage; Home Fed and the contractor selected for copying had to maintain a document control log; copying had to be supervised by a Home Fed employee with knowledge of the books and records of the institution; each copy had to be compared to the original; each copy had to be certified by the supervising Home Fed employee; and the document had to be maintained in the same order in which it was kept in the bank's files. So complicated was the copying process, in fact, that we had compiled a two-inch-thick Document Control Procedures Manual, our photocopying bible.

As I rattled off all these facts and procedures, I could see that Donaldson was following me every step of the way, if I could judge by his nods and murmured "yes" and "oh, I see" comments that periodically punctuated my saga of Home Fed.

In any event, I explained that all this labor resulted in a significantly more complex and broader scope of work than had been originally anticipated. Home Fed's records could not simply be bundled up and delivered to a copying service. We were compiling and maintaining records for evidentiary purposes.

"Many thanks for your explanation," Donaldson said, putting his pencil away. "It certainly casts a whole new light on the issue."

"The damn sixty-seven cents wasn't for *copying*, Sam. It was for preparation, copying, verification, quality control, and quality assurance. I should add that in a gesture of good faith, Price Waterhouse — who have done a helluva job on Home Fed, by the way — has initiated discussions with us to lower the fees called for in the original contract, and they voluntarily lowered their charges by $4 million, which reduced the individual copy charge from sixty-seven cents to thirty-seven cents. They were under no obligation to do so."

Sam thanked me profusely for my clarification, we shook hands, and he left to rejoin his camera crew, who'd been waiting outside my office. I was sorry I had had to go into such detail, but I figured the cause was worth it. I was looking forward to hearing Sam Donaldson rectify that overblown story on the nightly news.

A couple of nights later, I tuned in to ABC News. There was Sam Donaldson, looking me straight in the eye courtesy of the magic tube.

"ABC News has been investigating possible cost overruns at the RTC," he said, his face dead serious, "and among our findings is one that may seem small at first glance but is clearly significant: the RTC has been paying sixty-seven cents — that's right, sixty-seven cents — for photocopying bank documents. . . ."

Furious, I turned off the television, only sorry that Donaldson hadn't really been looking me in the eye personally, right there in my living room.

The next day I put in a call to him at ABC News.

"I'm sorry, Mr. Donaldson is unavailable. May I take a message for him?"

"Tell him Mr. Casey called. Al Casey. Please ask him to call me."

When after two days he hadn't called back I put in a second call, only to learn — not unexpectedly — that Mr. Donaldson was still unavailable. But the person who took the call promised — absolutely — that he *would* return my call.

I'm still waiting.

By the time I left the RTC on March 15, 1993, we had recouped 93 percent of the book value of the assets of the failed banks and thrifts we sold. Some 850 failed banks had come under our control — more than double the number of troubled thrifts than had been anticipated when the RTC was first set up — with combined assets of $415 billion. Of that, we had realized $385 billion in asset sales. I would gladly have stayed on for another year or two, since my ultimate goal was to squeeze out that remaining 7 percent. But a new political team was in power in Washington by then, and, understandably, they wanted their own people in key positions. I left with only that slight, 7 percent regret, but feeling I had done as good a job as I could, and thankful that, with the support of countless devoted and selfless people throughout the fifty states, we had helped the country avert a potential major disaster.

One basic misconception about the RTC I should like to correct, for it seems to persist even today, is that the much maligned and misunderstood agency was set up to "bail out" the savings and loans institutions. It was not, but rather to protect people, the depositors who were in danger of losing their life savings. The term *S&L bailout* that the media loved to bandy about is a complete misnomer. Every dollar appropriated by Congress — reluctantly, I might add, for the "scandal" was a political hot potato for virtually everyone in government — was used to pay off depositors. None was used to "bail out" stockholders, bondholders, or thrift executives.

An RTC update:

In July 1996, the Supreme Court ruled that some banks had been encouraged to take on large liabilities in order to save some savings and loans. The government had asked that they take over the failed institutions, and in return they were given favorable accounting treatment. The decision interpreted the contracts to which they had agreed as promising that the government, rather than the savings and loans, would assume the financial risk of any regulatory changes that might deprive the savings and loans of those advantages. The federal regulators had persuaded healthy savings and loans to acquire failing ones under an accounting method permitting the liability they assumed to be carried on their books as "goodwill," an asset that could be amortized over thirty-five or forty years. These deals were favorable to the assuming savings and loans, because this paper asset permitted them to make more loans than they could have otherwise.

In 1989 Congress had removed "intangible assets," including goodwill, from those that could be counted toward a savings and loan's minimum capital requirements. Thus many savings and loans fell out of compliance.

Several savings institutions sued the U.S. government in the federal claims court in Washington, D.C. Their cases were successful in the claims court in 1992. The government argued that its contracts should never have been interpreted to bind it to a promise to exercise regulatory authority in a particular way unless such a promise was unmistakable on the face of the contract.

Justice David Souter said that the savings and loans had never argued against Congress's right to change the law, but that the government had assumed the risk of paying damages for any financial injury the savings institutions might suffer from any changes that took place.

There are nearly one hundred instances of institutions that have breach-of-contract cases pending against the government. The actual amount of damages will be decided in the lower courts. In January 1996, the government used the figure of $10 billion to persuade the Court to hear its appeal of a federal court of appeals ruling that found it liable for breach of contract.

In this end-of-the-century world of ours, we move so swiftly from one crisis to the next that for many people the RTC is already a fading memory. That pleases me, for had that geometrically progressing problem not been dealt with boldly and forthrightly, it might well have had a more devastating effect on this nation's financial system than the Depression of the 1930s.

15

SLOW REVENGE AT HARVARD, "DRUGS DON'T WORK," A REVIVAL OF ETHICS

SOMETIME BACK IN THE 1960s my name was put on the ballot to become an overseer of Harvard College. The Board of Overseers at Harvard is the equivalent of the Board of Trustees at other universities. The election is a popularity contest; ten people are nominated, and the five with the largest number of votes are elected. I suppose it was a great honor even to be chosen for the ballot. But I lost, and I don't enjoy losing. Old friends would come up to me and ask, "Say, Al, how did that Harvard election ever turn out?" and I, not wanting to answer, would tell them something to the effect: "I can't say; only sixty percent of the precincts have reported in so far."

A few years after my defeat, Harvard president Derek Bok called. "Al, I have a great idea," he said. "You know, some of the people elected as overseers these past few years have neither the experience nor commitment we need. So I'm proposing to run a slate of 'losers,' people who were nominated in the past and lost who I really think would make more of a contribution. That way I'll gain five on the board of overseers that I really want. Will you allow me to include your name?"

"Derek," I said, "that first loss was humiliating, but I ran against a lot of recent graduates, and probably most of my classmates who might have voted for me were in the lost and found at the time. Still, a second defeat would be hard to take."

"I understand, Al," he replied. "But will you at least take two phone calls from people who admire you very much and would like to see you accept?"

"Who are they?" I asked.

"Andrew Heiskell and Hooks Burr," he said. The former was the chairman of Time Inc., and the latter a senior partner of Ropes & Gray, a Boston law firm, and a longtime member of the board at American Airlines. I said I would be happy to talk to them.

Heiskell called first and gave a long list of reasons why I should support Derek. I didn't argue but heard him out, then asked: "Andy, if I agree, will you vote for me?"

There was the standard long silence, then Andy said, with a quick but profound sigh, if I heard rightly: "Well, Al, as you know it's a very strong slate. There are several of my own close friends on it."

Next Hooks Burr checked in, and we did the same ritual dance before I popped the same question: "Hooks, if I agree to run, will you vote for me?"

Again there was a moment if not of silence certainly of hesitation before Hooks replied: "As you know, Al, I'm a member of the Corporation, and we are the only alumni not permitted to vote."

In fact, Hooks was a long-standing member of the elite, seven-member Corporation Board, a post he had held for twenty-eight years, the longest service of anyone since the founding of Harvard.

Despite the lukewarm response of my two "buddies," I decided to run, and I was to my (slight) surprise duly elected, and served for six years. I enjoyed every year of it.

In 1968, at my twenty-fifth class reunion, I had been plucked as a reluctant volunteer to argue in support of American involvement in Vietnam in a debate with Norman Mailer, a classmate. Mailer argued brilliantly, presenting reason after reason why America never should have meddled in Vietnam's affairs and why it should get out as soon as possible to avoid any further losses. The issues surrounding the Vietnam War were so intertwined and

complex that, while not in agreement with Mailer, I had a difficult time devising a convincing defense. My arguments floundered
against Mailer's rapid-fire attacks, and at the end of the hour, I
wound up humbly accepting defeat.

Usually I'm quick to let go of the past and focus on the future, but something about my defeat by Mailer lingered in my
mind. Not for very long, though; only about twenty-five years. In
1993 I had my chance for revenge. The program committee for
the reunion wrote and asked if I would be willing to speak on a
panel that would deal with the future role of my classmates, as
most were retired or facing retirement. I presumed the invitation
had been made because someone decided I had found the magic
answer about making one's "golden years" — a term I detest —
meaningful and productive. At first I was reluctant, because I felt
that all of my classmates probably had a pretty good idea what they
wanted to do (or not do) with their lives at this point, and to try
and generalize would quickly run the real risk of pontificating.
Anyway, it was then that the Mailer memory came surging back. I
told the organizers that if they could get Mailer to come on another panel with former *Washington Post* editor Ben Bradlee and
me, I would both attend and expound upon the virtues of retirement. Mailer was approached and hesitantly agreed to be on the
discussion panel, the subject of which was: advertising: a force for
good or evil in modern society?

Shortly before the discussion began, Mailer approached me
and, with a slightly confused look on his face, asked why I had insisted he be part of the debate. I looked at him straight-faced and
said, "Just be patient, Norman. Be patient."

Mailer argued that advertising was socially immoral, that it
convinced consumers to purchase unnecessary products, that advertising was infused with cynicism and advertisers eschewed the
truth in touting a product's virtues and benefits. This idealistic appeal sounded good, but in a nation where business is the foundation of an economy that 250 million people depended on, his
condemnation of marketing strategies seemed weak and uncon-
vincing.

When it came my turn to speak, I explained how, in my long experience, advertising and marketing had allowed the companies I had worked for to generate more profits, which were reinvested into the corporation for expansion and developing new projects, which in turn provided more jobs for people and generated more tax revenues to fill both state and federal coffers. I showed samples of ads from Times Mirror and American Airlines, even the Post Office, to show how they could carry a simple, straightforward, honest, and informative message to the public. Compared to Mailer's largely theoretical arguments, my defense seemed logical, well thought out, and, I must humbly confess, superbly intelligent. In any event, that was the consensus. When I finished, Mailer looked a little surprised, but I think he also understood why I had asked him to be there. The slate had been cleaned; it took me twenty-five years, but I had evened the score.

I hope, from that anecdote, no one will come to the hasty conclusion that I am in any way competitive. Or that I don't like to lose. Nothing could be further from the truth.

Today, though I am no longer a Harvard overseer, I serve on the board of three commercial companies and three pro bono companies. I am also chairman of the Washington-based national Drugs Don't Work Program.

One of the largest problems facing businesses today is the growing use of drugs in the workplace. While large corporations have the funds to initiate drug-free workplace programs, many small-to-medium-sized businesses, which employ over 80 percent of all Americans, do not have the resources to provide more than mere lip service to drug-free initiatives. The Drugs Don't Work Program was designed to assist smaller businesses with developing effective strategies for creating their own drug-free workplaces.

Formed under President Bush's Drug Advisory Council, on which I served, and the Partnership for a Drug-Free America, the program started as a pilot program in Connecticut under the leadership and vision of Bill Kaufmann, a former senior executive with Chase Manhattan Bank. This first pilot project became one of the most comprehensive and effective private-sector-led drug-prevention programs in the country. After another successful pilot in Florida, Drugs Don't Work became a national effort.

In the spring of 1994, my close friend Jim Burke, who was then chairman of the Partnership for a Drug-Free America, asked if I would be willing to chair the nationwide Drugs Don't Work Program. I learned that by one estimate 71 percent of drug users work. Every day they go into offices and factories and stores and try to do their job. That knowledge helped me realize that the drug problem depicted on the nightly news clips was vastly more complex than it seemed. So I accepted the position. Resolving the drug crisis no longer seemed a Washington priority, and the only way progress could continue was if the private sector took the initiative to continue the fight against drugs.

The problems are not just in the inner cities among the un-employed. Drugs are being used from Wall Street to Main Street, in the poorest ghettos and the most affluent suburbs. While it's easy to blame social ills on the youth of the country, I believe that they are more often the victims than the cause. The priorities and values of the nation are set at home, in school, and in the work-place. If adults are not convinced of the pressing need to eliminate substance abuse, it is highly unlikely that young people will change their own attitudes and behavior.

I hope I have made the case by now that I am not one who dwells on the past or who wishes, nostalgically, for the "good old days." But my participation in the Drugs Don't Work Program, which has taken me the length and breadth of the country, to cities and towns and farmlands, has convinced me that there is a distinct and undeniable relationship between the drug problem and a serious decline in ethical values.

The ethical quality of our society or any society is the sum of the separate actions of parents and their children, teachers and their students, employers and their employees, public officials and their staffs, professionals and their clients, individuals and their friends. At some point in our lives, each of us is inevitably in one or more of these roles, so our decisions and conduct are important to the whole.

Since it's embarrassing to discuss our own ethical behavior or that of our friends, it has become common practice to discuss ethics generically by attacking the "ethical behavior" of corporations and their officers, of government and its officials. By any poll, the majority of Americans believes business is primarily motivated by greed. Similarly, our elected officials are continually exposed to investigations for unethical and criminal actions. This is a matter that requires a certain historical perspective.

The founding fathers developed the concept of the separation of powers, which formed the basis of our Constitution two hundred years ago. Earlier, the French political philosopher Montesquieu explored the relationship between peoples and their governments. He said a dictatorship depends upon fear, so that when fear disappears the dictatorship is overthrown. A monarchy depends upon the loyalty of the people and dies when loyalty dies. Obviously, the most desirable form of government is a free republic; but in Montesquieu's analysis, a republic is also the most fragile form of government, because it depends upon a virtuous populace.

What did he mean by a "virtuous" populace? To me, *virtuous* means living by high ethical values. In turn, what do we mean by ethics? One of the best definitions was given by Dr. Albert Schweitzer. "In a general sense, ethics is the name that we give to our concern for good behavior. We feel an obligation to consider not only our personal well-being, but also that of others and of human society as a whole."

Montesquieu meant, therefore, that in a free republic the leaders and a majority of the people are committed to doing what is best for the nation as a whole. When that commitment breaks down, when the people consider only their own personal well-being, they can no longer be depended upon to behave in the best interests of their nation. When this happens, the result is laws, regulations, red tape, in other words, controls designed to force people to be trustworthy. These are instruments of bondage, not freedom.

In the mid-1750s, about the time of Montesquieu, a Professor Alexander Tytler of the University of Edinburgh made the following prophetic statement:

~ From bondage to spiritual faith;
~ from spiritual faith to great courage;
~ from courage to liberty;
~ from liberty to abundance;
~ from abundance to selfishness;
~ from selfishness to complacency;
~ from complacency to apathy;
~ from apathy to dependency;
~ from dependency back again into bondage.

Throughout most of our history, basic ethical values were considered fundamental to the nation and to the people who made up the nation. These values were passed on from generation to generation in the home, in the school, and in religious institutions, each reinforcing the others. We had a consensus not only on values but also on the importance of these values, and from that consensus we knew who we were as a people and where we were going as a nation.

Now, just what were the ethical values upon which our freedom was based? Honor, duty to God and to country, service to others, loyalty, kindness, generosity, hard work, self-reliance, and, above all, honesty and integrity. However, today, throughout America, far too many homes, schools, and religious institutions are no longer fulfilling their traditional roles as protectors and promoters of ethical values. Far too many people are growing up with almost no exposure to the values that once united Americans of all backgrounds. And, with a few exceptions, people in business and government have done little or nothing to express, much less stress, the ethical values that our young people at one time brought to the adult world.

Look at the large number of special interest groups today that put their own narrow concerns above those of the nation. Consider, too, the complacency and apathy of the majority of voters who fail to turn out on election day. Are we a complacent society? In a typical presidential election, less than half the eligible people vote. In other words, a president elected with 51 percent of the vote is actually the choice of only one quarter of the electorate. Democracy deserves better than that.

Are we a selfish society? In the federal budget, a huge percentage goes for entitlements, a monumental example of voting ourselves largesse from the public treasury. To an alarming extent, America has become a complacent nation, people concerned only with their own well-being. Our government has responded with an avalanche of laws, regulations, and controls; it has wrapped us in red tape like mummies, greatly diminishing the freedom that made America the greatest nation in the world.

Am I beginning to sound like Murphy? I hope not. I remain eternally, unequivocally optimistic. I believe that today millions of Americans are beginning to realize the importance of ethical values; in my travels throughout the country, in my classes at SMU, I have clearly sensed a growing awareness of the need to adopt and apply codes of ethics in our homes, our schools and colleges, our religious institutions, and especially in our places of work.

I've always had a considerable amount of self-confidence; whether I owe that to my genes or my upbringing, I'm not sure. I've felt I could, if I tried hard enough, do anything. I wouldn't say that it's faith that gave me the courage to act. I think it was a sense of right and wrong that my parents instilled in me. Everything was black and white. It was the "Irish thing," I guess. My mother used to say, "Just imagine that what you're about to do or say is going to be the headline in tomorrow's paper. Would I be proud of you, Albert?" It was a tried and true question, but Mother constantly impressed it on us.

"I'm not going to be there to help you all the time," she

would say. "But you must always do the right thing. And you must never shame your parents or your family."

Everyone in the business world ought to be able to agree that treating customers, employees, and suppliers ethically is good business. But corporations often put tremendous, sometimes impossible, pressure on their employees to improve the bottom line. Now they must learn to put equal pressure on their employees to take the ethical high road in meeting their goals and objectives.

"Only a virtuous people are capable of freedom," George Washington once said. "To understand personally and maintain the American way of life, to honor it by his or her own exemplary conduct, and to pass it intact to future generations is the responsibility of every true American."

Each of us must decide how we can best discharge that responsibility. As a nation we have great resources, great facilities, great transportation, and great technology. No country is better equipped to survive and prosper than America. However, machines and technology are not what makes the difference between nations, any more than they are the difference between one corporation and another. A successful society is a people business, and the heart and soul of this nation are the men and women who understand and believe that if something can go right, it should. And then do their damnedest to make sure it does.

CASEY'S COROLLARIES

A Selection

Numbers in brackets indicate pages in the book where examples of the corollary occur. When the wisdom comes from others their names are noted.

1. Repeal Murphy's Law.
2. Be of good cheer and small ego.
3. Time is precious; use it wisely and well. [Mother]
4. Create a climate of trust in the workplace.
5. Identify problems; simplify solutions. [2]
6. Create a structure in which everyone is important and all ideas count.
7. Progress means taking risks.
8. Being a winner means winning more times than losing. [31]
9. Total integrity should always be the basis of your dealings with others. [64]
10. Being successful implies having compassion for others. [John Walsh, 34]
11. Delegate responsibility as well as authority.
12. Virtue is an empty In box.
13. Memo writers are a social menace — okay, a *business* menace.
14. Values are more important than credentials; experience is more important than education.
15. You don't have to be mean to be tough. [3]
16. When negotiations get testy, use humor.

17. We learn more from our failures than we do from our successes.
18. Never do or say anything you wouldn't want to read about in tomorrow's paper. [Mother]
19. Solve problems face-to-face.
20. Motivate through respect.
21. Have the confidence to be kind.
22. Be confident, even when the odds seem stacked against you. *Especially* when the odds seem stacked against you.
23. Hire talented people; hopefully, one of them will be your successor.
24. Play fair. Too many people forget the first word, and often the second.
25. Never slam a door so hard you can't open it again. [Father, 3]
26. When people enjoy their jobs, hard work comes easy. [157]
27. The harder you work the luckier you get. [188]
28. Don't agonize over a problem; once you have all the information you can gather, act.
29. In any new situation, look for similarities from your past.
30. The greater the challenge, the greater the potential reward.
31. Greet bad news with a smile, then work to put it behind you. [185]
32. Look before you leap; listen before you lead.
33. Learn to focus completely on the person you're with at the moment.
34. Not every decision has to be based on the bottom line.
35. A bad decision is better than no decision.
36. Nothing in business is static; recognize change and don't hesitate to reprioritize.
37. Always question people, starting with yourself.
38. Weigh the pros and cons of any situation; choose the greater good for the greater number.
39. Leadership lasts only as long as it's exercised.

40. Meet weekly as a group with all who report to you; meet one-on-one each week as well.
41. In setting goals, be certain that everyone has a clear understanding of what you expect of them. [2]
42. Balance out social situations; if you invite one key staff member to your home, invite them all.
43. Be demanding as a manager, but never to the breaking point. [20]
44. Never abdicate your real self, no matter what the pressures; it will only do you harm and may even do you in.
45. Take your responsibilities seriously, but don't take yourself too seriously.
46. Take all constructive criticism seriously. [294]
47. Even after you've made what you know is the right decision, don't assume it's the final decision. [284]
48. If life ever offers you a chance to play God, seize it. [168]
49. This I know: the learning process never ends. [293]
50. When all else fails, get down on your knees. Amen.

SOME DOS AND DON'TS ON TAKING ON A NEW JOB

1. Become an involved observer of the passing scene.
2. **Listen, listen, listen.** If your mouth is open, you are not learning.
3. Mentally challenge all assumptions but keep your conclusions to yourself.
4. Your peers are your best resource; watch them.
5. Do everything possible to help your boss raise his/her status.
6. Allocate your time and resources — develop calendar checkpoints.
7. Your availability is your best asset — it should be directed up, down, and sideways.
8. Be sensitive to the feelings and goals of others, and make sure they know it.

9. Get an organization chart of your department showing names and titles.
10. Walk the halls; introduce yourself.
11. Ask for help and show that you appreciate it.
12. Don't try to impress people too quickly with your talents and accomplishments. They will all become known in due time.
13. Do what you say you will do. If you can't, say so.
14. Your first assignment is to become part of a team, not its leader.
15. Arrive early and stay late. Plan no social lunches for the first six months.

INDEX